THE CLASH OF CULTURES

THE CLASH OF
CULTURES

Managers and Professionals

JOSEPH A. RAELIN

School of Management
Boston College

HARVARD BUSINESS SCHOOL PRESS
Boston, Massachusetts

Harvard Business School Press, Boston 02163

Portions of Chapter 3 originally appeared in "The Basis for the Professional's Resistance to Managerial Control," *Human Resource Management*, vol. 24, no. 2, summer 1985.

LIBRARY OF CONGRESS CATALOGING IN PUBLICATION DATA

Raelin, Joseph A., 1948–
  The clash of cultures.

  Includes index.
  1. Professional employees. 2. Personnel management.
I. Title.
HD8038.A1R33   1986   658.3'044   86-14227
ISBN 0-87584-145-7

To Abby
This One's For You

Contents

List of Illustrations

TABLES

FIGURES

Preface

Managers have no lack of choice when it comes to books on managing professional employees. The majority of these accounts, however, deal with technical professionals, such as scientists and engineers. Although the literature on the professions and on various professional occupations abounds, these accounts tend to be dated. Today, there is a growing interest in the so-called salaried professionals, those professionals who carry out their craft in organizations rather than in private practice, although recognition of their particular difficulties in integrating into the bureaucracy is relatively new among the general management audience.

To date, there has not been an attempt to link the peculiarities of the salaried professional culture with the corporate culture of management. Thus managing professionals is essentially a mimicking process in which management uses its best instincts when working with professional rather than nonprofessional employees. Standard management practices are merely superimposed on strategies for managing salaried professionals.

We know too much about the corporate and professional cultures to let this continue. We know that both managers and professionals are affected by the wider social culture, which has slowly changed the attitudes and behaviors of people in the working world.

In this book I have endeavored to put these critical cultural variables together to produce a volume that can be applied specifically by managers, or management students, who already understand that dealing with professionals is qualitatively different from managing the general work force. After going into considerable detail on the idiosyncracies of the corporate and professional cultures and the wider social culture, I offer a set of managerial strategies informed by an understanding of the parties and their respective cultures. As readers will quickly appreciate, there is a natural conflict between management and professionals because of their differences in educational background, socialization, values, vocational interests, work habits, and outlook. For some, the differences are more emphatic than for others. There are reasons why this is so, and these are pointed out. But instead of letting management practitioners grope for a workable combination of strategies, this book helps them make a selection on the basis of a deep understanding of professional motivation and behavior. Management does not have to put up with the clash of cultures. There are definite ways to achieve the purposes of management in service of the organization and allow professionals to achieve technical proficiency and satisfaction.

This book, then, provides the manager with a recipe for managing the professional staff effectively. As with all good recipes, any number of variations, substitutes, and instinctual preferences can be followed. The core strategies for mediating professional/management conflict, however, can be observed reasonably closely, because they are based on a knowledge of professional experience.

The material covered in the book, as I have indicated, is based on research into the cultural backgrounds of managers and professionals. As baseline information, I use traditional sources in arranging my arguments. I have made liberal use of my own experience as a consultant and teacher of both managers and professionals, however, to supplement the coverage with live examples of both effective and ineffective handling of the organizational problems of professionals. Also, while on sabbatical from Boston College during the spring of 1984, I interviewed in great depth thirty professionals, professional-administrators, and managers to obtain their reactions to the preliminary ideas I had been formulating for this book. In addition, over the past few years, I carried out survey research of salaried professional behavior and published a number of studies I use in this account.

I wrote this book, however, not so much for an academic audience as for management and the management education community. Hence I do not observe all the canons of professional academic usage, such as comprehensive citation and full data back-up. I want the coverage to be very readable and accessible to managers of salaried professionals and to professionals themselves who desire greater understanding of their predicament within the bureaucracy. Nevertheless, the concepts covered here are often complex, as is all human behavior, so I ask readers to make use of their intellectual curiosity.

The reason for any confidence I may have in the value of the presentation to follow rests with my students and clients who in their own way and often without their explicit foreknowledge have contributed so much to my understanding of professionals in organizational life. I wish I could thank them all individually. I would also like to acknowledge the time and thoughtful insights generously provided by my interview respondents. I am grateful to my research assistants, Sue Fay and Dave Donelan, who helped me ferret out the literature relevant to some of the critical points presented, and to Caryl Oliphant, who prepared in good humor and with worthy dispatch the bulk of the manuscript.

I owe most to my family, who had to put up with my time away from them while I was either interviewing or writing. I have dedicated this book to my wife, Abby, who can tell you a lot about living with and managing a cosmopolitan salaried professional.

Joseph A. Raelin

Boston, Massachusetts
January 1986

Introduction to the Management of Salaried Professionals

1

The Problem: A Clash of Cultures

As a manager of professionals, how often in your career have you had to confront attempts by your professional associates or subordinates to challenge your authority? As a salaried professional, how much longer can you put up with managers who interfere with your right to work autonomously on the problems to which you have been assigned?

The inherent conflict between managers and professionals results basically from a clash of cultures: the corporate culture, which captures the commitment of managers, and the professional culture, which socializes professionals. Both cultures are further sustained by the wider social culture. Briefly, professionals who are salaried, namely scientists, engineers, lawyers, accountants, teachers, and the like who work in organizations rather than in private practice, are socialized through their disciplines and culture to carry out their technical responsibilities as members of a professional group. Their educational background and resulting socialization, however, typically cause them to experience difficulty, especially early in their careers, in conforming to the direction of management either. Managers, on the other hand, undergo a different kind of socialization. Their formal education is typically of shorter duration and emphasizes interdisciplinary and practical approaches to problem solving. Managers are further expected to learn the bulk of their craft on the job. The corporate culture, which strongly influences their socialization, defines the managerial role essentially as articulating the goals of the organization and devising procedures to meet them.

The root of the conflict between managers and professionals, then, stems from a more basic conflict regarding employees' roles. This role conflict, however, is not always clear-cut. Some managers and professionals simply buy into the other's culture; plus there is the complication of professionals becoming professional managers. Nevertheless, role differences between professionals and managers become particularly apparent within the confines of bureaucratic organizations. The manager expects the professional, as an employee, to follow the procedures of the organization and to abide by the manager's directives. Although all professionals deviate from managerial expectations from time to time, some find it especially difficult to reconcile their role as employees with adherence to the principles and methods of their profession. Furthermore, many professionals were deeply influenced by the social revolution of the 1960s, which pressed for quality of working life based on independence of judgment and a healthy suspicion of authority. These more "difficult" employees are referred to in this book as "cosmopolitan"[1] and are known to have widespread problems integrating into both the formal and informal structure of their organizations. They maintain marginal loyalty to the organization, preferring instead to align themselves for purposes of recognition and evaluation with their professional colleagues and associations.

The development of the cosmopolitan notion in studies of professionals has a rich sociological tradition. At first, it was thought that professionals could be characterized as either cosmopolitan or local, the latter professing loyalty to their organizations to the point of using an organizational reference for their social and esteem needs. We now know, however, that professionals can be cosmopolitan or local on different personal and organizational levels, and that they may also change their orientation on the basis of career stage, organizational setting, management style, or other circumstances. Moreover, it is possible for some professionals to have dual loyalties, in other words, to be committed to both profession and organization simultaneously, or even to be indifferent to both. The case has been made that depending on the work of the organization, it is useful to have at least the first three types.[2] For example, in research organizations, it might be beneficial to have cosmopolitans to produce technical discoveries, locals to administer the work of the cosmopolitans, and "combineds" to further the use of the technical discoveries.

Unfortunately, although sociologists know quite a lot about professionals, this knowledge has not been disseminated to the management community in a way management can use to develop effective strategies for allowing professionals both to reach their potential and to contribute fully to their organizations. This is especially true for those professionals who are either exclusively or partly cosmopolitan. Even locals, however, who may make excellent professional-administrators, are also occasionally mishandled, either by being aligned with professionals who have different orientations or simply by being unnoticed.

The point is that except for the most local of professionals, management and professionals are different. They occupy distinct roles in the bureaucracy. They often misunderstand each other and, as a result, come into conflict. The main purposes of this book are to explain the basis for this conflict through an examination of differences in culture, and to suggest strategies for dealing with it. Chapter 2 looks at the corporate culture, Chapter 3, the professional culture, and Chapter 4, the social culture. These three streams of culture serve as the explanatory framework for understanding the differences between professionals and managers. Clearly, not all professionals are the same, nor are all managers. Yet the differences between the cluster of occupations and orientations constituting management and that constituting professionals are proposed as being significant—indeed, as clashing. Chapter 5 describes in detail specific managerial strategies that can serve to mediate this clash of cultures. Readers who are pressed for time can go immediately to Chapter 5 to learn about these specific responses. Another reading strategy, under time constraints, might be to read selectively those portions of the foundation chapters (2 through 4) that treat the specific conditions the reader encounters in day-to-day work. As I shall point out shortly, potential for conflict between management and professionals depends on a number of factors that may or may not apply to the reader's particular circumstances.

In any event, the mediation strategies discussed in Chapter 5 are grounded in a firm understanding of the mutual needs of the parties. Their selection is also based on the desire ultimately to shape organizations that reward both professional accomplishment and managerial proficiency.

The book, then, although of interest to professionals, is directed to the management and management education communities as a guide to developing more informed or rational approaches to managing professionals. It treats salaried professionals as very distinct organizational employees. Some of the familiar management tools and strategies depicted in popular management texts (and unfortunately superimposed in some "management of professionals" accounts) simply will not work with professionals once the cultural predispositions of professional life are understood.

Before going much further, let us take a first glimpse at the contributions to the explanation of professional/management conflict afforded by the three streams of culture. These descriptions, although cast somewhat in their extremes, set the tone for our subsequent discussion seeking accommodation of these cultural differences.

Corporate Culture

American corporate culture was depicted originally as a progressive model of organizational practice compared with bureaucratic models of the late nineteenth and early twentieth centuries, and later as a regressive model in comparison with the more successful organizational and economic systems of Germany and Japan. Substantively, it has been characterized as performance- and efficiency-based, formal, competitive, and exceedingly individualistic. These characteristics describe a culture that breeds task and career specialization that in turn decreases organizational loyalty and employee retention. Young professionals, in particular, join an organization to practice their professional craft, which, having its base of knowledge and learning outside the company, can be carried out across many organizations. The corporate culture conforms to this model by limiting professional employees to particular assignments that restrict their internal mobility. Promotion is a matter of movement up a confined technical hierarchy. Of course, the professional can avoid trying to climb the technical ladder by choosing the always attractive alternative of transition to management. Otherwise, opportunities are expected to crop up at competing firms that can use the same professional skills for assignments not altogether different from those mastered at the original firm.

Professional Culture

American professional culture meshes perfectly with the corporate cultural phenomenon just described. It associates the expert, specialized, and technical knowledge of the professions with professionalism itself. An individual becomes a professional only when recognized as having mastered this knowledge and its associated skills. Professional preparatory schools initiate the process by segregating students from other professional disciplines and instilling in them the norms and values expected of those who practice in the profession. Students are expected to look up to the great figures in their chosen profession. They are taught the basic knowledge and principles of the profession before they are allowed even to think about practicing. Once they enter the work world, professionals, by keeping in touch with their educational institutions and by joining their respective professional associations, become socialized to maintain their skills, values, and standards and not to be compromised by their employing organizations. This can produce almost immediate strain as these new professionals, trained to pledge unremitting loyalty to their profession, are now asked to extend first loyalty to their organization.

Social Culture

The explanation of professional/management conflict would remain incomplete without tracing effects attributable to the wider social culture. Most professionals working in large organizations today either grew up in or were substantially affected by the 1960s generation, which is synonymous with the "baby boom" cohort. During the late 60s, a minority from this cohort, mostly college students, began a transformation in American culture that featured such new values as a willingness to question authority, a rejection of material standards, and a demand for fulfillment and enrichment in work. As part of two of the most prominent issues of the day, civil rights and the antiwar movement, the protest of the 60s incorporated a strong social ethic that sought fulfillment in a higher quality of life. By the mid-70s, as the cohort came to adulthood and as recession hit the country, the prior values were coopted and were themselves transformed into a less social, more individualistic, almost narcissistic, cultural system. We were in the "me" generation, characterized by a need to live for today, contempt for any form of delayed gratification, and total absence of self-denial.

The net effect of these cultural changes has yet to be gauged precisely, but it is clear that the interest in enrichment and intrinsic satisfaction in one's work has not disappeared. The social ethic may also be coming back into vogue. Professionals demand to be treated as sensitive human beings and expect involvement and participation in their work. Otherwise, they will go elsewhere if they can. If the first half of the 80s has revealed one persistent trend, it is a willingness to forego other benefits for the sake of job quality and friendship.

In sum, salaried professionals, especially those having a cosmopolitan orientation, have particular difficulties integrating into their organizations, mainly because of their strong adherence to a professional culture that places professional standards above organizational exigencies. The wider social culture, and especially the values of the 60s that have been diffused into today's culture, also affect these professionals. In particular, there is emphasis on individual identity, combined with a strong interest in quality of working life. Finally, the American corporate culture, with its orientation toward competition and efficiency, reinforces the conflict between professionals and their managers by formalizing roles, relationships, and procedures that are largely inimical to cosmopolitan predispositions.

Who Are These Professionals?

Before delving further into the nature of the potential role conflict between managers and professionals, let us pause to take a closer look at these salaried professionals. By salaried, I refer to professionals who work inside an organization rather than in private practice. In 1984,[3] salaried professional employment had stabilized at nearly 75 percent of total professional employment. Professionals in some occupations, such as law or medicine, may choose whether to work for an organization or not. Others, such as engineers and nurses, have little choice because the locus of their work is almost exclusively within organizational borders. Salaried professional employment has become the predominant form of professionalization for several other reasons. Owing to the increasing complexity of our society, in particular the emphasis on specialization of work as well as advances in technology, today's professional is trained to work in organizational settings such as courtrooms, hospitals, laboratories, and universities.[4] Specialization also makes professionals more interdependent. To serve the client better, but also as a practical matter for the professional, many specialists locate within the same organizational setting. The professional also needs to supervise the work of many paraprofessionals as well as control sophisticated technological apparatus, activities that essentially constitute part of the system of professional service. Today, even those from the so-called old professions, such as law and medicine, in order to affiliate with other professionals but also to work in areas that cannot support private practice, are turning more and more to group and organizational forms of practice.[5]

Having isolated and explained the "salaried" part of the professional label, let us now consider the term "professional." It is not uncommon to encounter any individual who has a technical specialty calling himself or herself a professional. What is it that distinguishes a professional from a nonprofessional? Traditionally, we think of professionals as having superior intellectual training, as maintaining their own standards of excellence and success, and as being supported by associations that maintain the quality of the profession. Seymour Sarason defines them more broadly:

> Individuals whose choice of work requires at least a college education giving them specific knowledge and skills, to be applied under supervision for a period of time at the end of which they are entitled to a label which carries credentials for independent activity.[6]

Definitional Approaches

The above definitions are functional; that is, they define professionals on the basis of what they do. Professional taxonomies are also built around occupational status. One may also use an individual level of analysis that can have structural and attitudinal attributes. Finally, a group or power perspective may be used to distinguish a professional group within the labor force.

The occupational approach simply selects occupations that are presumed to fall into the professional category. Most of the extant occupational classifications are based on either prestige or socioeconomic status. There is little agreement, however, on the classification criteria to use in selecting the professional occupations, and further, occupations are subject to change over time. Nevertheless, I offer below an arbitrary list of some of the common professions:

Accountants
Airline pilots and controllers

Architects, artists, and writers
Clergy
Doctors
Engineers and computer scientists
Foresters
Lawyers
Nurses
Pharmacists
Psychologists, counselors, and social workers
Scientists—physical, mathematical, and life
Teachers, librarians, and professors
Urban planners

Because the occupational approach is limited by the crudeness of the criteria used in defining membership in the class, the functional approach may be used to make the classification more precise. This is done by describing the functions professionals perform. Although the functional approach is subject to some arbitrariness, considerable research supports the listing of characteristics. Steven Kerr, Mary Ann Von Glinow, and Janet Schriesheim,[7] in reviewing this research, found six characteristics the literature has acknowledged as representing professional status:

1. **expertise**   engaging in prolonged specialized training in a body of abstract knowledge.
2. **autonomy**   possessing the freedom to choose the examination of and means to solve problems.
3. **commitment**   showing primary interest in pursuing the practice of one's chosen specialty.
4. **identification**   identifying with the profession or with fellow professionals through formal association structures or through external referents.
5. **ethics**   rendering service without concern for oneself or without becoming emotionally involved with the client.
6. **standards**   committing oneself to help in policing the conduct of fellow professionals.

The functional approach may be used to draw up an occupational listing. The revised occupational approach may still be inadequate, however, at the individual level of analysis.[8] Some individuals who lack professional traits may be engaged in a supposed professional occupation; conversely, individuals who act like professionals may not be members of a recognized professional occupation. Hence, in every presumed professional occupation, some individuals are more professional than others.

The individual level of analysis may be further broken down by structural and attitudinal aspects. The structural attributes consist of such aspects as formal education, standards, and entrance requirements that are part of the structure of the profession, whereas the attitudinal attributes represent such aspects as disposition toward other colleagues in the field, sense of autonomy, and the like.[9] These structural and attitudinal attributes may also be applied at the occupational level of analysis.

The more recent power or group approach to professional classification suggests that professional groups band together to preserve their status by maximizing their social and economic benefits in the labor force.[10] Specifically, professionals attempt to exchange their supposed scarce resources, i.e., their special knowledge and skills, for social and economic gain. Reports using the group approach concentrate on the political and social behavior used by the profession to advance its cause as a labor monopoly. Recent accounts disclose that the salaried professions may advance their status by attempting to maintain occupational control within their organizations.[11] For example, they may attempt to show that their technical contributions are sufficiently indeterminate that no one else can make them. They may also be relatively successful in fending off incursions from other occupations or even from state regulatory bodies that may attempt to substitute for or control their practice in some way.

Professionals and Quasi-Professionals

Professionals have consistently been rated by public opinion polls as having the greatest amount of prestige in our society, although this is not necessarily reflected in their financial remuneration. Some occupations, therefore, may attempt to gain professional status—perhaps by using the power approach—even though the majority of their members do not fulfill the functional conditions outlined in the previous section. Yet such occupations qualify as professions on many of the key functions or may have enough professional-leaning members to qualify them as emerging or quasi-professions. Among the previously noted occupations that might fall into this middle-ranking category are accountancy, engineering, library work, and urban planning.

The truth of the matter is that, using the functional approach, one could probably scale all of the occupations in order of their increasing professionalism, suggesting that professionalism is a matter of degree and cannot be defined as a discrete category. Nevertheless, it is useful to consider the quasi-professionals as a separate group, since their organizational adaptiveness may be different from that of the professionals. In fact, a number of researchers have found a variety of differences between these two groups. Most of the studies have looked at engineers as representative of the quasi-professional category and scientists as representative of the pure professional category. Kerr et al.[12] used the six functional characteristics to differentiate the two occupations, so their work is again referred to in what follows.

1. **expertise**   Engineers are found to have a less rigorous educational background. In fact, some studies have found practicing engineers with less than a four-year undergraduate engineering degree. Engineers are also thought to treasure the practical and pragmatic components as opposed to the basic components of knowledge. Finally, engineers value interpersonal skills more highly than scientists.

2. **autonomy**   Scientists are unrelenting in their support of this characteristic. Hence they tend to look with disfavor on conformity

or adherence to organizational norms. They consequently seek the freedom to select the problems they will study, whereas engineers are typically given the problems and even the procedural guidelines for solving them.

3. **commitment**   Scientists are interested in pursuing a career in their field, whereas engineers think in terms of a career in their company. Similarly, career dissatisfaction or alienation among scientists might manifest itself through a lack of autonomy to pursue their work, whereas among engineers, it typically results from lack of power and participation in organizational affairs. This characteristic, then, has implications for career progression in the two occupational categories. The transition to management is much more accepted among engineers, whereas scientists have a tendency to remain with their technical specialty.

4. **identification**   Engineers do not maintain an identification with their profession, in terms of dealings with associations and external referents, to the same extent as scientists. However, engineers with PhD degrees were found to participate more actively in professional activities than those with less formal education, although engineers with doctorates constitute under 5 percent of all practicing engineers.

5. **ethics**   Given their socioeconomic origin, specialization, and fragmentation, engineers are not considered to have as strong a foundation in the ethical values of professionalism as scientists. Smaller percentages of engineers would seek to make a contribution to society than to contribute to their organization. Engineers, however, are committed to the value of service.

6. **standards**   A number of both formal and informal mechanisms exist in the sciences for certification, review of practitioners' competence, and censure; yet these activities are typically beyond the power and interest of engineering associations. Further, it is not evident that engineers value peer control. In fact, many feel that their manager, if technically qualified, might be an acceptable judge of their professional performance. Yet, in spite of the fact that

the forces of change in a given profession may come from leaders who do not fully represent the membership, there are pressures in the quasi-professions, such as engineering, to police themselves more, to strengthen their professional associations, and to express a community orientation and code of ethics.[13]

The foregoing differences between professionals and quasi-professionals notwithstanding, it is clear that the individual approach must apply in determining the ultimate criterion of membership. Some engineers will act like professionals; others may not. In the material that follows, readers will have to keep these distinctions in mind and determine for themselves whether certain viewpoints are applicable to the management of particular professional groups. The so-called quasi-professionals are considered to be professionals in this book. Nevertheless, since we are addressing the audience of professionals *within* organizations, there will be limits, regardless of degree of professionalism, on how much autonomy and external identification are feasible.

Growth and Erosion of Professionalism

Nearly every professional occupation is growing. In the last few years, even teaching professionals have come back into demand. Professionals are now approaching 16 percent of the civilian labor force (up from 8.4 percent in 1950) and some projections have forecast a proportion of 20 percent in the 1990s. Another statistical indicator of professional growth is the explosion in the demand for services, which now account for 70 percent of all U.S. jobs and 60 percent of the gross national product (GNP). Projections are that these figures will stand at 85 percent or more by the year 2000. Professionals will continue to occupy a central position in the service industries, as suggested by Marvin Cetron of Forecasting International, who believes occupational emphasis will be on creative insight and imagination, technical skills, the ability to handle increasingly challenging work, and a facility for working with computers—all characteristics that, except for the last, have traditionally been associated with professionalism.[14]

Because the prestige associated with professionalism has caused so many occupations to claim this status, it is an intriguing question whether the classification of "professional" has grown to a point where the label has become meaningless. Conversely, since most professionals can now be found working in organizations, which by their nature threaten professional autonomy and ethical standards, one could also wonder whether the professional classification might erode to a point where its membership would be insignificantly small.

In terms of the first challenge to professionalism—its insurmountable growth—Harold Wilensky in his classic piece, "The Professionalization of Everyone?"[15] argued convincingly against such an occurrence. A number of threats, according to Wilensky, exist to dampen such growth. For example, pure professional status is unlikely to be conferred on occupations where the work is supervised largely by non-professionals. In other cases, such as real estate brokerage, professionalism cannot ensue since the service provided is so commercialized that the meaning of the service ethic is reduced. Other occupations, such as sales on the one hand or technical specialties on the other, rest on a base of knowledge that is either (1) too general or vague, or (2) too narrow or specific for the practitioners to achieve autonomy. Finally, Wilensky, although applauding the development of associations that establish higher levels of training and standards of performance among a number of occupations, suggests that these structural adaptations fall short of the expertise typically obtained in programs of higher education, which are associated with the traditional professions.

As for the erosion of professionalism, it is simply not the case that most professionals who happen to work in large organizations will be swallowed up by those bureaucracies. Although management needs to integrate the services of the professional with the other activities of the organization, management also depends on the professional for those services and recognizes its limited control over the regulation of technical performance. Further, as I shall demonstrate in detail in Chapter 5, a number of accommodative mechanisms, such as the creation of the role of professional-administrator, have alleviated the potential conflict between the need for control by management and the need for autonomy by the professional. Yet to the extent the results of professional expertise and research depend on market strategy, the professional's autonomy and independence are necessarily curtailed. However, if the productivity of our society in recent years has indeed been thwarted by a research lag[16] or a dearth of creativity, the role of the professional will be protected, for our policymakers are coming to understand that the vital search for knowledge depends on the integrity of professional endeavors.

Factors Mitigating Professional/Management Conflict

Having defined the professionals who serve our organizations, we can return to our original contention: professionals imbued with the norms of the professional culture and the wider social culture have difficulty integrating into organizations guided by the different norms of the corporate culture. There are, fortunately, mitigating factors that curb the potential for widespread conflict.

These mitigating factors can be reviewed at three levels: the individual level, the job level, and the organizational level.

Individual Level

Not all professionals are the same. They undergo different types and lengths of training, sustain different prior work experiences, have different attitudes and aspirations, are different in age and sex, and so on. Among the critical individual characteristics, I have already referred to cosmopolitanism as a work orientation that makes integration into an organization particularly difficult. A cosmopolitan professional is located, according to Alvin Gouldner,[17] at one extreme of a continuum, with the so-called local at the other extreme. Each is differentiated by varying degrees of organizational loyalty, commitment to specialized skills, and orientation to outside referent groups. The cosmopolitan, being low on the first of these traits but high on the latter two, is obviously a ripe candidate for conflict with the employing organization.

On the basis of my recent research, I have developed a simple checklist to help determine whether a professional has a cosmopolitan orientation.[18] Whether the reader is a manager seeking to determine the nature of the professional staff or a professional looking to explain uncertain feelings with regard to his or her adaptation to an organization, this checklist might provide a preliminary indication of cosmopolitanism. "Yes" answers are indicative of emerging or actual cosmopolitan predispositions and thus suggest that greater care has to be taken in understanding and managing the respective professional.

Cosmopolitan Checklist

Yes No

___ ___ The person believes he should be able to make his own decisions in regard to what is to be done on the job.

___ ___ The person would probably stay in the profession even if her income were reduced.

___ ___ The person's best friends tend to be members of his profession.

___ ___ The person has little interest in moving up to a predominantly administrative position in the company.

___ ___ The person believes her professional colleagues or professional association are better equipped to evaluate her performance than management.

___ ___ The person is primarily interested in advancing his professional reputation rather than a corporate reputation.

Another common individual characteristic that can influence professional/management conflict is the occupation itself. The question here is whether certain professions are more or less prone to bu-

reaucratic conflict than others. Some professions are clearly more represented within organizations than others. Engineers, for example, are
found almost exclusively inside organizations, whereas dentists are still
predominantly in private practice. Moreover, quasi-professionals are
primarily local in orientation, and hence can be expected to experience less conflict with their managers than pure professionals. Many
quasi-professionals can become quite loyal to their employing organizations and may even aspire to eventual managerial positions. The
intermediate position of project manager, popular in so many technology-based organizations, is a virtual gateway for engineering professionals to enter the managerial ranks.

Among the critical individual-level mitigating factors, length of
training has been found to be strongly related to conflict because it
affects the professional's organizational expectations. As is detailed in
Chapter 3, length of training is indicative of the strength of socialization into the norms of the profession. PhDs, for example, enter an
organization with expectations of making unique contributions. Thus
they expect to have both the freedom and the resources to do the job
for which they were hired. The job initially is seen as an extension of
one's professional practice. Indeed, most organizations and their managers respond to this heightened sense of self-importance by granting
professionals considerable individual freedom. Unfortunately, the
honeymoon cannot last forever. Sooner or later, most professionals
will be expected to conform to the organization's mission by working
on products or providing services that will ultimately increase the rev-
enues of the enterprise.

Age and tenure are two other interrelated individual factors that
condition the professional's response to the organizational environment. Researchers have found, for example, that older workers develop stronger work values than younger ones and learn to appreciate
the realities of bureaucratic life.[19] Older professionals begin to realize
that their upward mobility may be thwarted by the hierarchical nature
of most organizations. Perhaps, on a pessimistic note, these professionals gradually adjust their aspirations to more "acceptable" standards. My own research[20] has confirmed these conclusions for profes-

sionals in the late stages of their careers. Integration within their organizations becomes much less a problem, since most of these individuals experience a gradual deterioration in their skills that, combined with more sedentary habits, lowers their interest in relocation. Their organization becomes, almost by default, a fact of life. There are certainly exceptions to this pattern. Some older professionals sustain their inherent professionalism, including updated skills, throughout their working lives. Many others express their professional commitment by serving as mentors to younger professionals just starting out in their fields. Mentorship, however, tends to entail advice to the protégé regarding organizational norms. Hence the older professional in this instance may find himself or herself in the position of fostering integration.

Besides the critical individual-level mitigating factors discussed above, many other individual factors that pertain to any kind of employee, whether professional or not, clearly affect socialization and ultimate integration into bureaucratic life. Some of these are internal considerations, such as the individual's values, attitudes, aspirations, gender, personality, or personal work ethic. Others are external circumstances, such as income, family responsibilities, and prior work experience. All the factors described here are likely to interact in affecting the ultimate disposition of the professional regarding organizational integration. For example, a young PhD scientist, although educated under conditions likely to create a cosmopolitan orientation, may have been brought up by parents who instilled in the youngster the value of rendering unswerving loyalty to institutional authority. In this case, the potential for conflict with management over work assignments and conditions would probably be moderated by the individual's family background and ingrained values.

Job Level

Job characteristics are important in mitigating professional/management conflict to the extent that for some professionals a satisfactory job may override other wider, organizational conditions. Of all the attributes that could be proposed, autonomy, or freedom to examine problems using the methods in which one has been trained, appears to be the most critical to professionals. Autonomy has indeed been cited as synonymous with the very concept of professionalism,[21] and hence is critical to the professional's role in the organization. In a recent account, the most significant issue for managing salaried professionals was depicted as the ability to resolve the dilemma between their need for autonomy and management's need for control.[22] This is a theme I shall refer to often in this book, as it can also be used to frame our ultimate purpose of mediating the clash of cultures. I examine conditions under which both managers and professionals might compromise their acculturated roles so as to serve both the organization and society. By the end of the book, I expect to have illustrated some strategies that might join the parties in fashioning a mutually rewarding enterprise—one that recognizes and approves of the professional's need for operational autonomy but also acknowledges the manager's right of organizational control.

Challenge is a second critical job characteristic that appeals to nearly all professionals. It signifies a job that allows the professional to use many skills, even some that have not been used before or have fallen into disuse. The nemesis of challenge is underutilization, which often arises out of micro division of labor. The professional typically wants to do as much of the whole job as possible so that the underlying competencies are stretched to the fullest. Professionals also tend to be interested in variety in their activities. This gives them a sense of keeping up-to-date with emerging fields of interest and not becoming over-specialized.

Besides autonomy, challenge, and variety, meaningful work is important to many professionals. They want to work on projects that will have an impact on the society around them. Some professionals even go so far as to ensure that their work has socially responsible or ethical consequences. Professionals also tend to prefer performance-based work, that is, jobs that are evaluated and paid on the basis of a final result, not by the process to produce that result. Thus accountants do not like to be told how to audit this or that firm. Given an assignment, such as examination of a firm's import and export operations, they like to proceed independently and receive feedback only when the job is done or, if it is a protracted task, at intervals.

Information the professional has about job prospects both inside and outside the organization can also mitigate professional role conflict. If a staff engineer, for example, discovers through his internal information network that the chances of his becoming a principal are minimal, he may need to lower his expectations or refocus them on opportunities outside his own organization.

Professionals are also typically interested in jobs that tap their creative or entrepreneurial instincts, that treat them in a personal way, that emphasize professional standards, and that allow them to operate without excessive supervision. These characteristics will be illustrated throughout the book, and as with the individual-level factors, I shall illustrate how they might interact and how some professionals are more affected by them than others. If a research manager notes that the professional jobs in her area are becoming more and more routinized, for example, she might find that on some of her projects the professional staff are sufficiently experienced that they can be let loose to fashion some unique approaches to their work.

Organization Level

Professionals can be found in a variety of organizations, some of which are more receptive to professional practices than others. Professionals are likely to obtain an acceptable level of control over their work in organizations in which:

— professional expertise is recognized and valued,
— professional services are in high demand, or
— administrators are knowledgeable about professional concerns (or even have come from professional backgrounds).

Specifically, greater professional identification is likely to be achievable in such organizations as universities, hospitals, government agencies, and professional service organizations, such as law, accounting, investment banking, architecture, and consulting firms, than in most industrial organizations. The former organizations not only are heavily populated by professionals but also tend to allow their professionals a fair amount of self- and peer control. Professionals in these organizations are typically vital functionaries, as is demonstrated by their contact with clients. Another distinction regarding organizational type is the degree to which the professional is subject to external jurisdiction.[23] Autonomous professional organizations, such as medical clinics or scientific institutes, are least subject to external control, followed by heteronomous professional organizations, such as public schools or social work agencies. Professionals can operate reasonably independently in these two types of organization, whereas in professional departments within larger organizations, their work tends to be largely structured by management.

Nevertheless, any organizational classification should also consider the unit within the organization where the professional works. All else being equal, size has been found to be strongly related to integration.[24] The smaller the unit, the stronger the identification with supervisors, resulting generally in reduced conflict with management and higher morale. In addition, the type of unit may affect integration potential. As an example, basic research labs are more amenable to demands for autonomy by cosmopolitan technologists than product-development or technical-service departments.

Large organizations do not automatically signify integration difficulties for professionals. Some managements, aware of the interest in autonomy among their professional staff, will purposely flatten the organizational hierarchy or decentralize by spinning off divisions which are then allowed to function rather autonomously. They may allow certain professional units to function very independently not only from other operational units but also from top management.[25] A team from a CPA firm auditing one division of a large corporation, for example, might operate very independently from another team from the same firm auditing another division of the same corporation. Both audit teams will also function without a great deal of supervision from top management. The personal autonomy of the auditors within each team may vary, however, depending upon their hierarchial level, their status, or other factors.

The managers of organizations also behave differently toward the professional staff, depending on the firm's stage of development. There is typically more tolerance for autonomous and innovative professional behavior during the growth phase of an organization. Conversely, during the mature or declining phases, and especially during times of economic insecurity, there is less tolerance of professional entrepreneurship and involvement. According to Tim Hall,[26] during times of organizational stress, most managers follow the wrong instinct of centralizing authority and consulting less with their staff. The result tends to be increased corporate control, more layers of management, more rules and procedures, and increased fragmentation of professional work.

Opportunities for professional development and integration also vary with how central the professional occupation is to the business in which the organization operates. For example, lawyers tend to become more associated with management in a financial institution than a technical firm. In the latter, their expertise may be seen as less central than in the former, where they may even be encouraged to consider line-career opportunities. Similarly, technical staff working for a commercial products firm may have a weaker basis for integrating than those working for a technical service organization.

Another organization-level characteristic mitigating conflict is the nature of the supervision given professionals. Professionals prefer to work for professionally oriented supervisors, that is, supervisors who either have professional training or who have a strong appreciation of the norms of professional practice. This can change, though, if a professional-administrator is perceived to have discarded his professional label and taken up the cause of management. Nevertheless, entree into management is another prominent method to avoid professional/management conflict, since for an administrator, the functional emphasis shifts from advising to directing, or stated another way, from staff to line. Even when a professional unit continues to perform analytic services for line management, the head of that unit, while still a professional, wears one hat—the corporate hat. The individual may even be a corporate officer. As one vice president put it, "I am an officer of the corporation who also happens to be a chemist."

Professional staff also appreciate managers who, even if uninformed about professional methods, use a laissez-faire management style. In other words, professionals will tend to respond positively to supervisors who allow them free rein to employ their professional processes, even if administrative regulations are imposed. Professionals may perceive the latter constraints as simply part of the supervisor's job.[27]

Organization-level characteristics comprise a host of conditions that in various combinations and interactions can mitigate professional/ management conflict. Many of these are discussed in Chapter 2, which explores the effect of the corporate culture on professional practice. Such familiar constructs as structure, strategy, technology, and environment are examined to the extent that they affect the expectations and resulting socialization of professionals within bureaucratic settings.

Reactions of Professionals to Conflict with Management

There are numerous conditions under which a professional can be successfully assimilated within an organization. The professional may have intentions of becoming loyal to the organization to begin with and thus will heed management's directives in spite of professional standards. The job itself may offer so many challenges that there will be little reason or time for conflict of any kind. The professional may also be assigned to a small and professionally competent unit in the organization that has been granted considerable independence in conducting its activities. The list of mitigating examples could go on and on.

Yet what about the professional who in spite of the mitigating factors continues to experience role conflict with management? To what is this conflict likely to lead? The professional first needs to make sense out of the conflict, leading to an ultimate intention, i.e., deciding whether to adjust in some way, to state one's case to management, or to leave the organization entirely. This reaction is cognitive in nature. The professional may also exhibit an attitudinal response. For example, he or she may become dissatisfied with his or her career progress, may begin to distrust the manager, or may feel less committed to the goals of the organization. I propose that the most severe reactions, however, are behavioral responses.

Elsewhere I have noted that cosmopolitan professionals, who in fact remain with their organization in spite of pressing role conflict, have the potential of exhibiting maladaptive or even deviant behavior.[28] By deviance I do not mean property deviance, which would be most characterized by theft.[29] Rather, I am referring to production deviance, which is signified by some kind of interruption in one's professional practice inside the organization. This deviance might be exemplified by doing only the work required, exhibiting busyness, focusing attention more on outside interests than on work, manifesting boredom and apathy, engaging in unethical practices, becoming truant, or continuously flaunting outside job offers.

Maladaptive behavior can be detrimental to both the individual and the organization. For the individual it represents a constant source of strain, because the behavior does not resolve the conflict causing it. Resolution would result either from an adaptive response, such as becoming less cosmopolitan, or from leaving the organization. Maladaptiveness keeps the individual in a holding pattern. The organization, meanwhile, though not losing the individual, retains a disenchanted member whose practice may now conflict with the accomplishment of organizational objectives. It too is frustrated in achieving successful resolution of the role conflict; indeed, the strain has the potential to spread to other organization members.

Thus maladaptive behavior, as well as negative cognitive and attitudinal responses, constitutes an undesirable result of professional/ management conflict. Professionals become increasingly resistant to organizational purpose, and their antipathy toward management may even escalate. Clearly, management needs not only to neutralize these unfortunate consequences of conflict but to anticipate and prevent them through strategies that somehow accommodate professional interests while sustaining organizational task accomplishment.

The professional who chooses to leave the organization will probably cease his or her maladaptive behavior for a time. Many of these same behaviors are likely to resurface in the next organizational position, however, unless the professional or the new organization has different role expectations or unless more suitable methods of accommodating conflict are found. Hence, there is a need for both parties to monitor expectations.

This book, then, is an attempt to isolate the potential sources of role conflict between the professional and management through examination of the express cultural differences between these two parties. Each has a different set of expectations from the other, and some of these expectations clash. Sometimes, especially with the presence of some of the mitigating factors discussed earlier, these expectations may become mutual. I shall orient the discussion, however, to those cases where expectations are discrepant. Thus, although I am concerned about everyday experience between salaried professionals and managers, I am particularly interested in ways to manage conflict before it causes maladaptive behavior and other negative consequences.

After presenting the cultural positions of the parties in the next three chapters, along with examples of conflict management and mismanagement, in the final chapter I shall explicitly consider remedial strategies directed to managers of professionals. Opportunities for professional adaptation will also be included, however. The book, then, will follow the scientific method of diagnosis followed by prescription. The final step of any problem-solving method is action. After concluding this account, the manager of professionals in conjunction with the professional staff should be poised to take action.

The Corporate Culture 2

In this chapter, I examine the critical corporate cultural factors affecting professional behavior. The factors explored here relate to the overemphasis by most American managers on control over their professional employees. Granted, the job of management has become extraordinarily complex as organizations and markets have grown and become differentiated. There is a need, consequently, to integrate the parts of the enterprise. But integration need not be converted into tight control, which has the unfortunate side effect of constricting professional practice. Nor is it advisable to isolate professionals from the mainstream of the organization. Rather, professionals need to be viewed as highly skilled potential contributors who work best when given considerable autonomy combined with a sense of corporate purpose. Management ultimately relies on its professionals to stretch the potential of the enterprise, to make the job of management more concise or easier, to develop new ideas, and to ensure that the organization adapts to the future.

The chapter looks at the corporate culture from the professional's viewpoint. Hence the intent is to describe the factors of the corporate culture that limit the opportunity for professionals to realize their potential in work and at the same time contribute to the organization. In the next chapter, the roles are reversed. There, I take management's point of view so as to explain the barriers to effective utilization and integration of professionals erected by the professional culture. In this way, I shall be building a case that, when combined with an understanding of the wider social culture, will make way in the last chapter for the elucidation of explicit strategies for uniting the parties.

This chapter begins with an exploration of the constraints imposed on professionals by overspecialization, a condition that obtains when the professional's job is so narrowly defined that the generic competency is lost. In a similar vein, I next show how management compounds the problem of overspecialization by overspecifying the professional's day-to-day activities. Yet while interfering with the actual details of the professional's work, management does not sufficiently specify the overall corporate mission: I refer to this shortcoming as underspecification of ends. Overspecification of means can also lead to close supervision, a corporate practice that is shown to produce considerable strain among professionals who prefer general supervision, especially by professionally trained administrators, supplemented by peer control and self-management. The subject of control is examined in a subsequent section on formalization, which is shown in many instances to have a dampening effect on professional performance and creativity.

The chapter then turns to some of the more human dimensions in the corporate work setting, beginning with a discussion of job challenge, the lack of which underutilizes the precise skills for which professionals are hired. In the ensuing section on organizational impersonalness, I suggest that while some companies treat their professionals with respect, they do not trust them sufficiently to allow them to make work-related decisions on their own or as a group. Similarly, lack of entrepreneurship occurs when professionals lose the freedom to work on their own projects without constant managerial interference. Finally, unstable employment practices constitute an extension of the problem of impersonal treatment of professionals.

Overspecialization

Perhaps out of the strong tradition of individualism, American corporate culture has stressed the need for professionals to master specialized skills so that the individual becomes recognized as a master of his or her personal contribution to the total package of product or service. Ironically, individualism throughout pre-twentieth-century industrial practice was converted to more entrepreneurial work pursuits. The craft mentality suggested a need to develop comprehensive skills associated with the entire product or service. With the advent of the factory system and the concept of division of labor, the craft mentality made way for the onslaught of mass-production principles based on economies of scale and specialization. The Scientific Management school, deriving largely from the work of Frederick W. Taylor,[1] popularized and even made respectable the principle of specialization by showing how tremendous efficiencies could be achieved by breaking down each job into a series of related tasks and subtasks. Applied mainly to unskilled and semiskilled workers, Scientific Management theory considered a worker to be merely an extension of a machine whose exacting performance of some carefully planned mindless tasks would lead to maximum production.

Although Taylor's work has been almost entirely discredited because of the extreme manner in which it treated workers, the notion of efficiency through specialization persists. The genius of American management practice, especially emphasized during the military build-up and management of two theaters of war in World War II, was the ability to coordinate diverse yet common parts of a huge machine. Infantrymen and artillerymen were taught the same set of procedures wherever they were located, and the centralized orchestration of this incredible mass of people in war resulted in a feat of management rarely, if ever, seen before.

The tradition has continued. One need not be semiskilled to engage in specialized practice. Indeed, it is expected that the special skills a professional learns in training will be made available for explicit corporate tasks. The professional need not worry about the ultimate aim of the enterprise. Professionals are hired to exercise their precise skills: it is management's assignment to worry about integration.

Industry works hand in hand with the professional schools to continue to emphasize the need for specialization. The corporation is not hiring a generalist. Again, managers perform that function (although most concerns also compartmentalize the management function, for example, by requiring specialization vis-à-vis location of clients, industry accounts, management function—operations, sales, distribution—and so on). If a professional hired to perform a given staff assignment does not work out, there are countless others equally well trained in the skill at issue.

One study of the career paths of fifty managers and professionals in some of America's largest firms over a thirty-year span found that financial and personnel specialists were unlikely to have worked in any other specialty in those thirty years![2] It is no wonder, then, that integration has to be provided by an external source. A professional devoting so much time to one specialty is highly unlikely to spend much time communicating with another professional trained and nurtured in a completely different specialty.

The concept of overprofessionalization signifies exclusive concentration on one's professional skills, to the exclusion of organizational considerations. Upon entering a new company, professional employees are expected to practice the precise technical skills for which they were trained (if fresh out of school) or that they mastered in their former job or jobs. Thus the socialization process in most American corporate cultures complements the practice of overprofessionalization. The electrical engineer is hired to work on circuit design, not fabrication or assembly. The accountant is expected to continue her auditing work with the oil and gas industry. Moves to other functions are infrequent in most American companies if one starts with a specialized professional skill. The way to avoid corporate overspecialization is to move into management, where corporate policy appears to be more flexible and enlightened. Management, for the most part, is seen as a broad task entailing leadership over the wide array of functions carried out within the enterprise. Professional practice, on the other hand, is by definition specialized.

The task of coordinating these professionals, who are socialized not to relinquish their specialty for fear of obsolescence or, worse, job loss, is left to management. Occasionally, managers are assigned to bring together a group of specialists to work as a team. Contributors stay with their function but are encouraged to broaden their skills to improve links with other members of the team. These teams can become quite productive, especially when professional members begin acting in a responsive and undistracted manner. They no longer require assistance in deciphering their new jobs and organizational surroundings, feel comfortable with one another, trust their technical manager, and can be less concerned with protecting their exclusive skills. Ralph Katz[3] reports, however, that such teams are relatively short-lived; they may last up to five years. Interpersonal and external factors gradually lead to a growing unresponsiveness, to more established and, hence, less innovative forms of behavior. Team members during this phase may return to their overprofessionalized response patterns.

The obvious implication is that it is important to keep these teams moving, changing their membership on a periodic basis. Constant resocialization of specialized members takes a great deal of time, however. Only if the corporate culture permits and even encourages skill enlargement can groupings form that offer potential for innovation and productive work.

Effects on Individual and Professional Behavior

Specialization can be effective in industrial practice only where there are means of coordinating the diverse parts. Yet this is quite difficult to accomplish in the case of professional employment. By tradition, professionals prefer to listen to other, like professionals. If management is not trained in the specialty, how can it offer advice, control procedures, and understand how one function really relates to another? Posing questions like these, salaried professionals will insist on self-management. They will insist on controlling their contribution to the production function. Only when they have completed their part will it be advisable for the manager to come forward to link this part with the next sequence of events in the production or process chain. The more the professional is willing to relax insistence on specialized procedures demanded by the profession, obviously the easier it will be to coordinate the parts.

The NASA Apollo program (the subsequent problems with the Shuttle notwithstanding) was a good example of effective coordination among specialized professional subcontractors who willingly relaxed rigid assumptions about professional practice for the good of a superordinate goal—landing a man on the moon. Countless examples can be cited of the reverse tendency—supporting analytical detachment and methodological rigor in one's field at the expense of the integrated whole. The result can be a severe loss of perspective in which technological development can go awry in its social and economic effects. Robert McNamara's "whiz kid" mentality, based on technical excellence in a manufacturing concern, led the United States astray in Vietnam. Technical malfunction at Three Mile Island, public and private bankruptcies such as New York City, Braniff, and Johns Manville, the U.S. government deficit, the chemical contamination of Love Canal, and other such events have shaken our confidence in the ability of professionals to advance our civilization. Certainly the blame for the economic component of any social malaise cannot be placed solely on the shoulders of professionals, but we may wonder whether our economic enterprises in particular have been capable of pulling together their human and capital resources to compete in the international arena. Hayes and Abernathy[4] found that excessive use of financial and analytical formulas may have contributed to timidity in our allocation of resources. Is it possible that in relying on this technical information management has given up some of its former intuitive insight? As professionals enshroud their skills with an aura of sophistication approaching the mysterious, it is no wonder that they have created a domain that their own bosses fear to enter.

The effect of overspecialization on professional behavior is quite predictable. A cultural contract exists that calls for a loose attachment between employer and employee. The professional is hired to provide specialized expertise in a given function within the organization. As long as the professional's expertise is needed, corporate officials will do whatever they can to retain that employee. If, however, the professional's skill is in high demand, he or she will not hesitate to entertain other offers. The original employer will understand this process and will reluctantly let the professional go if the offer cannot be matched. To stay marketable, it behooves the professional to keep up-to-date in the technical area in which he or she specializes. It is vital that one's professional reputation remain intact. Maintaining one's reputation can be furthered by keeping in touch with the professional network and publishing in professional journals.

The net effect of this cultural contract, however, is to discourage the development of intimacy and loyalty to one's organization. Intimacy and loyalty suggest a tighter attachment to the employer than what might be in the professional's best interest in the marketplace. The longer a professional stays with one employer, the less attractive he or she may appear to other organizations, which suspect two forces associated with longevity: 1) the professional is gradually becoming socialized to the original organization's way of doing things and may be less capable of adjusting to a new climate; or 2) the professional's original expertise may be becoming obsolete.

Hence, professionals need to keep moving. One never knows when a better opportunity will emerge or when an employer will no longer need one's services. It is important continually to nurture new contacts and to stay professionally active. There is a paradox in all this, however. Overspecialization often creates the precise conditions that lead to obsolescence. Obsolescence has been defined as "the degree to which organizational professionals lack the up-to-date knowledge or skills necessary to maintain effective performance in either their cur-

rent or future work roles."[5] Since specialization requires the performance of tasks largely governed by fixed and standardized procedures, it
is quite likely that professionals will become redundant as they apply a
constant set of skills. They may also become increasingly compart-
mentalized as they become functionally and even geographically separated from other professionals. The only ways out of this dilemma are
to enlarge the job or to leave the organization for more challenging
opportunities elsewhere. Since management expects professionals to
do the precise work for which they were hired, the latter alternative
offers the greatest hope for returning to state-of-the-art practice. Of
course, organizational transitions are not always available or even personally desirable.

Exceptions

Not all American companies insist that their professionals remain specialized in the technical skills for which they were hired. Some recognize that professionals need continuous growth and challenge on
the job and thus encourage transition to other operations in the same
field or even to completely different technical fields. These companies, then, are more interested in hiring the individual who, though
trained in a specialty, can be a broad contributor to the organization.
They recognize that this individual's growth will be converted to a lim-
itless fountain of potential for the organization. So, they unleash the
individual to try new things. They are willing to invest in continuous
training and development. As long as the professional is willing to devote his or her energies to the business, management encourages
rather than blocks the expansion of professional skills and interests.

At 3M (Minnesota Mining and Manufacturing), a phenomenally
successful company that has been widely written about as a model of
the American corporate form, although the best chemical engineers
are sought to serve its diverse product line, the company does not allow
them to remain isolated in their specialty. They are almost immediately transformed into "3M engineers" and stripped of any prior distinction as university stars or former corporate specialists. These

professionals soon all belong to 3M, held together by a common thread of technology, 3M's basic bonding and coating technique. Moreover, like the research engineers at Bechtel, they are shunted off to the line to learn the principal businesses of the corporation. This ensures that any applications they may be working on will be sufficiently practical to be manufactured and to be marketed to the company's customer base.

Once socialized in this way, however, the professionals are constantly given opportunities to develop, to try new things, to expand their knowledge. Each division has many small, independent new-venture teams whose principal assignment is to try something new. There is also a New Business Venture Division at 3M, which further institutionalizes the freedom to test and expand on one's professional knowledge.[6] The company clearly recognizes that its success depends not only on the loyalty but also on the creativity of its professional work force.

Underspecification of Ends, Overspecification of Means

Perhaps the most critical problem management faces in its association with professionals is how to handle the professional's insistence on autonomy. This desire for autonomy clashes with the expectations of management regarding the proper role of the employee. Employees are hired presumably to conform to the basic goals and procedures of the enterprise. For the most part, management will not tolerate professionals establishing their own agendas and being controlled by their own peers.

The problem of autonomy is best addressed by breaking it down into two distinct parts: autonomy over ends and autonomy over means.[7] Autonomy over ends, or strategic autonomy, is the more traditional view, encompassing the freedom to select the problems to examine independent of directives from anywhere save the precepts of one's discipline. Lotte Bailyn[8] found relatively few professionals in the R&D

labs where she conducted detailed interviews who wanted this kind of autonomy. Her sample was more interested in autonomy over means, or operational autonomy, i.e., the freedom, once a problem has been set, to attack it by means determined by oneself but within organizational resource and strategic constraints.

I will show in this section that although professionals may not be interested in autonomy over ends, they do wish to have the ends defined. However, management sometimes makes the mistake of concentrating more on specifying the means of the professional's practice than the ends. This conflicts with the professional's desire for operational autonomy.

Underspecification of Ends

With the exception of those working for universities or for government and industrial laboratories in basic research, most professionals will accede to the right of management to establish the goals for the organization and to specify how the units in the organization will interact to achieve these goals. If professionals are given the authority to develop proposals on their own, these proposals are typically reviewed for their conformity to the organization's mission. Of course, enlightened managers, recognizing the value of a strongly motivated professional staff, will go to great lengths to sponsor the pet projects of their talented professionals as long as they fall within the company's general strategy. In a similar vein, some organizations allow their professionals to refuse to work on certain projects that do not coincide with their professional interests.

For the most part, however, corporate management expects its professional staff to work on assignments that are determined to be valuable. In some of the research organizations in which I conducted interviews, I found that some professionals were allowed to allocate a small portion of their time (say 10 percent) to projects outside their current assignment. Unfortunately, I got a sense from the professionals that they were so busy they typically never got around to working on these sidelights. Further, those that did still ended up working on projects of practical interest to the company.

The nature and management style of the organization aside, professionals may retain strategic autonomy in two circumstances. One is when they hold advanced degrees, doctorates in particular. Companies seem interested in accommodating the strategic interests of these professionals. Research has found, for example, some marked differences between engineers with and without doctorates regarding professional values and behavior, such as interest in advancing scientific knowledge[9] or the likelihood of participating in determining work assignments.[10]

Second, corporate management can become quite tolerant of professionals who have amassed a record of successes in the projects in which they have been involved. One technical manager whom I interviewed stated that especially when business conditions are good, his company always makes room for so-called new-project crusaders. These people have shown, however, that they can translate their theories into practice, and that the projects ultimately developed will benefit the company in some way. At another high-tech company, I was told that the corporation had released several million dollars of resources to a professional to start up a new telemarketing operation. This professional had achieved this level of autonomy, however, because of a proven track record both in his own company and previous jobs, because he was trusted and well liked, and, finally, because he was considered senior enough to manage the sums involved. Hence, to release a spark of innovation that might lead to a major new market, corporate management may be willing to grant enormous responsibilities to certain proven contributors. This indulgence of key professionals, however, is rarely without some self-interest on the part of the corporation. On the one hand, management often recognizes long-term potential in sponsoring the projects of these talented individuals; on the other, it realizes that without such support, many of these professionals might simply go to work for other companies or perhaps even start their own businesses, either of which could lead to subsequent competitive pressures.

Outside of these exceptions having to do with duration of training, quality of performance, and organizational nature and style, professionals on the whole are willing to abide by the principles and purposes of their organizations. Working in a totally independent fashion would promote isolation and contribute to very limited personal or social ends. On joining an organization, the professional recognizes the give and take of the psychological contract ironed out with the employer. Each party wishes not only to advance his or its own needs but to contribute to the achievement of the other's goals. Problems arise mainly when there is confusion about the goals each is striving to reach.

This is where underspecification of ends can lead to difficulties in managing professionals. Professionals, like all employees, need to know what the organization is about. Management cannot afford to get so caught up in day-to-day operational details that it forgets what the enterprise stands for. Unfortunately, it is sometimes much easier to work on details than on the guiding values that inform the organization's spirit and purpose. This latter pursuit, which I refer to as specifying the ends, has been communicated by consultants to the corporate community as a need to identify one's corporate culture. According to the corporate culture advocates, there is no more important job in management than shaping and enhancing the values that guide the behavior of everyone in the corporate community. These values need to be communicated in a variety of ways, from explicit statements to implicit symbols, to ensure that people know what the company is about and what the acceptable standards of behavior are. Unfortunately, in some complicated organizations that are, for example, multidivisional and multiproduct or that operate in fast-paced technological environments, it is unfair to expect management to produce a cultural vision on cue. Strategy is sometimes a property that emerges rather than is intended and may benefit from occasional non-conformance to current directions.[11] Yet management can seek to define broad boundaries around what the organization is doing. Organizations that have strong cultures, in this sense, do not need to rely on excessive rules and procedures. After an intensive period of socialization, i.e., learning the ropes, professional employees simply know what to expect. They can maintain a balance between conformity and autonomy because they know what the standards are and how far they can stretch the boundaries of acceptable behavior.

Exception: Specifying the Ends at IBM

IBM is a prime example of a company with a strong culture which, through its legendary presidents, Thomas Watson, Sr. and Thomas Watson, Jr., specified its beliefs and values for all its employees. IBM's beliefs can be found not only in its *Orientation Booklet,* but in the hearts and minds of its devoted employees. There are three strong beliefs: 1) respect for the individual, 2) customer service, and 3) excellence. Beyond these beliefs, IBM also issues a set of fundamental principles to guide its employees' conduct. These principles deal with such issues as managerial talent, technological development, employee development, stockholders' return, and social responsibility. Watson, Jr., in his McKinsey Foundation Lectures, suggested that these beliefs and principles were more responsible for the company's success than its technological and economic resources or its organizational structure, innovation, and timing.[12] They also constitute absolutes in the sense that whatever else may change, they remain constant.

To an outsider, these beliefs may seem vague or overly general. Inside the company, however, they are reinforced through countless practices that embody the IBM culture. Professionals at IBM learn quickly what is appropriate and what is not. They know how much autonomy they can carve out within the confines of the corporate value system. The values do create some constraints on professional practice, but few would say they are overly constraining. The first and third beliefs, for example—respect for the individual and excellence— militate against the establishment of an overly conforming organization. Indeed, IBM is known for its tolerance of professionals who can come up with new ideas and who are willing to take the risk of challenging untested assumptions.

Symbolic of this tolerance, Watson was known to have told a "wild ducks" story countless times to spur the risk-taking behavior of his professional and managerial staff.[13] The story was about a nature lover who enjoyed watching the wild ducks fly south each fall. Out of kindness, he began to put food for them in a nearby pond. Lo and behold, some of them, relying on his food to get through the winter, no longer bothered to fly south. After several years, some even grew so fat and lazy that they found it difficult to fly at all. The moral of the story, according to Watson, was that you can make wild ducks tame, but you can never make tame ducks wild again. At IBM, he wanted to be sure that the company never tried to tame its wild ducks.

As an addendum to this story, on one occasion an employee reportedly told Watson that even wild ducks fly in formation. Watson, agreeing with this point, used the information to draw a further analogy to the IBM culture: "We're all going in the same direction." Nothing could better demonstrate IBM's commitment at the top to specify the ends.

Overspecification of Means

While management can often be accused of vagueness in communicating its values and beliefs to its professionals, it can also be guilty of overcontrolling the means of professional practice. Professionals desire autonomy over many of the operational decisions associated with their work. For example, a project engineer would most likely prefer to:

1. initiate modifications in project policies and procedures
2. have final approval with project management on engineering, design, and construction methods
3. review project progress reports and make corrections if necessary
4. participate in selecting the junior engineer, technician, and design personnel for the team
5. prepare final cost reports for headquarters
6. review customer-organization scheduling progress
7. act as arbitrator of team-member technical grievances[14]

Professionals are hired to apply specialized knowledge to a host of unstructured problems. Solutions to such problems are ordinarily developed through individual problem-solving processes.[15] No amount of administrative procedure or regulation will necessarily cause the problems to be solved more quickly or more efficiently. Yet professionals are sometimes obliged to report very specifically on their activities.

Their preference is that control be exerted at the point of results. Given a schedule, the professional simply attempts to get the job done.

Accordingly, he or she will seek to establish personal, systematic methods for approaching and solving the problem. Of course, consultations will be sought, sometimes quite frequently, with colleagues at similar or higher levels who therefore exert implicit control over the professional's activities. In a law firm, for example, a senior partner might provide an associate with a small research assignment, upon completion of which there will be a discussion of the merits of the attorney's work. As mistakes are gradually eliminated, the associate will work with increasing operational autonomy.

Management is reluctant, nevertheless, to allow professionals—and even professional-administrators—to control the means of their practice unless they can become convinced that the professional staff understands the full economic purpose of the entity. One way of developing an interest in a business is to promote contact between the professional staff and the users of the organization's products or services. In research laboratories, scientists and engineers might be encouraged to maintain contact with clients even to the point of promoting new business. In one lab I visited, this practice was thought to be the principal reason there was so much loyalty to the organization. Each professional staffer had a stake in the company through the promotion of a project. The professional was given a great deal of latitude in working out details of the project with the client, so that success or failure rested heavily on the professional's own initiative.

Companies often hold periodic planning meetings to discuss particular product lines with which some of their research staff may be associated. These meetings are attended by representatives from marketing, sales, and production, as well as R&D. For companies that are not organized on a project or matrix basis, these meetings are essential to give professional researchers a sense of the results of their efforts. Problems surfacing on some of the company's current products are ironed out, and the researchers' ideas about some of the firm's new ventures are solicited. Especially where research professionals are relatively isolated in their day-to-day functions, it is critical to expose them to internal users, whether through formal meetings or through informal channels of communication.

Professionals can also minimize difficulties arising from managerial incursions on their autonomy by working with their managers to obtain the most appropriate placements in the organization. Some jobs in any organization require more independence of thought and action than others, even at comparable levels. Professionals who wish to take more responsibility for their own work and who have proven their ability to use their discretion in a dependable manner can be assigned to some of these positions. If jobs of this nature do not currently exist, perhaps some positions can be redesigned or enriched.

In industrial research organizations, there are typically clear differences in autonomy between jobs in research, in development, and in technical service. Research projects generally allow the most discretion, since they are primarily concerned with the discovery of new knowledge. Professionals work relatively unhampered by operational constraints. They keep themselves up-to-date, typically through intensive collegial interaction and external contacts.

Development projects, on the other hand, involve more operational control, since they tend to be tied to the organization's particular markets, interests, language schemes, and cultural norms.[16] These projects translate ideas into tangible outcomes by making use of the company's existing strengths in technology, marketing, production, and so on. Professionals here need to stay in touch with technical developments outside their organization but also must maintain close ties with other internal functions. There is less opportunity to deviate from established procedures than in the pure research setting.

Finally, technical service projects tend to be extremely local. Since they deal with existing product lines, they rely heavily on established practices and procedures. Professionals performing service work face the least operational autonomy.

Management usually has no trouble filling its research and development slots, but may find some difficulty in recruiting professionals to do service work. Further, some managements do not like to segregate the three research functions completely, because there are obvious benefits in keeping the activities interdependent. Basic research, for example, has to be at least generally tied to existing technical capabilities, something the other two functions know a lot about. Therefore, professionals may occasionally be asked to blend their responsibilities, or at least if they are doing research, to be available to perform vital service duties when necessary. In most of the technical organizations I interviewed, research professionals reported having to switch hats from time to time to provide back-up to emergency service projects. Many complained that this process constituted an incursion on their work and said they would prefer not to be interrupted. Nevertheless, they did appear sensitive to management's need to interrupt them in this way.

Perhaps no activity illustrates more clearly the conflict between professionals' desire for operational autonomy and management's need for control than the project-termination decision. Projects are terminated for any number of reasons. A given project may simply appear less desirable, given available resources, than other competing projects. As a project proceeds in development, more accurate information can be obtained than was available at inception. Projected returns from the project, as well as cost and time constraints, may make it appear less attractive than it was originally.[17] Market and technical factors may also change the complexion of the project. R&D management recognizes these constraints on its research projects and is usually willing to take the risk of promoting long shots. This is done, however, with the knowledge that few of them (in some companies, no more than one of ten) will ever reach the marketplace.

It is one thing for a manager to accept the inevitability of project terminations but another to expect a professional who has committed extended time to a project to turn away gracefully. In my own research, I have found it is ordinarily factors outside the professional's purview that lead to terminations.[18] For example, the sheer number of projects in the R&D portfolio, the innovativeness of the research, or the lack of specificity in the target markets are associated with project abandonment. On the other hand, human factors such as professional and managerial commitment and the presence of a project champion are associated with project successes. Hence, as Peter Mullins pointed out,[19] the willingness to cooperate among technical professionals is critical to R&D success. He advised management to avoid cutbacks in

R&D budgets as a way of convincing the professional staff of the firm's commitment to research. He also called on management to allow the professional staff more discretion in the selection of research projects.

As I shall detail more precisely in the next chapter, professionals, rather then communicating their dissatisfaction with a lack of operational autonomy, tend to seek ways, usually through indirect means, to gain greater control over their work. The resulting behavior is often adaptive to the circumstances, but can it become maladaptive. For example, some professionals may respond to management's insistence on a precise accounting of their project activities by purposely making their reports vague. Although the reports are filled out, the professional hopes to create sufficient latitude that he or she can deviate from the original course of the project should circumstances demand it. Professionals also engage in bootlegging, undertaking projects on their own time and without the clearance of the manager responsible for the budget. Bootlegging constitutes a prime example of the professional's thirst for autonomy. Fortunately, much bootlegging, although initiated out of the professional's own interest, can eventually be incorporated in the company's business, resulting in some cases in highly successful ventures. On the other hand, bootlegging carried to the extreme can pull the professional away from the company's strategic interests and result in mediocre performance on key corporate projects.

Close Supervision

We have concluded that professionals generally desire autonomy over the means of their work but not necessarily the ends. Similarly, they wish to work under general and not close supervision.

In most organizations, supervision occurs through two channels. Executive supervision takes the form of directives from top management. Top managers set the overall corporate policy and perform vital coordinating functions, such as linking the operating units with each other and with headquarters or, interacting with other organizations in the company's environment. For the most part, this executive guidance is experienced by the professional employee as general supervision. Only rarely does it become specific, as in the case of a salary exception or a major infraction of company policy. Executive supervision, then, falls into the category of specification of ends, which most professionals are quite willing to accept.

What is known as first-line supervision, or direction from one's immediate supervisor, can fall within the category of specification of means, and it is here that the difficulty lies. Professional work typically requires a great deal of flexibility, creativity, and intellectual analysis. It is filled with exceptions. Further, in some settings, the professional needs to maintain close contact with the client, which requires flexibility of response. Hence the classic notion of supervision as "bossing," in other words, requiring the professional to adhere to prescribed rules and standards, is not always valid or appropriate. Essentially, many of the traditional supervisory functions are transferred to the professional employee in the form of self-supervision and peer control. The supervisor's job becomes basically developmental and coordinative. The supervisor is responsible for providing resources and support for the professional's work and for ensuring integration among the relevant operating units. Supervision does not have to be close, since the methods for doing the work are established by the professional. Supervision of professional employees should focus more on results than process. This means that the first-line supervisor becomes responsible for setting the goals to be achieved within reasonable time limits and for setting the general norms of behavior.[20] Day-to-day operational problems are handled for the most part by the professionals themselves. It is better to have professionals solicit the help of their managers when necessary to resolve resource or personality conflicts than to impose explicit rules or norms on them. In a fluid work environment, any rule or norm can quickly become outdated or inoperable.

What besides development and coordination do professionals look for from their supervisors? My research suggests they prefer professionally oriented to administratively oriented supervisors.[21] That is, they want supervisors who either belong to the profession or who, if not professional by training, have somehow managed to make themselves technically competent. The reason is simply that professionals want to concern themselves with technical rather than administrative problems. They do not object to rules and regulations designed to address professional concerns. As long as the supervisor can display an appreciation for the professional's problems and act in a way that helps resolve them, prospects are good for a compatible working relationship. Fortunately, there are many supervisors who are professionally trained and secure in their professional reputation and who also see their supervisory role as promoting the interests of the profession in their organizations. This is, of course, the best of all worlds, since the supervisor in this instance embodies the integration of cosmopolitan and local orientations.

Some organizations, acknowledging this approach to professional supervision, select their supervisors strictly on the basis of professional, rather than administrative, competence. Universities, research laboratories, and professional service firms tend to select supervisors or managers from the ranks of professionals. There is a growing trend, however, among other professionally based organizations, such as hospitals and schools, to find administrators who are specially trained in management, in addition to or even beyond their technical competence. Most of the professional graduate schools, for example, have added administration-oriented departments, and this has become a very popular field of concentration. It is now common to find departments of educational administration, health-care administration, public administration, and even human-services administration. Perhaps this marks an attempt to professionalize management, suggesting that there are principles of administration for these various professionally based enterprises that should be systematically taught to potential supervisors.

Professionals do not object to this management trend in their professions, but only insofar as new supervisors are first well grounded in the precepts and practices of their profession. In too many instances, professional supervisors have little or no experience in the profession before they become managers.

Young professionals, in particular, need the technical and gatekeeping experience of sound professional supervisors. It has been reported, for example, that young CPAs in accounting firms suffer from a lack of fixed superior-subordinate relationships among partners and staff.[22] In fact, supervisory relationships are infrequent and where they do occur, they center largely on paperwork outside the firm. Having to handle a variety of assignments, the young CPA often has to "punt" in his or her relations with the client, since there is not enough time for supervisory consultations on the appropriate technical skill to apply.

The gatekeeping function, sometimes performed through a mentor and/or one's supervisor, is critical to the young professional. The gatekeeper can assist in the socialization process, ensuring that the professional learns the ropes, especially when it comes to understanding and interpreting the reality of the new setting in order to function more effectively.[23] Gatekeepers also can introduce young professionals to outside contacts. Naturally, the critical gatekeeping role can only be filled by a supervisor who remains professionally active. The supervisor who chooses to extend loyalty exclusively to the organization and who simply maintains his professional memberships without active participation or involvement may be viewed as having "sold out."

Apart from the supervisor's substantive contribution, there are style considerations. This is where the notion of close supervision really comes into play. Close supervision is usually considered an end point of a continuum, with something called general or loose supervision at the other end. It cannot be defined precisely in terms of number of hours per day, because it will obviously vary depending on the setting, the task, and other contextual factors. Yet most professionals could tell you whether their supervisor uses close or general supervision.

An extreme form of general supervision is laissez-faire supervision, in which the supervisor virtually leaves the professional alone except to receive the results of the completed assignment. Close supervision, on the other hand, also referred to as tight or direct supervision, involves frequent requests for explanation of and control over the professional's work.

Another continuum used to describe supervisory styles, depicted in

Figure 2-1, extends from authoritarian control to participation. The authoritarian, or "tell," supervisor assumes that, being fully responsible for the professional's work, he or she must tell the subordinate exactly what to do on any assignment. The professional is then expected to follow the supervisor's commands. The participative, or "join," supervisor, at the other end of the continuum, acknowledges the professional's technical expertise and invites his full participation in any decision about the work at hand. Together, supervisor and subordinate work out the parameters of the professional's assignment.

As in any continuum, there are intermediate styles. For example, a supervisor, after personally examining a work-related problem, may attempt to "sell" or guide the professional toward a preconceived solution. This style is obviously to the right of the pure tell type, since the supervisor allows for some input into the decision, although he or she will most likely attempt to persuade the professional to go along with the preconceived solution. A supervisor may also "consult" with the professional staff, honestly consider its viewpoints, and then make the final decision. This type of style is to the left of the pure join type, since it does not accord the professional staff responsibility for and full participation in the decision. Studies of professionals have concluded that they prefer general and/or participative supervisors.[24] Few profes-

Figure 2-1   A Four-Style Supervisory Continuum

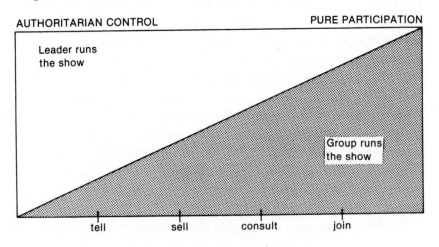

sionals have ever expressed an interest in receiving close supervision except when the task at hand is new or unfamiliar.

Peer Control

Peer control and self-management can substitute for supervision in evaluating the performance of professionals. Supervisors who lack technical competence may simply not be qualified to evaluate technical performance. In addition, unless supervisors engage in inadvisable close supervision, it is nearly impossible for them to assess important social or interpersonal skills, such as willingness to cooperate, loyalty to one's colleagues, or initiation of ideas.

Peer control is a particularly appropriate method of supervision for professionals working in homogeneous groups or teams. Indeed, the group in this setting becomes a very powerful socializing agent. Professionals dealing with others in the same discipline are subject to very subtle pressures to perform, and—provided the reward system is based on group rather than individual performance—to help one another. Peer evaluation becomes more complicated in interdisciplinary teams. In these situations, not every professional may be willing to submit to evaluation by coworkers. For the method to work effectively, there must be a high level of trust, respect, and sharing among the peers of the group, as well as a noncompetitive reward system. Interdisciplinary team members may allow peer evaluations under these conditions but probably will insist that the evaluations be limited to nontechnical aspects of their work performance.

One comparison of peer and supervisory evaluations in R&D revealed that peer evaluations were more specific, could discriminate better between technical and social skills, were no more lenient, and were not affected by friendship or enmity among colleagues.[25] As expected, peer evaluations were most effective where the professionals participated in setting the assessment criteria. Peer evaluation, then, can be a very effective way of establishing control in a professional work group, whether the system in effect is formal or informal. It can also free the supervisor to spend more time interacting with his or her own peers (i.e., other department heads), rather than having to worry constantly about the performance of the professional staff. This is not to suggest that the criteria for effective evaluation of professional work are always succinct and universally accepted by one's peer group. In such fields as education and psychotherapy, professionals may not even agree on what constitutes a successful outcome for the student or client. Nevertheless, professionals desire to work out these criteria of performance among themselves.

Self-Management

The preceding discussion raises the possibility of professionals, as mature people, relying on themselves to gauge their performance. Many of their methods have built-in checks that require almost a programmed learning style of practice. The physician, for example, in narrowing down a diagnosis, will have the patient undergo a series of tests that essentially serve to evaluate a rational set of hypotheses about the suspected cause of the illness.

Nevertheless, self-management can rarely be relied upon as the sole means of control. A well-known research study of scientists by Donald Pelz and Frank Andrews[26] found that those who were influential in their companies and who worked on diverse problems profited the most from self-management. Most of the scientists in the study performed best, however, when other sources such as colleagues, senior professionals, or supervisors helped them formulate their work goals. These findings are consistent with our earlier discussion regarding the professional's interest in operational rather than strategic autonomy. Once the supervisor or professional-administrator has discussed expectations regarding the product or outcome of the professional's work, the latter prefers to work autonomously; i.e., to develop independently the necessary procedures to reach the mutually agreed-upon goal. Self-management, then, is critical to the process of the professional's work. The exception to this is Pelz's and Andrews' finding on specialization. Scientists who concentrate on making new discoveries in a specialized area need the assistance of colleagues to corroborate or refute their theories. On the other hand, those who cover broad areas tend to do best on their own. Some of this is of course explained by experience. The specialists often tend to be younger, while the generalists tend to be the older, more experienced, and more senior professionals. The latter have amassed the necessary organizational and professional experience to work more independently.

The Chairperson—A Thankless Job

In the academic world, the role of the supervisor is played by the department chairperson. I have talked with scores of such individuals and only rarely have heard someone say he or she really enjoyed the job. Most report that it is a task that has to be done by someone, and it is their turn.

This relatively prestigious position is unpopular for a number of reasons, including excessive time constraints, paperwork, lack of sufficient authority, and so on. The issue of supervision, however, clearly contributes to the ambiguity and resulting dissatisfaction associated with the job. Surrounding themselves with the cloak of academic freedom, professors prefer to make themselves immune from teaching supervision. Unless the chairperson is a highly respected scholar, the same may be said for research supervision.

There are few clear-cut criteria that chairpersons can use to evaluate the performance or control the behavior of their staff professionals. Some respond with a laissez-faire style. They simply leave their colleagues alone and direct their attention to the administrative chores of the job—conducting searches, coordinating class loads, teaching schedules, and the like. Others adopt a close supervision style, trying to improve the teaching quality or research productivity of their faculty, especially their more junior members.

The laissez-faire style is tolerated and even preferred by self-motivated faculty. Some of the junior faculty, however, if unable to find a mentor, suffer under the laissez-faire style, since they are unlikely to learn the norms of the school or how to play the publishing game in time to earn tenure. Yet, of all possible styles, none is likely to be resisted more than close supervision. One well-intentioned chairperson was reported to have had his secretary track down a potentially wayward junior faculty member who had not met his office hours on a particular day. The junior faculty member was incensed that the chairperson had acted so "unprofessionally." The secretary's call to him was viewed as a direct insult to his professionalism.

Most professors I have spoken with prefer a consultative chairperson—someone who consults with them on administrative matters and who is available to assist in academic or research matters. For the most part, professors manage their own schedules and professional behavior; indeed, this is reputed to be one of the principal assets of the profession. They also rely on peer control, broadly defined as the wider academic community in their area of scholarship, to assess their research, and collegial control, defined more narrowly as their university or department associates, to assess their teaching. Although student evaluations are common in most universities, they appear to be given less weight than peer assessments. Indeed, some faculty view these student evaluations as an indignity foisted upon the academic profession. How often, they might argue, do physicians submit to patient evaluations?

Formalization of Control and Practice

Classic theories of management called for administrative procedures to control military and basic manufacturing institutions. The notion of bureaucracy referred to the operation of large organizations through formal reporting mechanisms. These reporting systems, however, whether designed for program review, product planning, budgets, job descriptions, performance evaluation, or other purposes, have come to be almost universally disliked by professionals. You cannot go into a company today and not hear tales of woe from managerial functionaries complaining about not getting this or that report on time or at all from the professionals. Perhaps some of this is human nature. It is like the college student's obligatory complaints about cafeteria food. No one likes to fill out forms. And yet professionals, who see themselves as having been hired to contribute their specialized knowledge to the task at hand, seem to feel particularly burdened by having to deal with forms and reports. These documents not only take them away from their work; they also pose a challenge to professionalism itself. They make the professional accountable to management on management's terms. Professionals prefer to be accountable to themselves and to their peers.

Formalization, then, which refers to official procedures that prescribe appropriate responses to recurrent situations,[27] has direct implications for managerial control and professional practice. Management needs a rational method to coordinate the diverse parts of the organization and hence relies on the reasonable administration of rules and regulations. Professional work, however, does not lend itself easily to standardized procedures. Professionals tend to believe that each case is unique. They also prefer to complete their assigned tasks without interruption from their superiors. This notion is not wholly unsupported by Max Weber's original conception of bureaucratic authority, which was based on both expertise and hierarchical position.[28] Salaried professionals today are likely to have more expertise or technical competence than their management. Management needs to retain the prerogative of control, however, since, as I discussed in the section on strategic autonomy (autonomy over ends), its primary function is to guide the enterprise toward its mission.

Having argued in favor of managerial control, I am nevertheless convinced that this control must be moderate or sufficiently flexible to promote the originality and innovativeness of the professional employees. Professionals should not have to feel that their daily work is constantly being checked. Most individuals will abide by long-term targets for volume, operating costs, or other measures of performance or contribution. Short-term multiple controls, however, are not likely to gain acceptance among professionals.

Perhaps the major drawback of excessive controls on professional behavior is their presumed negative relationship to autonomy and entrepreneurship. Professionals do not mind being held accountable for their actions but prefer that the accountability follow a steady period of work. Much of their work requires cycles of activity, reflection, and revision. Short-term controls may interrupt the cycle before the job is done. They also have the potential to interrupt concentration, which is an absolute necessity in entrepreneurial endeavors.

Richard Pascale and Anthony Athos[29] depict the negative consequences on entrepreneurship of short-term multiple controls in their comparison of Japan's Matsushita Electric Company and the United States' International Telephone and Telegraph Company (ITT). At ITT, former Chairman Harold Geneen was enamored of the use of interlocking controls to keep tabs on corporate operations. To get to the "unshakable facts," Geneen established multiple reporting systems. If a manager did not pick up a problem, undoubtedly some system would. One of the effects of this system was to discourage the individual entrepreneur. Too many people were getting into the act. One simply could not push a new venture for long before being brought back to the main office to account in full detail for its strategic and financial merit.

Matsushita, in contrast, exercises extraordinarily tight control but only over a few critical variables. It uses such "soft" constraints as style or values to indoctrinate its personnel in acceptable corporate practices. Hence, there is less need for the multiple checks and balances used by ITT and consequently more scope for autonomous decision making and entrepreneurship.

Geneen reviewed performance constantly—at the division level, once a month. Reportedly, he even called people at odd hours of the night to ask about this or that item on a report. Likewise, executives were known to have called Geneen during the wee hours of the morning to get his approval on critical corporate matters.[30]

ITT's success under Geneen was short-lived. Managers and professionals alike either quit or handled the stress imposed by the controls by occasionally resorting to short cuts to meet deadlines, quotas, or budgets, some of the short cuts outside the bounds of accepted business practices.[31]

Rather than attach gross financial and operating measures to the performance of professionals, except in the long run or where the professional may be in a position to affect directly the performance of an operating unit (in the capacity of professional-administrator, for example), it may be advisable to have professionals set their own performance objectives. In this method, known also as MBO, or management by objectives, the professional identifies the behavior that is critical to the performance of a set of tasks and the criteria for determining whether an objective has been met. Care must be taken, however, to allow the professional ample time to get the job done and to have him or her focus on only a small set of challenging yet attainable objectives to maintain his or her interest.

When it comes to the enumeration of job responsibilities, although job descriptions have considerable merit in promoting human resource management policies, they should not be rigid. Too precise job descriptions can leave little room to maneuver and can stifle the creativity of professionals. Often, the job description communicates a prescribed chain of command when it details to whom the incumbent must report. Although satisfactory as a general map for operating, the organization chart and its accompanying documentation through job descriptions should also not be cast in concrete. Professionals need to have some leeway. More harm than good is done when someone is told she cannot take a certain action because it is not part of her job.

One way to ensure this less formal pattern of control is to keep operating units relatively small, allowing professionals and management to get to know each other. Johnson & Johnson has broken up its huge organization, for example, into no fewer than 150 independent divisions, thereby giving each division manager a chance to really get to know his people and his division's activities. Such a decentralized approach, although not always appropriate for companies operating in less consumer-oriented markets, certainly allows for greater freedom of movement by professionals because division managers can accept some ambiguity when they have the opportunity to know their operation more personally.

The Advantages of Formalization

Although the Johnson & Johnson approach has been quite effective, I do not want to leave the impression that every company needs to devise some method to thwart formalization in order to free up its professionals. Not all formalization is negative. Some technical procedures are called for as part of professional practice.[32] Difficulties tend to crop up around burdensome administrative procedures. Resistance to administrative procedures, however, varies by type of professional and also by the nature of the organization. Lawyers working in law firms, for example, may be less subject to bureaucratic constraints than corporate counsel working in legal departments of large corporations. Yet staff attorneys may acquire more authority and expect less standardized procedures than accountants working for the same company in an auditing department. Lawyers like to point to the indeterminate nature of legal knowledge, which relies on informed estimates of the arguments that will be persuasive in specific jurisdictions under particular circumstances. By its very nature, then, the practice of law, dictated by factors often extrinsic to the law itself, cannot be entirely standardized.[33] Auditing, however, in large measure because of its inherent function, needs to abide by more formalized practice (even acknowledging its own situational idiosyncracies). The formalization prescribed by the accountants is sanctioned by the profession, however, and thus is promulgated more because of technical need than managerial control.

It is nevertheless conceivable that some administrative procedures may actually permit some professionals to do their jobs better or even to grant them a greater degree of autonomy.[34] Certainly procedures covering seniority and due process, for example, may prevent some of the capricious or coercive elements of supervision, such as using deference rather than competence as a means of advancement, transferring professionals without their foreknowledge, or placing individuals under excessive stress or workloads. Administrative regulation, however, can be a two-edged sword. After a certain point, the procedures can turn against the independence of professionals, who soon discover there is a rule for everything. Further, rule making, as a prerogative of management, can be used to weaken professional autonomy, especially when it is used to serve only corporate, and not professional, interests. One young scientist complained to me that she could not transfer to a plant from her headquarters research position because of a rule that the boss's permission was required. Her boss bluntly told her that he simply could not afford to lose her right then.

Finally, formalization as an administrative practice may depend heavily on the nature of the unit within a large organization. In large technical corporations, for example, one might find a variety of laboratories and testing facilities, some devoted to applied and development work, and others to basic research. Basic research labs tend to be most productive when operating with a relatively free hand. Consequently, management will make concerted efforts to minimize paperwork requirements. Development units will face greater information requirements owing to their need to coordinate with mainstream corporate functions, particularly marketing and production. Also such units typically need to coordinate with one another in an effort to share resources, unless they are structured to be purely competitive with one another. In any event, professionals working in applied and development units will need to keep other units in the company informed about cost and time schedules, personnel needs, expected margin of contribution, future resource requirements, and so forth. To the extent professionals can select their own assignments, those who wish to avoid administrative regulation should try to get themselves placed in units oriented to a higher level of purely professional practice, such as basic research labs. Management should promote the internal mobility of its professional staff along these lines to the extent the company's overall staffing requirements allow.

It is evident that the need for information systems to coordinate the tasks of the professional work force is greater in some instances than in others. Professionals also differ in their receptivity to control systems. Organizational type matters too. Nevertheless, as a general rule, professionals need to have rules and regulations kept to a minimum. Managers need to ensure that any formalized process they are contemplating is reviewed for its importance. There is an ever-present danger that a planning document, for instance, may precede proper planning. Procter & Gamble is famous for its insistence that all planning documents and proposals be limited to one page. Although not always practical (and as a result now undergoing a modification known as the talk sheet that incorporates preliminary collaboration among several levels of management), the one-page memo did force P&G staff to reflect on how to reduce any initiative to its essentials. The more a company can promote this thoughtful practice of keeping control to a minimum, the more its professionals can spend time concentrating on work that will benefit the company.

Project Evaluation—A Special Case

Where management determines, after careful reflection and scrutiny, that particular administrative or technical procedures are warranted, it should be equally careful in using these procedures when evaluating decisions. Rational and objective processes tend to supplant intuitive processes. Both components, however, are critical in corporate decision processes. It is not uncommon that companies using project-management structures employing a large number of technical professionals will establish critical performance measures for each project. Among the available measures, profit margins typically predominate as the ultimate indicator of the project's contribution to corporate operating results. On the expense side, the project might have to account for a good many services and resources provided internally. These may include engineering staff from other projects and divisions, training and development, capital equipment, market research, personnel services, and so on. Corporate information procedures may, for example, require that each service or resource be expensed in the form of transfer prices.

The difficulty arises when because of heavy initial expenses, projects do not show a sufficient profit margin early in their development. Some projects obviously require greater initial investment for subsequent but longer-term payouts. If management becomes infatuated with the numbers, the company's project managers will gradually learn how to manipulate the figures. Further, the competition among company projects may become unhealthy as units learn to avoid sharing resources if doing so will be reflected negatively in their quarterly reports. A short-term emphasis may develop within technical management, and projects that do not show early profits may be prematurely terminated. Professionals may be pressed to bend standards to get immediate results. Long-term endeavors that allow them to sharpen or expand their skills will be dropped in favor of short-term projects that may require the application of overworked, repetitive skills. The result in terms of professional practice may be the anathemas of overspecialization, lack of challenge, and lack of entrepreneurship.

This scenario has, in fact, occurred in one company with which I am familiar. Rational, objective processes simple got away from management, overwhelming its extremely sharp gut instincts. Especially where professional talent is concerned, patience is required to let good ideas develop. This may necessitate a lesser reliance on short-term objective measures of process and performance and a greater reliance on sound reasoning based on a thorough understanding of the business. In the case cited, it was not the measures themselves that were bad, although they had reached excessive proportions. The real culprit was the encroachment in the managerial mind of reliance on short-term criteria. In this case, information systems became almost more important than the business for which the professionals were hired.

Lack of Job Challenge

Most managers understand that professionals desire challenge in their work. Why, then, are there not more opportunities for enrichment on the job? There seem to be three underlying reasons. First, American corporate culture is fascinated with size; it believes that its success has been tied to economies of scale. From a structural point of view, this translates into the creation of large units of people working on specialized parts rather than small units of people working on wholes. Second, to supervise the work of these large units, elaborate control devices have been constructed that require detailed reports of time and resources expended. Finally, although the span of control may have widened in terms of the number of workers reporting to any one supervisor, freedom of action has not followed suit. Managers are now even more under the gun to ensure that their units are functioning properly. Hence, they rely increasingly on information systems and less on personal contact with professionals. Each of these conditions lessens scope for creativity in the performance of one's job.

Job challenge refers to the opportunity for professionals to make fullest use of their skills. The nemesis of challenge is underutilization of time and talents. Professionals, by training and inclination, want to stretch their intellectual abilities to the limit. They desire, particularly early in their careers, to be involved in their work, and to make use of every minute. They also want to identify with the whole product or service on which they are working. They want to be able to see their contribution.

Challenge has two dimensions for professionals. On one hand, it signifies a horizontal expansion in job duties. This can be achieved in two ways: 1) by giving the professional more of the complete job to be done or, 2) by allowing the professional to spend more time working with teams that are given the opportunity to decide how they will complete the whole job. In each instance, the professional has a chance to do more and different things. In the teamwork option, the individual may choose not to change the specific assignment he or she is working on, but in this case the element of choice presumes sufficient challenge in the job to begin with. When the assignment no longer provides enough challenge, the individual may request from his team members an opportunity to try something new.

For some professionals, it is not enough to do more and different things to experience challenge. A systems analyst may not see any benefit in being given additional responsibilities in inventory control. A construction engineer may not derive any additional satisfaction from assignments in safety and maintenance. What many professionals truly want in their jobs is authority over the task at hand. This suggests an interest in the content of the work. The word used by Frederick Herzberg[33] to describe this dimension of job challenge is "intrinsic." Intrinsic satisfaction is derived from the work itself; hence, it is necessary under intrinsic motivation to have a high degree of self-control over one's work agenda. The result is a greater sense of responsibility, achievement, and self-actualization.

Job challenge derived from intrinsic satisfaction comes not from horizontal expansion but from vertical expansion of one's job duties: not doing more things, but having more responsibility for the things one is assigned to do in the first place. So, the systems analyst working in the area of quality assurance, for example, now begins to establish the standards of inspection. The construction engineer now becomes responsible for setting the parameters of the strength tests to be conducted. In each instance, the professional remains with his technical field but seeks to expand his knowledge in that field.

Of all the motivators of performance for professionals, job challenge stands at the top of the list, precisely because of its association with professionalism itself. Management needs to understand that the professional is by nature a mature worker, and challenge goes with maturity. Maturity may be defined in two ways: job maturity and psychological maturity.[36] Job maturity relates to ability or the knowledge and skill connected to the performance of the job at hand. It can be viewed as almost synonymous with the concept of professionalism. Psychological maturity relates to the willingness, motivation, or commitment to do the job. Psychologically mature workers wish to take personal responsibility for their tasks. They are self-confident in their work and do not need extensive encouragement to get the job done. Many, in fact, also associate psychological maturity with professional status.

Examples of Challenging Environments

Some companies recognize the value of designing jobs that allow for both horizontal and vertical expansion. At The MITRE Corporation, the core group of professional personnel, referred to as the technical staff, or tech-staffers for short, is undifferentiated by title, level, or job description. Roles in any given project are extremely flexible. Hence, the professional is not encumbered by position in deciding whether to assume more responsibility for particular assignments. Further, the climate in the company encourages lateral moves, referred to as soft-shelling; tech staffers can transfer temporarily to any number of different project assignments. Supervisors can restrict the movement of indispensable professionals by appealing directly to their department heads, but this does not happen very often, since they too are seeking technical assignments on their own projects. In addition, the professionals at MITRE have the opportunity to expand their knowledge and interests by applying for new positions through a job-posting system or staying on a project or series of projects for a longer time in order to deepen their knowledge in a particular area.

At 3M, professionals are allowed to join the many new-venture teams operating at any given time on a full-time basis. If they and their team succeed, they may stay with their new venture and receive commensurate position and salary recognition. If they do not succeed, they are allowed to return to their former job.[37] The challenge, therefore, is always available to the professional who wants it and is made even more attractive by the absence of employment risk. This sends a message to 3M professional employees that challenge and innovation are central to the company's mission.

Barriers to Job Challenge

A professional may create a barrier to challenge by refusing to extend his or her technical skills to other fields. Further, some professionals simply do not want challenge on their job. Research has found, for example, that older professionals, somewhat worn out by the politics of organizational life, tend to lower their aspirations and professional commitment and become more interested in the salary and benefits that accompany the job.[38]

Nevertheless, most professionals still value job challenge. The barriers are more managerial and organizational than personal. Some managers resist redesigning jobs to be more challenging because their training emphasized the need for job fragmentation and rigid control. These managers simply have not adapted to more enlightened management principles. Managers resist mainly, however, because they fear that vertical redesign will shift control from their hands to those of professionals. They fail to recognize that redesign will give them more time for tasks other than supervision, such as cross-functional communication, customer contact, or market analysis.

Organizationally, as the MITRE example demonstrates, all parts of the organization have to cooperate if design changes incorporating challenge are to be implemented. Lateral transfers, for example, will not be effective if allowed to operate in one direction only. Second, as the 3M example demonstrates, challenge schemes need to dovetail with other organizational support systems such as wage and salary administration. Challenge has to be rewarded and nurtured. It also has to be approached with patience, since it takes time to pay off. Before it can be successful, organizations need to withstand and support an initial period of professional and management reorientation.

Organizational Impersonalness

Besides responding well to challenge, professionals flourish in work environments that treat employees as mature adults rather than numbers. Unfortunately, managements have not always adopted a personal approach to supervision. Two schools of management have evolved to respond to the plight of employees faced with organizational impersonalness: the Human Relations school and the humanistic school.

The Human Relations School

A theme of the Human Relations school of management, which developed in reaction to Frederick Taylor's Scientific Management principles, is that workers must always be treated as people, not cogs in a machine. Originating in the famous Hawthorne studies at the Western Electric plant in Chicago between 1927 and 1932, the Human Relations school rebuked Scientific Management's dim view of human nature. Some of the early studies revealed that when workers were treated like people rather than machines, productivity increased. Workers respond to motivators other than money. The social setting, leadership style, and such intangibles as attention, recognition, and responsibility govern performance. At least four principal findings from the Hawthorne studies serve as a foundation of the Human Relations school:

1. An organization is not a machine but a social system made up of people, with all their hopes, fears, envy, desires, and needs.

2. Noneconomic rewards have as much bearing on productivity as economic rewards. Friendship and collegiality are important parts of the job.

3. Productivity cannot be achieved simply through the direction of management but requires concurrence by the worker group in the form of social norms.

4. Workers cannot always control decisions about their work. Groups make decisions about jobs, and sometimes these group decisions may not conform with those of the formal organization.

Although the Human Relations approach was formulated primarily in response to the conditions of factory workers, its principles apply to salaried professionals today. These principles emphasize the role of the group or team in the total effort. Indeed, professionals seldom work completely alone. They depend on the advice, feedback, and informal evaluations provided by their peers to give them the impetus to move to progressively higher levels of competence and productivity. Technical professionals, in particular, work on projects together. Although each individual may be relied on for his or her specific expertise, the contribution of each professional is incremental to the total effort of the team.

In this context, seldom can one individual be counted on by management to control the decisions of the group. A project manager may speak for the group but cannot control the group. Attempts at total control of a professional group are doomed to failure because professionals by nature are not manipulable. Their contribution to a group decision must be recognized. Hence, the professional group is a complicated social system encompassing many of the same personal issues found in social systems outside the workplace, such as the family and community. Individuals have to learn to deal with each other's personal idiosyncracies, habits, and styles, as well as cope with the tensions and frustrations that crop up from time to time in the group. Multiple bonds are formed for different purposes, some technical, others purely personal. Yet the group must perform, and most individuals realize that that is their main purpose. Management needs to recognize the subtlety but also the positive value of this system. Group performance based on results more than process is a very important concept for management to grasp. The effective manager realizes that the professional group, when left alone to accomplish an assigned objective, can be one of the most powerful vehicles for achieving productivity within the corporate arsenal of resources. The manager's job is to further the growth and development of the group, not to interfere in its efforts through useless process constraints or individual productivity incentives that discount the contributions of others. The manager should also realize that the group can help control selfish and deviant behavior on the part of individual contributors.

The Hawthorne studies revealed the challenge imposed on management by workers who, when allowed to set their own standards, attempt to loosen standards so as not to work too hard. Can this slow-down process occur within professional ranks? It is important to remember that the managerial philosophy in effect at the time of the Hawthorne studies was based on the notion of man as machine. But man has always been considered more unstable than machines. Therefore, the manager had to set unrealistic standards for workers to get them to produce at the desired level. Left to their own devices, they would choose not to produce. Workers were viewed at the time as instinctively lazy and unreliable. Most people would agree that professionals, by virtue of their investment in human capital, are not inherently lazy and unreliable. Yet, as people, they are capable of working to rule. As a group, they can still choose to set loose standards of production or service. However, when they are challenged and allowed to decide how they will complete a task and when they are committed to the work at hand, they are unlikely to behave in this fashion.

Some companies have long recognized the importance of the human group to corporate success. At Hewlett-Packard, a company that is legendary for its treatment of workers as people, many informal policies emphasize the need to work as a team. Project engineers, for example, routinely leave whatever they are working on on their desks so that others can play with it, which may result in some incremental or even major improvements. H-P has a well-known open-lab-stock policy. Professionals are encouraged to go in and take whatever they need. They can even bring some of the stock home. Management obviously believes that whatever the employee will work on will benefit the company in some way. But even beyond that, a culture is promoted. Contributions for the good of the company and the group are expected. Abusers of the policy are simply not tolerated. One might assume that in this open-stock policy the norms of trust go so deep that one would have to be desperate to abuse them for personal gain.

A more transient yet compelling example of the use of teamwork in corporate culture took place at United Air Lines between 1970 and 1976 under the leadership of Ed Carlson. Before Carlson took the reins, morale had plummeted as the company became mired in a huge, centralized bureaucracy. Decisions were made from the top down and workers at all levels, even the pilots, were discouraged from offering their views on corporate issues. Carlson initiated many changes to reverse both the financial and human relations predicaments at United; among them was the institution of teamwork principles. By becoming highly visible throughout the company and insisting that his executive staff be the same, he gradually proved to the work force that their ideas and concerns would be addressed. He virtually flattened the corporate hierarchy, thereby pushing decision making down to the levels where it had the most immediate impact.[39] If a decision on route structures, scheduling, safety regulations, or aircraft purchase affected the pilots, for example, they were brought into the decision. The company under Carlson began to act like a team. Not all of the teamwork principles, however, survived beyond his tenure.

The Humanistic School

The humanistic school of management, though very close in guiding philosophy to the Human Relations school—indeed, some of its proponents have also cited the roots of their propositions in the Hawthorne studies—offers some new insights into the treatment of professional workers in organizations. One of the early architects of this school was Douglas McGregor, who developed the now-classic notion of Theory X and Theory Y.[40] These so-called theories represent managerial assumptions about human nature. Theory X assumes that workers are unreliable and inherently lazy and, as a consequence, will do their jobs only if either coerced or convinced that they will receive a commensurate reward for their efforts. Theory Y, on the other hand, assumes that employees are inherently creative and are interested in directing their own work and taking responsibility for its outcome. McGregor believed that most people have the potential to behave in consonance with Theory Y, hence, that it behooves managers to adapt their management style accordingly. Assuming there is a continuum between X and Y, professionals clearly fall into the Theory Y range. How do the humanists suggest such people ought to be treated inside an organization?

Chris Argyris[41] answered this question in his development of the humanistic approach to management. He reasoned that most workers today are still treated as if they were immature, even though there is compelling evidence that they are able to behave according to Theory Y. Corporate life simply has not given them opportunities to meet such needs as self-esteem, a sense of responsibility, achievement, or challenge. As a consequence, they feel uninvolved in their work, a state that has led to feelings of submissiveness, dependence, and psychological failure. To reverse this predicament, management needs to recognize the potential in all of its workers. This would entail adhering to humanistic values. Opportunity should be created to develop trusting and authentic relationships, work should be made challenging and exciting, workers should be allowed to develop to their fullest potential, and, finally, people in the organization should be allowed to influence the way in which they relate to work, the organization, and the environment.

As I see it, the humanistic school rests on four principles, all of which can be found in one form or another in Argyris's work. The first principle, however, derives directly from earlier work by the Human Relations advocates. It is that any decision should be made by consensus among those individuals directly affected. As United under Ed Carlson illustrates, this bottom-up, consensus decision-making approach can be the first step toward creating intimacy and involvement among the work force. A second by-product of consensus decision making is the next principle, trust. Trust among workers in an enterprise is essential if people are going to feel free to express themselves, take risks, and work in a sharing fashion to keep the organization responsive to its internal and external challenges.

Trust has another important function in an organization. It allows individuals to take initiative without others fearing that hidden or illicit motives guide their efforts. It signifies an environment in which all members are working toward the same ends. It allows for some relaxation of the need for close supervision. Finally, as was demonstrated so well by Pascale and Athos,[42] it allows for relaxed communication, characterized as much by metaphor, joking, occasional abstractness, and nonverbal cues as by brute frankness. Perhaps because of misuses of the T-group methodology in the 60s and early 70s, humanism occasionally became identified with nondefensiveness—with the practice of being forcefully honest or open with one another. Although there are occasions when frankness is called for, i.e., when an auditor must reveal his past and present relationship with the client or when an engineer's decision to work with a new group may be affected by a past dispute with the project leader, a climate of trust allows for some indirect communication. It lets people hold onto their defenses, foibles, and weaknesses but in so doing, affirms their acceptability. It judges people's effectiveness, not their personalities.

The third principle of humanism, after consensus decision making and trust, is egalitarianism. Egalitarianism suggests a breaking down of formal roles between individuals in the organization. Managers do not act as if they are superior to their professional employees simply because they outrank them. As explained by William Ouchi in his *Theory Z*,[43] managers show broad concern for their subordinates, relationships tend to be informal, and people relate to each other as individuals, not as superior to subordinate. Consequently, there are no real class distinctions among group members; rather, differences are based on competencies and the diverse talents of the membership. When people relate to each other in this way, there is more opportunity to develop trust. One professional I talked to pointed out that a symptom of depersonalization in his organization was when people in engineering, for example, said something like, "Marketing decided to forego this end use for our product," rather than "Neal decided." Referring to Neal as "marketing" depersonalizes Neal, removes him from the group, and targets him as a role player rather than a person. Of course, it is quite possible that that is what Neal wanted to accomplish. The psychic gain he may experience from a temporary feeling of superiority, however, will be quickly offset by negative attitudes and mistrust among the professionals in the engineering project group.

No better example of the egalitarian principle can be found than the Friday afternoon beer busts held at the Tandem Corporation, a highly successful Silicon Valley computer company.[44] This ritual allows individuals from all levels of the corporation to shake off their roles and relate to each other as individuals. At events such as beer busts, managers may act frivolously and in so doing become part of the crowd. The beer bust is by no means out of character at Tandem. The company openly proclaims that people matter. Tandem goes to extremes to emphasize its egalitarian orientation. It has no formal organization chart and few formal rules. It seldom holds formal meetings. Jobs, duties, and hours are flexible. There are no name tags or reserved parking spaces. Although some of these practices may not be appropriate in larger organizations working in better-defined, more stable markets, or where strategies at later stages of the product life cycle require more organized procedures, the message from Tandem, applicable across all organizations, is that workers respond enthusiastically to being treated like people.

The last of the humanistic principles is that one of the most critical organizational goals is to satisfy human needs. Although this principle can be viewed externally (producing goods and services that meet consumer needs), the humanists focused more on the organization's responsiveness to internal human needs. They saw a direct parallel, however, between external organizational effectiveness and the inculcation of humanistic values in the work force. Argyris, for example, has shown how organizations that attempt to develop the potential of their workers are responsive to change and hence more adaptable to the vicissitudes of the marketplace. The human needs Argyris spoke about were the higher-order needs addressed by one of his predecessors, Abraham Maslow.[45] Maslow believed that, after meeting such basic needs as security and friendship, people shift their focus first toward self-esteem, represented by such attributes as responsibility, achievement, challenge, and recognition, then toward self-actualization, represented by such attributes as self-acceptance and the realization of one's potential. Argyris applied these ideas to the organization, seeing as management's principal responsibility the provision of opportunities for workers to grow and mature in the direction of higher-order needs.

This principle of humanism differs from the philosophical base undergirding Ouchi's Theory Z. Based on the theoretical work of Emile Durkheim, Theory Z sees the principal purpose of management as creating a stable social order, somewhat akin to Durkheim's industrial clan.[46] By providing stability, the industrial clan ensures the satisfaction of its workers, who, as a consequence, may then aspire to meet higher-order needs. The latter result does not seem to constitute Theory Z's main focus, however; indeed, it is possible that some professionals in a Theory Z firm may wish to satisfy only their lower-order needs for security and in so doing preserve the organizational hierarchy as it currently stands. In the humanistic firm, it is the explicit goal of management to provide not only an opportunity but a challenge to its professionals to develop to their fullest potential.

Exceptions

Many organizations do act on humanistic principles. Indeed, the field of organizational development is dedicated to helping companies evolve in this direction. Companies that have not been oriented this way require many many years of systematic, planned change before they can truly treat their workers as people. Some companies, however, in large measure because of the foresight of their founders, began with and then sustained humanistic values.

Two companies, each employing a large number of professionals but in totally different industries, that are recognized for their humanistic orientation are Hewlett-Packard and Delta Airlines.

Bill Hewlett and Dave Packard recognized the value of humanistic management from the start. From the beginning they insisted that people call each other by their first names. They also did away with time clocks and saw that their professionals' work schedules were adjusted to the demands of their personal lives. As the company grew, Hewlett and Packard passed on this humanistic culture through consistent policies that reflected the so-called HP Way, which has come to stand for a celebration of the value of people working to their fullest potential. They also nurtured their humanistic values through a formal Statement of Corporate Objectives, which contains a section on *Our People*. In this statement, there are direct references to the need for employees to share in the development of the company and to the need for management to see that workers obtain a sense of personal achievement and accomplishment in their work.[47]

Delta Airlines is so unabashed in its belief in the value of people that it has promulgated a slogan, The Delta Family Feeling. Delta is one of the most successful airlines in the business, and it passes much of its success on to its employees, not only in higher salaries than the industry average but also by working hard to develop their "family" trust. During the last recession, while other airlines cut back, Delta held the line on employment and drew the "pint of blood," as senior management put it, not from its employees but from its stockholders.[48] The latter would have to realize that management was not going to destroy some members of its family during times of hardship. Rather, the whole family would stick together. Indeed, professionals at Delta are known to have manned ticket counters and handled luggage to get the company through difficult times.

As a final example of the development of trust and teamwork in an organization, top management in a company with which I am familiar decided it would try to eliminate depersonalization in its job-posting policy. One of the principal difficulties in job posting is that often the department head who puts out a requisition already has a candidate or two in mind. The job is "wired," so to speak. The problem becomes how to handle a candidate who is rejected out of hand. In most organizations, department heads typically treat a rejected candidate by making up an excuse or using some other impersonal method to shield the truth behind the matter. In this case, senior management simply decided to encourage department heads facing this dilemma to be frank about a wired position. Other candidates would be invited to apply (and might even win the job from the preselected candidate), but at least they would know what they were up against. Rejected candidates would then be granted a feedback review at which the department head could feel free to discuss how they stacked up against the successful job bidder. The net effect of this policy has been to make even the company's competitive personnel practices more humanistic.

Lack of Entrepreneurship

Entrepreneurship is typically treasured by the cosmopolitan salaried professional. It refers to the opportunity to gain resources for and work on a favorite project. Three elements are typically associated with entrepreneurship: the freedom to choose one's own project, freedom to implement it on one's own, and freedom to work without the interruption of day-to-day supervision. A derivative of entrepreneurship, known as bootlegging, has a pejorative connotation, because it consists of entrepreneurial activity *outside* the principal business of the company. Further, bootlegging is often engaged in solely for the benefit of the professional, with any corporate benefits being secondary or incidental. Nevertheless, some managers see some benefit in permitting bootlegging by a selected few.

Companies that afford limited entrepreneurship are for the most part inimical to professionals. Probably few top managers would express outright opposition to entrepreneurship, but many frustrate it by failing to provide a work environment that accepts risk, change, and even failure. Management needs to encourage innovative attitudes to create an atmosphere that is supportive of entrepreneurship. Such an atmosphere is characterized by a willingness to accept both the risk involved in entrepreneurial activity and the changes entrepreneurship may create. This willingness may be conveyed to the professional work force through statements and publications, but professionals are more apt to believe it when they see resources being committed to entrepreneurial endeavors. These resources signify not only financial support but encompass allowance of adequate work time, equipment, personnel, and so forth. Executives who behave in this way are sometimes referred to as executive champions. Thomas Watson of IBM was an executive champion in his firm commitment to and tolerance of so-called deviants who could disrupt the conformity or standard practices of his company. Lewis Lehr of 3M often articulated an acceptance of failure; for example, quoting from a 3M publication, he stated:

> Management that is destructively critical when mistakes are made kills initiative and it's essential that we have many people with initiative if we're to continue to grow.[49]

This statement is further backed at 3M by an expectation that every division obtain 25 percent of its sales from products that did not exist five years earlier. Hence, entrepreneurship can be expected to produce as well as draw on resources. Far-sighted managers are able to see the long-term benefits of supporting entrepreneurial activity. It not only is financially beneficial to the company, but, as was found in a major study of entrepreneurship, it provides for greater integration of professionals into corporate life.[50] Organizations that allow and encourage entrepreneurship tend to breed professionals who experience less tension between their research interests and organizational demands.

Although executive sponsorship of entrepreneurship is critical, a distinction should be made between sponsorship of the process and the product of entrepreneurial activity. Some top managers can become so committed to particular projects that they refuse to consider other alternatives or objectives. Even at 3M, it has been well documented that some managers originally discounted projects that later proved valuable because they had become overly involved in their own pet projects. Fortunately, the risk-taking climate was sufficiently pervasive that some overlooked projects became successful anyway. An oft-quoted story at 3M concerns the fellow who was fired because of the apparent failure of a roofing granules project.[51] This entrepreneurial wizard, however, kept coming to work anyway and eventually turned the project into one of the company's most successful divisions. Incidentally, this notable named George Swenson was rehired!

The process of entrepreneurship, then, calls for tolerance of risk taking and recognition of the value of long-term success. Warren Stumpe,[52] in an amusing essay on new-product psychology, warned that failure to inspire this risk-taking orientation among corporate employees could lead to a new classification of the R&D cycle:

Stage 1 —Euphoria
Stage 2 —Disenchantment
Stage 3 —Chaos
Stage 4 —Search for the Guilty
Stage 5 —Punishment of the Innocent
Stage 6 —Promotion of the Unemployed

Support for entrepreneurial activity does not mean that management should not insist on consensus in the overall corporate mission. Top management has an obligation to define the business the company will engage in, including its product or service market segments and/or its technology. Professionals need to know, and then adhere to, the objectives of the corporation. This can come about only where management informs them about the types of projects it is willing to engage in and support. Once the corporate mission is articulated, however, professionals should expect unwavering support of their entrepreneurial efforts. For example, a policy of making an R&D department responsible for product innovation without allotting the department an adequate budget would clearly send mixed signals about entrepreneurial support.[33] Indeed, even bootlegging can be tolerated where the professional's principal work conforms to the overall corporate mission. In this way, the company's product line is sustained while the chances of achieving a significant breakthrough are increased.

Role of Project Champion

The R&D literature has attributed great importance to the role of project champions in fostering entrepreneurial activity. Typically, a project champion is a professional who is symbolically identified with a project and takes charge in seeing it through to completion. My own research has revealed that management needs to encourage the emergence of project champions, while allowing them a certain degree of independence.[54] Although the champion must be totally committed to the project to sell it to top management and to compete with other possible champions for scarce corporate resources, Carl Heyel[55] warns that he or she must not contract "projectitis," which results in maintaining too narrow a view of corporate needs. The success or failure of any entrepreneurial venture may hinge on the project champion's ability to balance "projectitis" with insight into the overall corporate structure, politics, and objectives.

Project champions, as links with management, must also be careful not to impose their will on a project until later on in its development. In one project with which I am familiar, which was undertaken to investigate electrochemical systems, the technological process was quite complicated. The project leader gave the professional staff ample elbow room during the early stages so they could work at their own pace. Finally, the project reached the development stage. At that point, a company with an ideal potential application expressed a deep interest in the product. Top management began to apply pressure on the project staff, even threatening to transfer it to another division. It was then that the project leader emerged to exert his influence to hold onto the project and see it through. Although he sacrificed a good portion of his current personal influence to keep the project alive, he did in fact see the project through to successful commercialization, for which he was ultimately rewarded.

Exceptions

Some companies recognize the need to foster entrepreneurship among their professional staff to release creative energies and talent for innovative and ultimately profitable work. Many companies simply recognize the entrepreneurial orientation of professionals and, in general, allow these employees free rein to try new things, provided they stay within the business objectives of the enterprise. Honeywell's Fellows Program, modeled after so-called dual-track programs that have been adopted by several predominantly technology-based companies nationwide, allows a small number of exceptional technical professionals to follow a career track equivalent in stature to the traditional managerial track. Further, these individuals are given time and resources to develop long-term ventures as long as they stay within the company's technological purview. Entrepreneurial activity is supported, for instance, by bringing the fellows together to exchange ideas, by soliciting their participation in technological reviews and forecasts, and by allowing them to gain national exposure by presenting and publishing papers.

Some excellent companies go even further by promoting bootlegging among a select few of their most entrepreneurial personnel. IBM's version of the Fellows Program gives forty-five so-called heretics a chance over a five-year period to shake up the system and try almost any new venture, to be backed up with appropriate corporate resources. At Texas Instruments, a program called IDEA (identify, develop, expose, action) was funded to finance long-shot projects. About forty IDEA representatives throughout the company were given authority to allocate funds, without any other approval from the top, for projects proposed by managers and professionals who otherwise would not have the influence to obtain funding from the traditional sources.

Admittedly, these programs involve only a fraction of professional employees in the respective companies. Yet even at a symbolic level, they display top management's faith and confidence in the potential of professional entrepreneurship.

Unstable Employment Practices

Although cosmopolitan professionals are more loyal to the profession than to the organization, they are not immune to organizational commitment. Indeed, it can be argued that professionals, when guaranteed reasonable employment security, will devote considerable attention to their professional practice inside their own organizations. Professional and organizational loyalty need not be mutually exclusive.

It is unfortunate that so few organizations use stable employment practices. Otherwise, the seeming incompatability between professional and organizational loyalty might dissolve. Most managers believe, however, that the best way to reduce costs during a slack period is to reduce the size of the work force. They fail to recognize that the development of stable production and employment practices can anticipate, prevent, and thereby cushion the shock produced by a sudden loss of business.

Essentially, a stable employment policy is a statement to employees that they will not be laid off after a certain period of employment. It would be pointless to guarantee any professional immediate security with the company at the time of hire. Both the individual and the employer need time to adjust to one another. Once the adjustment period is over, however, the company should be able to extend an offer of guaranteed employment for as long as it stays in business. The condition imposed here constitutes a managerial right to rescind guaranteed employment status upon reasonable notice and upon submission of proof that the business is likely to fail. To my knowledge, this condition has yet to be invoked in companies with stable employment policies, probably because the commitment to stability requires and is therefore accompanied by superb managerial practice.

Managing for Employment Stability

Once managers become convinced of the positive relationship between productivity and job security, they need to explain the benefits and liabilities of employment stability to the professional staff. The latter will share in productivity growth during upswings but will have to tighten their belts during downswings. Cooperation throughout the business cycle, however, will be rewarded by a promise of employment security. Meanwhile, management will do whatever it can to smooth the fluctuations in the business cycle through better strategic and operational planning.

The use of a fair bonus system symbolizes this process. Professionals should be rewarded with a bonus during productivity-growth phases. The bonus should be tied to individual performance where possible, but if performance is based strictly on group effort, members of the group should split the bonus equally. If the company should suffer a loss of business, however, for whatever reason, management should feel free to institute, and professional employees should accept, a temporary suspension or reduction in the bonus. That way, all corporate members share the burden, much as family members do when working together in a family business.

Beyond the bonus, other management strategies can contribute to the development of a policy of employment stability. James Bolt[56] argues that the sine qua non of such a policy is the meshing of the organization's human resource planning with its strategic planning. Once the company can reliably project its ventures into new markets, products, and technologies, it can plan for the number and types of employees it will need. Less ambitious but equally important among human resource planning strategies are so-called buffer devices. Overtime and temporary help, used mainly with nonexempt and paraprofessional workers, are effective approaches when not used to extreme. With large numbers of professional workers, vending and subcontracting can be considered to avoid having to hire an excessive number of full-time employees. Xerox has at times filled the equivalent of 150 jobs through a contracting arrangement it calls networking. The organization can also use flexible or reduced work schedules to ease the pressure of economic downturns. Working fewer hours per day or fewer days per week, for example, resulting in a trade-off of leisure for work, may actually be appealing to some professionals who have come to appreciate more fully other aspects of their lives beyond work, such as family, community, or even self.

Retraining and redeployment constitute two other effective mechanisms for avoiding layoffs.[57] Training, of course, should not be instituted only to ensure stable employment. Corporate and professional needs are constantly changing, as is the marketplace. Management needs its professional staff to be up-to-date and sufficiently versatile to respond to changing business patterns. Some professionals will also want to try new things, particularly where they are encouraged to take charge of their own career development.[58] It makes sense to offer them wide opportunities to retool and retrain. Redeployment, defined as moving an employee to another location and perhaps a different job capacity, is a riskier strategy, since it not only represents a great cost to the company but may uproot the professional's family. Nevertheless, following the 1969–1970 recession, Texaco successfully redeployed sixty-five professionals (mostly chemists and chemical engineers) in its five U.S. laboratories. Most of these professionals moved from R&D into such operating departments as refining, petrochemicals, engineering, environmental protection, and oil exploration.[59]

Stable employment can also be pursued through a variety of company-specific policies. A commitment to keep a lean staff, selective hiring, and early retirement incentives are among an array of measures that can be used, but in each case they must be fitted into a rational human resource policy. Keeping staff too lean, for example, eventually might be perceived as taking advantage of one's professional employees, especially if the professionals become overworked or where their assignments cannot be easily contracted out. On the other hand, stable employment practices should not be interpreted as promotion of the status quo. Professionals are still expected to perform; indeed, the guarantee should provide a base of security that releases the professional's creative instincts. The individual knows that he or she will not be fired for trying out some new ideas or methods. Also, employment stability by no means obliges the professional to remain with the organization should better opportunities become available elsewhere.

Ultimately, management's commitment to a policy of employment stability should be guided by an overall philosophy of personalness, as discussed earlier. In a research-oriented company I visited, the vice president of administration accounted for his company's outstanding reputation for employment stability in this way. He said professional employees in his company all know that if they do a good job on their current project, they will be reassigned to another challenging project when their current assignment is over. In the interim, efforts are made to keep people on their present assignments. In most instances, the professionals are even encouraged to develop a long-term relationship with customers. This policy of challenge and stability at the project level, according to this vice president, is translated into a broader corporate policy of employment stability. Staff professionals tend to like their work, and even some of those who leave seeking greener pastures come back.

Beyond demonstrating a general commitment to the intrinsic work interests of its staff professionals, management can support efforts to maintain professional contacts. Extending loyalty to a professional association is not synonymous with being disloyal to one's own organization. In fact, stability on the job allows the professional more time and energy to concentrate on professional development. The professional will probably attempt to try out any recently learned professional skills in his or her current work setting. Hence, the organization can become the beneficiary of the new skills and techniques.

The Management of Retrenchment: A Special Case

A special case of employment-stability management occurs during a corporate retrenchment, for it is under this condition that the policy of stability faces its most rugged test. Under conditions of retrenchment, it is difficult for management to allay fears of massive layoffs or to reduce the growing sense of uncertainty that pervades the work force. Dissatisfaction with the job, with one's colleagues and superiors, and ultimately with the organization may emerge. These attitudes can ultimately stimulate a variety of maladaptive responses, such as greater attention to minute details; overcontrol of minor aspects of one's job; initiation of, transmission of, and actual belief in false rumors; and reluctance to engage in cooperative activities. Workers may expend only minimal effort, perhaps just enough to avoid being fired for lack of performance. During or even after the crisis, disheartened professionals will seek to leave the organization as soon as an attractive alternative opens up elsewhere.[60]

Although employers may at first glance applaud such turnover as a means of solving their retrenchment problem, my observation is that this solution is very shortsighted. Typically, it is the most talented professionals who leave, since they are most in demand. This causes the employer to expend otherwise needed resources in replacement and training costs. Meanwhile, the former employees may be ensconced in competing organizations, making use of the skills and knowledge acquired in the original organization. Finally, any lack of commitment among the remaining professional staff may reduce the adaptability of the entire organization. Traumatized workers, in an effort to cling to whatever stability may remain in their lives, resist further changes initiated by management, even when they may be beneficial. For example, management may develop a retraining or retooling program to prepare some of the professionals to move into new businesses. Mistrusting management's motives, some of these professionals may resist such a change by openly deploring an attempt to transform their professional skills. They may cling to their original skills and refuse to try to adapt, raising the banner of commitment to professional standards. Management may then respond with further threats and even more layoffs. Both parties become increasingly intransigent, closing off the available means of communication and thus confirming negative expectations and attributions. The company by this time enters a cycle of despair and further job insecurity.

Management can lessen the strain of retrenchment on its professional staff first by being especially alert and responsive to the professionals' needs. It must continue to provide open information about the organization's troubles. There is a temptation during retrenchment to replace long-range objectives with short-run performance targets. For example, management may put more pressure on supervisors to show paper gains or divert resources to projects that can produce quick operating results. This temptation needs to be avoided unless professionals can be convinced that the changes are only temporary. Resorting to these methods deflects management from the practices that made the company an effective and trustworthy employer to begin with. If professionals begin to see resources dwindling that previously supported their personal and professional development, they are naturally going to begin to separate psychologically from their managers, a process that will gradually sever the trust management has worked so hard to earn.

Exceptions

Some companies and agencies have maintained stable employment practices through good times and bad as part of an overall approach to human resource management. Managers in these organizations have long recognized that the benefits of stable employment outweigh the short-term financial gains accruing from layoffs. In particular, they realize that the commitment to the company by the professional staff stimulated by enlightened employment policies will be converted into productivity growth.

Lincoln Electric Company,[62] the world's largest manufacturer of arc welding machines and electrodes, issued a formal guarantee of continuous employment in 1958. This announcement followed a successful seven-year test of a no-layoff policy. Lincoln Electric's commitment promises employees forty-nine working weeks of at least thirty hours each per year. The commitment extends to all employees having at least two years of continuous service with the company.

The policy has been an indisputable success. Even during the 1974–1975 recession, when market growth slackened and attrition and resignations fell below the industry average, the company not only laid no one off but also paid annual bonuses of over 90 percent. A year later, during an energy and snow crisis when the plant was closed for two days, incredible as it may seem, the company's employees took their employer to task for trying to pay them for four days of work!

Lincoln Electric has accomplished its feat of continuous employment with the help of sound business and human resource practices. The company has continuously stressed the importance (and, consequently, influenced the growth) of arc-welding technology. It also has managed to smooth production flows by finding and developing reliable vendors. It has combated sales fluctuations through such approaches as price- and cost-cutting, expanding its reconstruction business, introducing new products, manufacturing for stock, and carrying out work during slack time that can be deferred during busy periods. From a human resource standpoint, the company uses overtime selectively, promotes almost entirely from within, encourages creativity and entrepreneurship at every level, hires with extreme care, and with the cooperation of the work force deploys its staff flexibly in terms of jobs, location, and time.

Although it is impossible to determine whether Lincoln Electric's continuous employment policy is uniquely responsible for the company's success, or vice versa, the relationship is clearly reciprocal. The guarantee induces worker cooperation, which leads to high productivity growth, which in turn enables the company to increase its earnings, part of which are used to pay for stable employment.

Although it has never expressly promised it, IBM has had a virtual no-layoff policy in the United States since at least 1941.[63] This policy is implied in the attention the company gives to overall human resource planning. Each operating unit submits a strategic plan that outlines employment growth into the future. The numbers are quite precise within a two-year period. Using this plan, IBM managers attempt to pinpoint their skill requirements and workload fluctuations. These projections are based on employment self-sufficiency within each operating unit within each division. The idea behind this decentralized approach is that if each division and unit can successfully balance its work force requirements, the job of maintaining full employment corporate-wide will be that much easier. The workload projections, however, are usually on the low side. The slack is taken up through overtime, subcontracting, temporary employment, and vending. The company also makes good use of its retraining facilities. Between 1972 and 1975, when IBM twice faced significant economic difficulties, 7,000 of its employees were totally retrained. Another 10,000 were deployed into different assignments. In 1974, a Corporate Resource Group was formed to oversee manpower-balancing efforts throughout the company. Made up of functional directors for manufacturing, finance, marketing, development, service, and personnel, this group reviewed internal staffing, redeployment, and hiring of all new employees and generally provided effective resource management for IBM worldwide.

Hence, there is little need for IBM to have a formal policy of stable employment. IBM professionals and their managers have simply grown up with full employment. As Theodore E. Grosskopf, Jr., director of the company's human resources, has explained, "They understand the commitment needed to make it work, and they are willing to do their share."[64]

The Professional Culture   3

Because many readers may be unfamiliar with the literature on professionalism, this chapter begins by reviewing the foundations of the professional culture, to wit, its historical roots, its education and training peculiarities, and the early socialization experiences of young professionals. After a look at the stages of development professionals experience within organizational settings, I turn to some of the idiosyncratic factors of the professional culture that appear to cause the most strain with management. These factors—overprofessionalization, autonomy over ends as well as means, overemphasis on professional standards of evaluation, disregard of organizational procedures, and lack of interest in real-world practice—should have a familiar ring to them. Indeed, in many cases, they are the obverse of factors considered in Chapter 2 as unfortunate by-products of the corporate culture. When combined with the values of the social culture presented in the next chapter, these factors reveal the conceptual basis of the challenge involved in managing professionals.

Historical Basis

Although the roots of the professional culture can be traced to the eighteenth-century philosophers of the Enlightenment, the tenets of professionalism as we know it emerged during the mid-Victorian era, between the Civil War and the turn of the century.[1] During this period people began to see the world as a rational place, where every person could discover his true self within the confines of space and time.[2] This was also the age of positivism, which, grounded in the earth-shattering discoveries of science and technology, advocated the use of scientific and technical rationality to solve the world's problems. Positivism became institutionalized within the American university, which created by the end of the nineteenth century a new kind of professional. Again relying on the logic of rationality, the professional asserted that science could be channeled to serve mankind and begin to reverse the failures of human beings, which were attributable to human frailty.

In the view of the positivist philosopher Auguste Comte, science could be reshaped to serve moral ends and could be used to cleanse the world of mysticism and superstition, which, as forms of pseudo-knowledge, retarded the advance of civilization.[3] The new professional, in service to this scientific rationality, could be relied on and would be evaluated for his competence, knowledge, and preparation rather than such earlier traits as sincerity, honorable reputation, or righteous behavior. The professional essentially became a detached scientist who could examine human problems through an empirical lens and prescribe solutions using the latest methods. Essentially, using the hypothetico-deductive system of the scientific method, the professional approached each new problem as an experiment that required the objective testing of competing hypotheses. As a body of knowledge evolved regarding cause and effect, certain standard solutions could be relied on for particular problems. Variations in or distortions of a problem were approached by submitting the causal agent to further experimentation based on known theories. The professions gained sufficient dominance even to propose solutions to moral dilemmas, using the same hypothetico-deductive system. Questions about sustaining life, for example, were deferred to the physician's proclamation of whether life-threatening agents could be controlled by modern science.

The interest in positivism in this country coincided with the rise of the modern university, which was strongly influenced by the German tradition. This tradition viewed the university as a multidisciplinary research institution interested in the advancement of knowledge through scientific examination. Professionals were not immediately assimilated into the universities, but as they gradually assumed positivist norms of practice, they were admitted not only to teach the applications of their craft but also to conduct scholarly research in their discipline.

By the late nineteenth century, professionals found themselves invested with enormous powers and autonomy, because their knowledge was considered beyond the reach of ordinary humans, including their clients. Professionals themselves, of course, fostered this view, but in many cases their status consciousness was an inevitable consequence of graduate training. Whether it be the bar exam, med boards, or the PhD dissertation, the rites of professional initiation severely tested both the intellectual and emotional resources of the candidate. Other activities, such as internships, professional oaths, paper presentations, framed degrees, and awards convinced both the public at large and the professionals themselves of their inflated importance.[4] The more imposing the professional symbols and tools, the more prestige and status the public was willing to bestow. Often, professionals chose to display the trappings of their discipline. Physicians, for example, did not feel secure opening an office without the requisite microscope on display. All of this, of course, exaggerated the client's fear, respect, and dependence on the professional.

Burton Bledstein[5] and Donald Schön[6] argue that this dependence led to some unfortunate consequences for professional practice. Bledstein believes that the professional culture exploited the weaknesses of Americans—their fear of violent, sudden, catastrophic, and mystical forces that could affect them but about which they had no knowledge. The professional became the scientific authority in nearly every sphere of American life, but his rational dispassion led to an elitist, albeit middle-class, isolationism. American medicine, for example, rationalized the quarantine of the poor in the ghettos by theorizing that diseases thrive in the dirt of tenements. Schön asserts that professionals misused their autonomy by advancing their positions illegitimately for private gain. Professional solutions produced consequences that in some cases were worse than the problems they were designed to solve. Professionals themselves delivered contradictory recommendations on problems of national importance.

Disenchantment with the professions has been gradual. The world wars stimulated scientific research, especially into the incredible powers that could be harnessed through the use of science. The Manhattan Project is the outstanding example. The Soviet launching of Sputnick in 1957 further mobilized American support for science and technology as the nation came to grips with the national shortage and inadequate preparation of its professionals. Yet lingering doubts about the use of professional knowledge were transformed into conscious resentment as the media played up the professional's role in such disasters as the Vietnam war, the Bay of Pigs, Three-Mile Island, the near-bankruptcy of New York City, and more recently, the Challenger space shuttle explosion.[7] Such incidents have undermined the image of professionals in their own eyes and the eyes of their clients. This loss of respect, coupled with a gradual loss of autonomy, has led salaried professionals even to consider unionizing as a means of retaining their professional rights within their employing organizations. Teachers have become militant in this respect, and although they have succeeded in retaining some benefits and privileges, one begins to wonder whether the process has tarnished their professional image further. Indeed, the transition to salaried from private practice, which occurred most dramatically between 1950 and 1975,[8] heralded a change that has been referred to as the bureaucratization of the professions.[9] Professionals in organizational settings now have to compete with other employees as well as among themselves for organizational rights and privileges. They are no longer instantaneously accorded special status owing to their professionalism.

So, the present day reveals a mixed bag of status, responsibilities, and rights bestowed on the professional population. The long tradition of autonomy and the claim to expert knowledge remain, although more firmly in some professional groups and settings than in others. The utility and effectiveness of professional intervention are no longer taken for granted but are scrutinized by other experts and by the general public. Professionals, in sum, may still hold a special place in our society, but today they must face the reality of being held accountable for their every action.

The Education of Professionals

Assimilation into the professional culture begins early in the professional's education. During this time the professional begins to identify with the profession and take on some of the personal attributes associated with it. These manifestations are in most cases premature and are largely imitative, but they are nevertheless important in fulfilling the ambitions of the individual. A person may aspire to a particular profession for myriad reasons. Substantive attitude, an image or stereotype associated with a particular profession, a sense of calling to the field or a service ethic, a yearning for status, or a desire to make money may be at work. Whatever the original reasons for the choice, they are likely to be altered once one actually goes into practice. During professional education, however, these bases for occupational selection are likely to sustain and nurture the young professional.

The choice to embark on a particular program of graduate study is likely to be accompanied by considerable anxiety. Except for the very few who are either disenchanted or who for whatever reason do not make the grade, the decision tends to be viewed as irreversible. This is because of what Seymour Sarason[10] calls the "one life-one career imperative." Youngsters in our society are exposed to an ever-expanding smorgasbord of career opportunities, but are told they must choose one. Career paths are linear according to this imperative, and one cannot afford to lose time dabbling in different occupations. A choice should be made and then receive all of one's concentration and energy.

Of course, the one life-one career imperative is a myth propagated by the strivings of the American middle class, which sees dedication to a profession as the road to success. The myth has been defied by countless examples of career wanderers, some of whom have distinguished themselves in several careers or in an ultimate career chosen after a long period of dabbling. Yet the linear career path is presented as a reality to a youngster about to embark on a professional career.

By the time one enters a university, the prospect of actually becoming a professional is within reach. Some of the professions, such as nursing and engineering, can be studied as part of one's undergraduate education, although graduate work is available. It is in part owing to their more limited term of study that these professions are sometimes referred to as quasi-professions. Most professions require some form of graduate education.

A number of characteristics of graduate education help students learn what life in the professions is about. The conditions of instruction differ from those in undergraduate schools. Generally, graduate schools are characterized by smaller classes, more seminars in place of lectures, and greater personal contact between students and professors.[11] The change between undergraduate and graduate instruction may take place only gradually, however. For example, the first two years of medical school are heavy on rote instruction, whereas the last two years provide increasing clinical exposure that clearly distinguishes them from earlier educational experiences.

Contact with professors during these first years is critical, since this provides the first opportunity to witness in action the professional the student hopes to become. The professor, in fact, may not emulate at all the characteristics of a practicing professional; nevertheless, students tend to copy their teachers' behavior and even adopt their outlook. Fortunately, most professors are willing to reveal some of the uncertainties and inadequacies of their field. They do not always command all the facts and willingly expose gaps in knowledge in the professional field under study. Students also discover differences of opinion among their professors. All of this contributes to a "philosophy of doubting,"[12] which is essential in reinforcing, though in a very subtle way, the students' commitment to the field. Appreciation of the profession's need for new ideas and more knowledge strengthens the students' vision of being able to make a contribution some day.

Peer groups, fraternal associations, and titles and dress associated with individual schools further strengthen students' identification with the profession they hope to enter. Both formal school traditions and informal relationships that develop under mutual pressures of work and study play a role.[13] Moreover, out of the need to experience total immersion in one's field, professional students tend to be segregated from those in other disciplines. They are bound by the unique concepts and language of their discipline as well as by sheer propinquity. As they face their rites of passage, marked by milestones of examinations, boards, and clinical trials, they naturally band together. Many of the relationships formed during this period become lifelong. Even if these young professionals lose contact with each other as their careers separate them geographically, they often establish new social relationships with fellow professionals.[14]

Professional education is also characterized by apprenticeship programs. Some schools require more formal practical experience than others. Social work preparation, for example, entails at least a year of supervised practice, whereas law schools, with the exception of mock trials, require little formal apprenticeship experience. Nevertheless, the apprenticeship is viewed as a vital link in the educational process. If it is not provided by the school, it usually takes place in the new professional's first job. For example, some young lawyers clerk for judges, and new physicians and surgeons must fulfill internship and residency requirements. In the sciences, apprenticeships take the form of lab work under the supervision of senior scientists. In apprenticeship, the student is finally disabused of any notion that professional training is merely an extension of undergraduate work.[15] Students now have an opportunity to practice their profession directly. For the first time they see themselves as practicing professionals, which gives them a firm basis for identification and eventual commitment.

A final and somewhat overlooked influential element in professional education is students' identification with great figures in the field. Whether it be Clarence Darrow in law, Florence Nightingale in nursing, or Jane Addams in social work, these figures personify excellence in one's chosen field. Usually a number of folk legends surround such figures, many of which are not taken too seriously. These legends express an ideal, however, that students can aspire to reach. On the negative side, their inability to meet these standards or others they may have set for themselves can cause serious problems in socialization, which I shall examine in the next section.

As their professional education progresses, students experience considerable ego satisfaction and become increasingly committed to their field. This commitment drives them toward the degree and ordained professional status and helps them over the humps. The aspiring professional's family, however, may suffer during this time. In particular, the spouses and children of student professionals, according to C. F. Cook,[16] typically have to sacrifice or delay satisfaction of their needs to help the candidate fulfill his or her degree goal. Yet family members do not really participate in or experience any ego satisfaction from this process. Often the candidate, totally committed to the education experience, is oblivious to this imbalance in need fulfillment. This can lead to turmoil in marital and family relationships.

The psychological needs of the student are fed by other relatives.[17] Many are distinctly proud of this individual's accomplishments, particularly if he or she is the first member of the family to earn an advanced degree. All this tends to inflate the ego, but the adulation can be important in getting the candidate through the long ordeal of professional education. Yet the attention of other family members can also lead to a misguided sense of self-importance. The student may begin to expect deferential treatment from others once he or she begins full-time practice. The educational experience is unrealistic in that it shelters the student from real-world problems during the term of study. True, the problems the student is learning to solve are real, but solitary devotion to these problems and their associated learning tasks, coupled with the deference shown the candidate by his or her family, heightens the status of the profession in the student's eyes. The result can be eventual strain not only within the family circle but also within the employing organization if the student chooses not to go into private practice.

Early Socialization

Once having fulfilled all degree requirements, the new professional must decide where to begin practice. Will it be in a private office or in an organization? The choice has been increasingly toward the latter. The decision to become a salaried employee, however, typically poses more difficulties than private practice when making the transition from professional school. The principal reason is that private practice allows the professional to exercise independence of judgment in applying his or her technical skills, a trait that was nurtured throughout the educational experience. Admittedly, the dissertation committee chairperson, faculty advisor, or even the curriculum made many decisions for the student. Further, the problems he or she worked on were chosen by someone else. Yet the process of professional education encouraged the assumption of increasing responsibility for one's own decisions. In an organizational setting, this independence of judgment may be curtailed or even denied in the first year or so of experience.

The main problem for professional novices choosing to work for an organization is that, although they will be relied on for their technical expertise, the application of their knowledge will be necessarily curbed by the operational exigencies of the organization. This may not be revealed in a formal way, but it will be explicit. For example, the boss may not be not be as directive as one's thesis advisor, but the requirements for shaping one's work along particular lines will be relatively clear-cut. A social worker, for example, might see individual therapy as the undisputed optimal treatment modality in a particular case, yet the exigencies of the agency may require group counseling or a self-help group referral.

The problems of transition to salaried work do not occur only during the first year on the job. For some professionals, they are never-ending. Below, however, I have chosen to focus on those problems that arise during the early socialization period.

Unfortunately, professional school does little to prepare students for bureaucratic life. Professional schools see their job as preparing students to practice their technical specialty.[18] There is virtually no formal attention paid to career concerns, or to the idiosyncracies of organizational life. Hence students receive little training in how to assess themselves, i.e., how to evaluate their goals and ambitions, their values, their skills, or their personality style. They are left to face without warning the difficulty of balancing work concerns with the pressures and demands of family, community, and other outside activities. They have little appreciation for the changes they are likely to face during the subsequent stages of their adult development. Although they may receive some help in finding their first job, they rarely are shown how that job connects with others to form a meaningful career path. In fact, they have few tools with which to evaluate their current job in terms of its satisfaction potential, skill requirements, communication patterns, advancement potential, connection to other key corporate functions, and so forth. Other than quickly discovering that their boss plays a different role than their thesis advisor, for instance, they know little about how to develop and maintain a relationship with the boss. They may also recognize the separate role of a mentor in their career, but here too, they are not sure how to go about finding a mentor and developing a constructive mentoring relationship. Finally, they know very little about organizational and political culture; hence they are quite often unsure about which questions they need to ask, what work habits are considered acceptable, whom to get to know, how and how much to talk, and countless questions such as these relating to personal and career behavior.

Cook[19] found from his experience working with young PhD science graduates that a predictable pattern of declining productivity and creativity occurred as a direct result of the strain accompanying the transition between graduate school and the research laboratory. For example, young PhDs have difficulty acculturating to a technical environment where older people seem more interested in such non-work and nontechnical matters as boating, camping, and teenagers than in the technical matters at hand. When they return to the lab at night to work, they find a tomb rather than the familiar night society they remember from school. Red tape seems to entangle them: the forms to be filled out, purchasing procedures, requirements to attend staff meetings, and so on. Meanwhile, their families, which had to play second fiddle during their education, now begin to demand more time and attention.

Some young professionals make the transition with relative ease, perhaps because of personality factors, a favorable first job, a concerned boss or mentor, or perhaps just a close fit between school and organizational experiences. Others find it difficult but adapt through any number of coping responses. Some, for example, may bury themselves in their work, attempting to learn their trade and the ropes as quickly as possible. Many seek support and reassurance from their peers as well as from their membership in what they are convinced is an elite professional group. Unfortunately, many others find ways to escape their problems by switching jobs prematurely, separating from their family, or becoming disenchanted with and in some cases even leaving, their profession.

What is it about professional education that causes these unfortunate responses during early socialization? Sociologists Nina Toren and Judith King[20] uncovered a number of reasons for transition difficulties. First, the degree itself confers professional status that translates into a powerful force affecting the young professional's normative commitments and work dedication. A good deal of research has found significant differences in professional orientation between PhDs and non-PhDs, for example. Among engineers, PhDs place greater importance than those with bachelor's degrees on having contact with colleagues, on belonging to a professional community, on contributing to knowledge in the field, and on challenges that are intrinsic to engineering work.[21]

The process of obtaining the degree itself influences subsequent behavior, particularly in its requirements of self-discipline, independent judgment, and self-direction. The sheer length of time devoted to the study of one's field must result in a certain amount of emotional attachment and commitment. The investment, in other words, produces an ethos characteristic of professional life, expressed through the values of contribution to scientific knowledge, freedom to do research, unlimited opportunity to use one's expert skills, service to humanity, and pride in upholding professional standards.

Ralph Turner[22] has coined a phrase, "role-person merger," that perhaps best captures the phenomenon being described. Once the individual has surmounted the barriers preventing all others from entering the profession, he or she begins to interpret the accomplishment as an exclusive rite of passage. The candidate now becomes one with the profession. According to Turner, this might even mean continuing to play the professional role in situations where it no longer applies. Continuing to play the role of academic researcher in an industrial setting is an apt illustration.

Subsequent Development within the Organization

Organizational career theorists view early socialization within an organization as a relatively consistent stage corresponding to one's first years in the organization, which, if successfully mastered, leads to subsequent stages of development. Hence, some of the problems I have described above are expected to confront most professionals during their apprenticeships. Organizational career theorists believe, however, that subsequent stages of development within an organization present new and different challenges to the more experienced professionals. My own research[23] has revealed different professional work patterns during three distinct career stages which I call finding a niche, digging in, and entrenched.

Finding a Niche

During this early stage, young professionals tend to be idealistic about their profession. They seek jobs that provide intrinsic satisfaction.

They also tend to be highly mobile, preferring to try different organizations if they do not find what they are looking for in the first.

Unfortunately, much of their initial work is routine.[24] Yet it is critical that they not get bogged down in this routine work. Indeed, although they must do a satisfactory job, they need to save time to search out and complete more challenging tasks. This need for risk-taking behavior is somewhat blocked, however, by the nature of the novice's early assignments. These tend to be part of larger projects under the supervision of senior professionals or a supervisor.[25] It is necessary, then, that the young professional show some patience, make the most of the experience shared with older professionals, and gradually take on more independent work as opportunity allows.

Gene Dalton, Paul Thompson, and Raymond Price believe it is critical that the young professional seek out a mentor during this early stage.[26] The mentor effectively bridges the gap between graduate and organizational experience by providing organizational savvy that can nowhere be found in the graduate student's textbooks. The mentor is usually an expert in the same field as the apprentice, but this is not a necessary condition. Rather, the apprentice relies on the mentor more for learning the ropes: how to structure the analysis so it gets done faster, who to talk to to get a request approved, how to requisition necessary equipment and travel funds, how to negotiate faster delivery from suppliers, and so forth.

Digging In

This mid-career stage, when many professionals are in their thirties to mid-forties, perhaps affords the greatest opportunity for expressing one's professionalism. Professionals during this time are committed to their work, and put in long hours, and their skills are at a peak. They tend to seek organizational environments characterized by small work groups, collegiality, and high pay. Having developed a fair degree of trustworthiness, they must adapt to the organizational culture and make their personal imprint without jeopardizing the essential norms of the organization. One way to make a mark is to become a temporary specialist in a critical area without becoming pigeonholed.

Professionals during the digging-in stage still need to reconcile personal standards with bureaucratic requirements. Although the school experience is now far behind them, there is still a tendency to resist organizational rules and procedures, to resist supervision, and to maintain only conditional loyalty to the organization. A number of tasks face these digging in professionals, according to developmental theory.[27] First, there is a need to develop a working relationship with peers from other disciplines, supervisors, and administrators. Although perhaps poorly prepared to do so, professionals need to learn to accept this human aspect of organizational life, including the need to politick and compromise to get their ideas across. They also need to develop trusting relationships with immediate colleagues to whom they might be able to turn for support and advice. In facing technical difficulties in their work assignments, they will need to cope with ambiguity as well as outright resistance to their ideas. Feedback on performance during this stage may be even less forthcoming than during early socialization. They will also need to establish an organizational identity, which is contingent on learning the reward system in the organization, that is, how to get ahead, whom to associate with, whom to trust. Finally, this is the period when many professionals choose to specialize and others begin a transition to management. It is also the time when professionals are most vulnerable to alienation and burnout.

Entrenched

This last stage of organizational career development raises the specter of obsolescence as the professional gradually loses touch with recent changes in the field. Yet this is also a time when professionals may decide once and for all to accommodate themselves fully to the organization's value system and expectations. This willingness to compromise may stem from recognition that one is less employable elsewhere than at an earlier stage in one's career, or it may come from a reluctance to uproot oneself and one's family. Nevertheless, by the entrenched stage, the organization and its management have conferred certain rights and privileges on the professional employee, such as steady salary increases, promotions, trust in the professional's performance and dependability, the sharing of organizational secrets and other manifestations of membership, the reliable support of a work group, and so forth. Those who have sustained their performance through many years may be given tenure status, wherein the individual is assured of a job except perhaps in cases of economic emergency. Although tenure outside academic institutions or organizations offering employment security is implicit rather than formally granted, it releases the professional for increasingly independent work.

The late stage of organizational development also entails less supervision of one's own work and more responsibility for the work of others. Two roles are possible: mentor and sponsor. The mentor guides young professionals who are finding a niche and may at the same time broaden his or her own expertise, developing skills that are applicable across the organization or even across the industry. Analytic programs developed by systems engineers, for example, may be used to respond to a range of organizational problems, even though they may initially have been designed for a customer. In fact, working directly with the customer or client is another characteristic of tenure status. Mentors typically maintain a wide range of outside contacts, including liaison with other professionals.

Sponsors differ from mentors in that they focus more on clearing organizational paths for younger professionals than on giving them direct technical guidance. Although such individuals may or may not be in formal line positions, they typically are highly influential in the organization because of their innovative ideas or direction. They also tend to be recognized through achievements and publications outside the organization.

Unfortunately, only a minority of older professionals become mentors or sponsors. Moreover, many entrenched employees do not stay up-to-date in their field. Some display inability to adapt to change. Management may strengthen the potential for obsolescence by assigning senior persons to secondary roles in the organization in order to make way for the presumed inspiration of youth. Older professionals may be assigned to routine work or jobs that lack intellectual demands, time pressure, or variety.

The stages of organizational career development affect the professional's response to managerial direction. In the remainder of this chapter I will describe the barriers to organization integration posed by the professional culture. In the context of developmental theory, it is safe to say that this description of average experience is most representative of professionals during their early and middle career stages. Since increasing age and seniority are known to produce gradual adaptability to environmental phenomena,[22] some of the factors described may apply less to older professionals, although this will vary by individual, organization, and occupation.

Overprofessionalization

Professionals of all stripes have a tendency to become overprofessionalized, i.e., to practice their specialized competencies and serve their professional interests to the exclusion of organizational considerations. It is a particular plight of cosmopolitans, however, because their self-esteem rests on their technical expertise rather than, say, their interpersonal or political competence. As I point out in Chapter 2, management encourages a complementary tendency toward overspecialization by segregating professionals within the organization and by designing jobs requiring finer and finer segmentation of skills. Banishing the professional staff to research and development labs in industrial organizations, institutes at universities, war colleges in the military, or monasteries serves to segregate professionals from the mainstream of organizational life, and hence reduces the likelihood of their integration into the organization.[29] Admittedly, these subunits are designed to allow professionals to retain their technical concentration without excessive managerial distraction and are often promoted by the professionals themselves. Then again, some of these segregated units are obliged to provide services to other line departments, as when research labs do service work for production or quality control departments.

This requires more frequent interaction with management. Overall, there is a tendency for organizational segmentation to produce professional overspecialization. As long as microspecialty is in demand, there are no adverse effects. Should market conditions change, however, requiring different skills, the professional may find that he or she has become redundant. At this point, the professional can be said to know more and more about less and less. Feeling insecure and seeking comfort with associates in a similar predicament, professionals such as these concentrate even more on what they do know. Each skill group begins to think of itself as superior and independent of others.[30] Coordination of these professional groups, by this point, becomes a management nightmare.

Although it is easier to maintain a specialized stance toward one's work when functions are segregated and hence professional values are reinforced by colleagues in a group, some professionals working individually continue to rely on their specialized expertise. In this instance, the pursuit of professional identity is a lonelier process and likely to produce greater role strain. Nevertheless, some professionals persist, owing to the powerful forces of professional socialization. The greater the insistence on narrow technical responsibility, however, the greater the possibility of eventual obsolescence and limited access to positions of broader responsibility. The lone specialist, in particular, risks being pigeonholed.

Evolution of the Problem of Overprofessionalization

Overprofessionalization has both an epistemological and a psychological base, and the two are intertwined. The professional seeks to advance knowledge in his or her field through use of a theoretical framework that represents a reliable paradigm of investigation.[31] Besides developing the framework, which includes concepts, laws, and other explanations, professionals add to knowledge through their acquaintance with a body of literature, proficiency in using specialized instruments, understanding of causal relationships, and a process of inquiring, that enables them to collect, organize, and interpret data.[32] With these tools in hand, professionals proceed in systematic, even pedestrian, fashion to solve problems. Although the search for solutions, using the professional processes described above, may bring its own intrinsic satisfaction, the professional also obtains the psychological reward of status. As perhaps one of only a small few who know how to attack particular assignments, the professional is relied upon to solve some of management's problems.

In some organizations, such as universities, research labs, and professional service organizations, professionals work predominantly with other like professionals and, hence, may lose their status as unique problem solvers. Even in these settings, however, because of increasing complexity in the various professional fields, further specialization occurs. Within a university, for example, the professor joins a particular department, e.g., organizational behavior, within a school, e.g., School of Business Administration. Within the department, the professor specializes in teaching only certain subjects and conducts research in a few specific areas. For example, the teaching specialty may be human resource management, and the professor may be particularly expert in performance appraisal, concentrating on research in BARS (behaviorally anchored rating scales). By narrowing the area of expertise, the academic professional can attain personal influence and authority within the university. Typically, status is earned more through research than through teaching. Research, however, requires entrepreneurial talent, whether displayed through links with colleagues at other schools, through grantsmanship, or through negotiations for reduced teaching loads. Entrepreneurial activity of this kind can potentially involve the professional in more contact with the administration of the university.

Problems arise not necessarily when one specializes but when one overprofessionalizes. Overprofessionalized professionals may attempt to set up an artificial barrier between themselves and lay persons. They may become arrogant and paternalistic in their dealings with so-called nonexperts who may attempt to help solve problems using their intuitive judgment or a trial-and-error method. It has been shown, however, that nonexperts can make significant contributions to technical knowledge in four major areas: 1) problem identification, causal awareness, and diagnosis, 2) traditional knowledge, as in folk remedies, 3) inclusion of cultural elements and community needs in evaluating interventions, and 4) intuitive and personal knowledge.[33] Architects, for example, in their design of physical environments, can be aided enormously by talking with residents who have walked and played in the streets or shopped in the stores. Agricultural scientists developing new seed strains find it advantageous to talk with farmers who have worked the land. The farmers, having an intuitive grasp of the regional ecology, can predict whether the new seeds will be vulnerable to certain predators, plant diseases, heavy seasonal rainfalls, or high winds. Finally, it is well known that biochemists and pharmacologists have developed some important modern medicines by studying folk medicines.

Nevertheless, some professionals persist in isolating themselves from lay persons. In organizations, this is a prime cause of conflict with management. Professionals are known to take exception to the commercial decision-making methods managers use. Working within the framework of business, managers reach decisions on the basis of partial information. Their problem solving is sporadic and deals with the exigencies of the moment. They are keenly aware of the importance of timing in responding to changing business conditions. This commercial orientation, though understood by many professionals, is not fully appreciated.

Managers have other than commercial motivations, of course. One of the manager's principal tasks is coordinating the diverse functions of the firm. The more professionals are willing to relax insistence on specialized procedures, the easier it is for management to coordinate the professionals among themselves as well as with other units in the organization. Further, though not always a technical expert, the manager typically has sharp intuitive insights into the work and potential contribution of the company's staff professionals. One of the most successful projects I have ever studied succeeded because the chief engineer developed a relationship with a procurement manager who was able to work out a special liaison with a particular vendor on some new integrated circuits.

Overcoming Overprofessionalization

It is a mistake for salaried professionals to believe that to achieve independence of action, discretion, or autonomy in their work they must narrowly specialize and thus make themselves indispensable. Pelz and Andrews[34] showed many years ago that autonomy and overprofessionalization do not go together. Indeed, the most successful professionals in their sample of 1,300 scientists and engineers were those who were highly autonomous but who also maintained a strong interest in a variety of research problems. Professionals need to focus their energies until they have mastered their discipline. Some may then wish to continue to specialize, if for no other reason than that they love their work. Others may wish to broaden their knowledge and skills. It is at this juncture that choice is critical. Professionals generally want to have some discretion over assignments that extend their competencies. At People Express,[35] pilots are known to engage in "cross-utilization," meaning they may double as schedule drafters, cargo specialists, or inventory managers. Although these tasks surely go a long way in helping them learn the airline business, there is undoubtedly less than unanimity in pilots' attitudes toward staffwork, which may take up as much time as flying.

One way of viewing the broadening process is through an organizational career perspective. Accordingly, it could be argued that one should specialize initially to make a mark on the organization. At some point, however, one should have gained sufficient confidence to let go of the specialty and expand one's horizons. As one becomes less dependent on others and succeeds in tackling a variety of problems and initiating new solutions, more autonomy should be granted by one's managers.

This process of first specializing and then generalizing was noted by Edwin Smigel[36] in his study of law firms. Associates typically begin by taking on special assignments and then concentrating on a narrow area of the law. If the young lawyer performs well enough in the specialty, he or she may next begin to receive assignments from some of the partners, a work pattern that begins the broadening process. Those who can pass the test of working for the most powerful partners may themselves make partner. Although partners may develop special areas of expertise or establish steady client relationships, they like to be flexible enough to entertain new assignments. The business environment affecting law firms is hardly stable. More and more large institutions are beginning to bring their legal work in-house rather than rely on a single law firm for all their legal needs.[37] Legal professionals have to be ready, therefore, to handle a variety of assignments if their firms are to compete successfully.

Autonomy over Ends as well as Means

The issue of autonomy, which was also addressed in the last chapter from the managerial perspective, is perhaps the most critical problem in the management of professionals. As was explained in Chapter 2, professionals wish to make their own decisions without external pressure from those outside the profession, including their managers. This right of autonomy, however, clashes with management's expectations regarding the proper role of the employee. Professional employees are expected to conform to the basic goals and procedures of the enterprise.

The problem of autonomy among salaried professionals may stem from the fact that they differ in some important ways from their counterparts in private practice.[38] The private practitioner, such as the doctor, for example, has exclusive responsibility for the patient's or client's welfare. This is simply not true of salaried professionals; although they perform critical functions for their employers, they are not indispensable. A bank, for instance, if not satisfied with its in-house counsel can purchase legal services from outside firms. There are also power differences to consider. Doctors have little dependence on their patients. Salaried professionals, however, rely on their managers to employ them. Even when the salaried professional's services are in short supply, there is a limit to the number of organizations that would hire this individual. Finally, private practitioners still seem to have higher status than salaried professionals. Indeed, by such organizational criteria as hierarchial level or salary, the latter have less status even than their managers.

As is detailed in Chapter 2, the problem of autonomy is best addressed by breaking it down into two parts: autonomy over ends, or strategic autonomy, and autonomy over means, or operational autonomy.[39] I have already established, furthermore, that professionals are primarily interested in operational autonomy. Most good managers will not quarrel with the quest by professionals for operational autonomy. Indeed, the *Cox Report*[40] found that managers at the supervisory level were interested in collaborating with subordinates on objectives and then measuring performance against these objectives. At the executive level, general managers of divisions and subsidiaries, as long as they had operational control, themselves abided by the need to submit to parent-company financial controls. Unfortunately, some managers persist in overcontrolling the means of professional practice. Whether it be the need to fill out small-order procurement forms, produce technical memos on every step of the process being worked on, submit to bothersome department reorganizations, or pass on a customer to the appropriate authority for fear of being accused of usurping the boss's responsibility, professionals by nature will object to process constraints. They prefer that control be exerted, if at all, at the point of output. All they need to know is when the manager wants the finished product, design, or process. Once the parameters are set, they will get the job done. Of course, consultations will be sought, sometimes quite frequently, with colleagues. This merely adds, however, a further, though more implicit, control on the professional's activities.

On the other side of the coin, salaried professionals may be equally guilty of usurping the managerial prerogative of autonomy over ends. It is clearly management's job to establish the strategic goals of the organization or at least recognize those goals and values that emerge to shape the embodiment of the organization. Management then communicates those goals and values that can guide behavior within the organizational community. But some professionals believe that their expert status gives them the right to decide what their precise agenda at work will be. I have seen this basic struggle over strategic autonomy played out countless times in technology-based organizations that have a defined R&D function. Problems typically arise in basic research or between research and development. Basic research scientists generally insist on freedom to select their own work assignments. Their managers, most of whom have scientific backgrounds, will not necessarily object to their insistence on autonomy but may try to curtail the number of projects they work on. Upper management, meanwhile, puts pressure on these managers to be sure that the scientists engage in projects of obvious strategic relevance to the firm. Debates about long-term versus short-term interests are likely to ensue.

Conflicts between research and development often take the form of power struggles. Those scientists committed to research may try to relegate development to a less substantial role in the company. Each group, meanwhile, faces different objectives: research may tend to emphasize quality and innovation potential, whereas development is typically more interested in cost and process constraints.

Individual scientists or engineers within either function, but typically development, may come into conflict with management or even with other professionals when attempting to champion a premature project. In a computer manufacturer, one product engineer attempted to push a disk drive project into the marketplace well before some of the other engineering specialists had cleared their own specifications. Relying on electric, mechanical, and magnetic technologies, a disk drive requires considerable integration within the project team and is usually the responsibility of the project manager. The young product champion in this case simply could not tolerate any delays, which the more experienced manager accepted as a reality of the development process. In another company, which basically handled defense contract work, occasionally some of the technical professionals became disgruntled when their company refused projects requiring new technologies and competitive procurements. Yet, as a reliable contractor expected to deliver certain products, the company could simply not accommodate these professionals, as it was not within its mission to enter competitive bidding markets.

Professionals obviously differ among themselves regarding the amount of strategic autonomy they require. As a general rule, engineers, having been socialized to adopt an applied view, require less autonomy over ends than do scientists. Physicians, owing to their supreme professional status, have historically insisted on complete autonomy over health-related decisions in the hospitals and clinics in which they work. If they have deferred to any bureaucratic requirements, these have typically been administrative concerns, such as scheduling or paperwork.[41] In recent years, however, physicians have seen their strategic autonomy deteriorate as a result of the rise in influence of such external forces as corporate health organizations, third-party payers, and government regulations.[42] Other exceptions, discussed earlier, wherein strategic autonomy may be granted, include the degree status of professionals, their track record, and the nature of the organization they work for.

Professionals also, learn to relax their insistence on strategic autonomy as they become encultured within the organization, i.e., as they realize the advantage of connecting their technical competence with the needs of their employer. As Robert Avery[43] pointed out, they need to become "idea salespersons" within their organizational communities to create enthusiasm and stimulate contributions. This may at first appear to be inimical to their identity, especially the need to negotiate with others in different departments; but many professionals find that some of the social and organizational constraints can be overcome if they are simply included as factors in their work. Although compromising on autonomy in this way is difficult, often because of inexperience, it is necessary to make one's organizational environment predictable.

Overemphasis on Professional Standards of Evaluation

On the basis of a set of expert, specialized skills and the resulting claim to autonomy as a right, professionals expect to direct their own activities in the workplace free from constraining regulations or interference by others. They desire, furthermore, to be evaluated on the results of their activities rather than on their conformity to the rules and regulations of the enterprise. It can also be argued that the professional procedures they follow are quite critical to their ultimate performance. Much of their training involves learning often exacting, systematic methods. Indeed, the scientific method, entailing rules for concept formation, conduct of observation, and validation of hypotheses, exemplifies the tradition of professional practice.

Professionals will thus submit to evaluation of their practice in the process sense, but they prefer that their peers perform this function. This entails a review of their conformance to professional standards as well as an opinion regarding their use of "professional judgment." Even when their administrators are also professionals, however, there is a limit to how thoroughly the individual's methods can be reviewed. In law, the methods of practice, categorized under the heading of due process, are largely affected by nontechnical factors such as local conditions, business sense, or intuition. Hence, legal administrators are hard-pressed to standardize work in corporate settings. Nevertheless, the activities of the lawyers, as specialists within the organization, need to be regulated to ensure that they are in conformity with the organization's mission, as well as coordinated with the work of others. Management, therefore, needs to establish minimum rules of conduct, some of which may interfere with professional norms.

Bureaucratic Versus Professional Standards

There is perhaps no greater source of strain between managers and professionals than the conflict between bureaucratic and professional standards. Subject to past commitments and current pressures from both internal and external interest groups, managers can rarely achieve the ideal standards upheld by professional groups.[44] Their training is categorically different from the training received by professionals. Classroom education emphasizes interdisciplinary, practical approaches to handling competing interests. The popular case method often works against an elegant or pure solution. This applied stance is further reinforced by extensive on-the-job training.

Professionals, on the other hand, are allowed to experience the purity of professional knowledge, without the contamination of bureaucratic conditions. Their exposure is predominantly confined to a single discipline, and their objective is to meet and even eventually raise the standards of excellence in that discipline. These standards are supported widely by others in the profession who occupy positions outside the organization. Where professional standards conflict with those used within the organization, professionals can muster support for their cause by recruiting the support of fellow professionals or their professional associations. This provides some help in resisting bureaucratic standards that may be considered ill advised.

One study found that social workers overwhelmingly resisted state bureaucratic standards, such as residence requirements governing client eligibility for assistance and budgetary ceilings governing the amounts of assistance.[45] Such standards defied the service ethic engrained in the social workers' code of professional behavior. Teachers have historically resisted attempts by their administrators to get them to resort to formal rules as a means of controlling student behavior.[46] They view such rules as antagonistic to their primary function as professional educators.

Managers occasionally press professional staffs to relinquish their insistence on strict observance of professional standards. In one company, a manufacturing division urged the in-house organizational training group to provide a quick stress management course to relieve some of the pressure on the first-line supervisors. The training group resisted, responding that it had no stress management course on-line, nor would it consider delivering one until it had properly diagnosed the situation confronting the supervisors. The division vice president said he could not afford the time for a needs analysis, so he simply contracted a stress management program from an outside consultant.

In another company, a computer manufacturer, a tremendous dispute erupted between marketing management and the engineering staff responsible for the next generation of micros. Marketing wanted to announce and display the new computer at an upcoming international sales convention. The design team resisted, saying it would not be able to deliver the computer with the speed rate it was working toward. Management felt that the product should be displayed anyway, with the advanced speed rate promised as an extra. The engineers felt that introducing the product before they had achieved what they hoped would be a significant breakthrough would compromise their integrity.

Whereas these scenarios depict professionals as the agents responsible for holding back information, the situation is often completely reversed when it comes to the communication of new knowledge. Professional reputation is based primarily on published work or patents. Although one can rise in the ranks of a professional association by being a good worker—for example, by planning meetings, publishing newsletters, and coordinating placements—most professional offices are reserved for the scholars in the field. Of course, some of the stars in a given profession may shun membership in a professional association. Nevertheless, their reputation will remain intact if they continue to publish or if they have already made important discoveries.

Management, however, considers new knowledge discovered by its professional employees under the organization's auspices to be its property and is loath to release it if the knowledge can give the organization a competitive edge. Industrial organizations attempt to patent discoveries from their laboratories, for example, but the patent process often takes too much time for professionals yearning to see their contributions in print. Beyond the patent, some companies require that any publication produced by a professional be first screened for confidential disclosures. Scientists and engineers are also usually required to sign an agreement not to divulge corporate secrets if they leave the company. It has been reported that restrictions are typically more severe for engineers than for scientists, since the former are more directly involved in unique products or processes of the firm.[47] Similarly, communication of development work is scrutinized more carefully than basic research.

In spite of these restrictions, professionals tend to seek employment opportunities where they can improve their status as well as their skills. Consequently, publishing, attending professional meetings, and having access to resources and facilities to aid in their research will be important to them. Aware of these criteria, some companies purposely encourage professional standards to attract high-caliber professionals. Moreover, gaining a reputation as a professional developer can help the firm from a public-relations and even capital-development standpoint.

Differences in Standards among Professionals and among Organizations

Standards differentiate both professionals and organizations. For example, we know that cosmopolitans tend to be predominantly interested in professional recognition through the usual professional outlets. Locals, in contrast, are interested in achieving rank and status within their own organizations. Since the professions as a whole may be roughly categorized on the cosmopolitan-local continuum, it is not surprising that engineers, for example, tend to be less concerned about being evaluated by their managers than scientists.

Other factors distinguish individuals within the same profession. Sharp differences have been found among nurses on standards, especifically adherence to hospital rules and procedures.[48] The differences are attributed to whether the nurse has been trained in a diploma or degree program. Diploma programs are designed by hospitals; degree programs are collegiate. The nurses with degrees, having been trained partially outside the institution where they practice, tend to be much more resistant to hospital standards.

Physicians, being among the most cosmopolitan of all professions, have a tradition of successfully resisting bureaucratic encroachments on medical standards, but this has begun to change. One salaried physician with whom I spoke told me that the disagreement rate between his hospital and Medicare regarding hospital admissions was up to 30 percent, compared with the historical rate of 5 percent. Doctors have relied in the past on a great deal of self- and peer regulation to control their practice, whether through specialty boards, their medical societies, recertification processes, or simply collegial consultation. Although external review procedures have begun to creep into the profession, another physician whom I interviewed believed professional standards were one area doctors would continue to hold onto. He reasoned that it was simply ingrained in the profession. He told me a story about an in-law of his who had just completed a musical recital. At the conclusion of the program, this young doctor, to the great dismay of his wife, bluntly asked the unsuspecting musician: "Did you make any mistakes?"

With respect to differences in standards among organizational types, nowhere is one as free to follow one's professional standards than in the university. Yet universities and schools, and even departments within a given university, differ dramatically in their emphasis on professional versus teaching and service standards. Hence, cosmopolitan professionals trying to build a reputation in their discipline will be careful to pick a university that stresses research over teaching. In fact, in some instances, scientists may choose to work in industry to avoid teaching entirely, even though industrial work may not offer as much independence.

Government agencies and professional service organizations offer the next greatest freedom from bureaucratic constraints on professional standards. Government, given its diversity of functions but in particular its unique role of trying to achieve the public interest, interferes less in the publication of nondefense material, for example, than commercial enterprises. Professional service firms also give their professionals considerable leeway because of the uncertain nature of their work flow and their reliance on entrepreneurial activity.[49] These firms also build reputations based on professional integrity. Indeed, one of the pitches a law firm can make in persuading a company to buy its services rather than hire in-house counsel is that the law firm can be more objective. Thomas Barr,[50] of the law firm of Cravath, Swaine & Moore, explains that a lawyer in an outside firm can turn to his partners and say, "Look, I have to say to the president of X corporation that if he does something improper, we'll resign." It is simply easier to fall back on your partners than have to sit there and do it yourself. Of course, no partner wants to lose a big client, either.

This example begins to explain why industrial concerns offer perhaps the least freedom to adhere to professional standards. The professional is simply more dependent on management when it comes to personal career decisions. Furthermore, because management's first concern is meeting the goals of the organization, professional standards will be accepted only to the extent they merge with bureaucratic standards. Often, however, managers and other nonprofessional employees approve of and follow the bureaucratic standards more readily than do professionals. Hence, rewards, such as salary increments and promotions, tend to favor the nonprofessionals over the professionals. Moreover, some professionals have reported in surveys that such intrinsic rewards as challenge on the job are more readily available in managerial than in professional positions. Dual career ladders, a corporate strategy I shall address at length in Chapter 5, have been constructed to respond to legitimate complaints by professionals about inequality of rewards, both extrinsic and intrinsic.

The Role of Professional Associations in Standard-Setting

One of the main reasons salaried professionals can push so strongly for adherence to their professional standards within bureaucratic contexts is that their professional associations will back them up. Through their publications and meetings, these associations and societies disseminate knowledge of the field and keep their members up-to-date on new developments. Through the meetings, professionals can keep up their contacts with colleagues in other organizations. This stimulates their feelings of importance and status within the profession. Through presentation of papers at these meetings, professionals acquire another outlet for appraisal and recognition of their work. Standards are upheld through other functions of the professional association. Through accreditation of educational curricula, standards of training are established. Through publication of codes of ethics, standards of conduct are defined. Registration and licensure set qualifications for membership and limit practice to the qualified.[51]

Some associations have also gotten into bread-and-butter issues, such as salaries and working conditions and have virtually taken on union status through collective bargaining. The National Education Association (NEA) is the largest association of this kind. Professionals in other occupations have resisted unionization and have even formed ad hoc unions to resist the unionizing efforts of nonprofessional unions; in some cases they have disbanded after a successful defeat of outside unionism. Among the reasons that have been cited for professional opposition to unionism has been the dampening effects on personal autonomy and initiative resulting from the union's operational values of standardization and uniformity. Professionals sustain an intense individualism and ambition, and hence fear any collective system that does not reflect the individual's responsibility, performance, or qualifications. As a result, they resist seniority systems—among the most popular of labor provisions—which are based on length of service rather than merit.

In an effort to combat unionism but nevertheless band together to present collective concerns to management, scientists and engineers in a limited number of firms have organized so-called sounding boards. These groups get involved in matters of direct concern to the professionals they represent. In the tradition of company unions, however, they seek to collaborate with management and hence draw the line on establishing an adversary relationship, which is more characteristic of formal unions.

In spite of the unique position of professional associations in fostering the professional standards of their memberships, officers of these bodies often have difficulty gaining support for their associations.

Professionals join associations for different reasons and hence may disagree on the importance of particular agenda items, such as technical versus career matters. Since professionals themselves differ in their orientation to the profession versus the organization, some associations may find it harder to attract and sustain their membership than others. A recent EDN (formerly *Electrical Design News*) magazine survey disclosed that more than half (51.6 percent) of its electrical engineering readers thought that the IEEE (the Institute of Electrical and Electronics Engineers Inc., the world's largest technical professional association) did a poor job representing them. Part of the problem in engineering, beyond engineers' notorious local orientation, is the fragmentation of their professional societies. Each technical specialty, e.g., civil, chemical, electrical, mining, and mechanical, has its own society, and each of these has its own regional and local affiliates, special-purpose organizations, and federations to which it may belong.[52] Finally, professional managers not only belong to these professional associations but often become prominent in them. This occasionally curbs participation on the part of the purists, who see any form of management, professional or not, as encroaching on the development of bona fide standards for their profession.

Disregard of Organizational Procedures

Since professionals are by nature individualistic and resist conformity to regulations imposed on them from outside the profession, it is no wonder that they tend to disregard procedures used to standardize some decision making in their organizations. Professionals may not disagree with the use of routine procedures to help get certain jobs done within the organization, as long as the procedures do not hinder their practice. And most professionals work in jobs that do not lend themselves to easy codification or reliance on rules. Nevertheless, some managers see value in routinizing professional work to the extent possible, primarily because it increases efficiency. In general terms, managers need to make choices about how their organizations will exploit their respective environments. Those who push for routinization tend to emphasize profits and efficiency; those who push for nonroutine processes tend to emphasize growth, innovation, and quality.[53] In the social work environment, for example, management may choose to emphasize the number of clients served or the quality of the services provided.

Where routinization does occur, i.e., where there is a preponderance of rules defining and enforcing what is to be done, professionals tend to react negatively. The research in this area has found that among their reactions are feelings of disappointment with career and professional development, disappointment over inability to fulfill professional norms, and even dissatisfaction in social relations with supervisors and colleagues.[54] W. Richard Scott[55] found in his sample of social workers that 72 percent believed their caseloads were too large to allow them to perform adequate casework with their clients, and 85 percent believed they were required to spend too much time filling out the various forms required under agency procedures.

There may be one classification that can differentiate organizations on professional procedures: government versus private organizations. In the United States, the combination of a public policy oriented strongly to fairness and equality of opportunity and shortages in the supply of services has led to the need to install procedures to assist professionals in making service decisions. In the area of law, Department of Justice attorneys face particular prosecution priorities that lawyers in private firms would consider overly burdensome.[56] For example, the actual conduct of prosecution is dictated by a 56-page operating manual written to standardize procedures in all jurisdictions. Conduct is further limited by a centralized decision-making structure that controls personnel, disbursements, and even the disposition of major cases. When I presented this finding to a young attorney working for a district attorney's office, he told me that many young lawyers will acquiesce in these procedures since, at least, they will have obtained some good experience prosecuting. The ambition of some of these lawyers, however, as implied in this remark, is ultimately to go to work for a private firm where they can practice more autonomously. Of course, many who are committed to civil service law do stay in the public sector. Further, some lawyers prefer the security offered by government work. Nevertheless, the procedures imposed in public bureaucracies, for whatever reason, are at best tolerated by professionals.

As another example, I was told by an exasperated physician that an electric company would allow one of his patients to defer payment of her utility bill because she had to care for someone seriously ill at home. What bothered him was that the company would not accept a phone call from him corroborating this fact. He had to write a letter, because that was the procedure the electric company had worked out through the state agency that regulated the bill-deferral program.

The antipathy toward procedures felt by professionals is in many cases understood by their managers, who can often make life easier for them by selectively applying particular regulations.[57] Indeed, some managers see their job as buffering professionals from outside interference so that they can do their work unhampered by unnecessary interruptions. Managers who behave in this way typically recognize and profit from the technical contributions made by their professional staff. A more subtle process of goodwill may also emerge in certain situations where the manager, in exchange for a reduction in interference, expects compliance on particular procedures that are of subjective importance. I have seen this occur in university academic departments, where, in exchange for a reduction in teaching load or a favorable teaching schedule, a professor volunteers to serve on a critical administrative committee organized by the dean or department chairperson.

Although administrative procedures often interrupt the professional's practice, they are at least tolerated when held to the bare essentials of managerial control. Technical procedures are a different matter. They are viewed as the domain of the professional staff, and interference is almost automatically resisted unless formulated through professional administration. Even then, professional managers need to be careful not to tread on professional prerogatives. For example, in hospital or clinic settings, a physician-in-charge may through chart review make comments on the treatment plan of an attending physician in order to maintain high standards of patient care. These comments, however, are interpreted as suggestions, leaving a wide margin for alternative behavior. In the administrative practice of scheduling, however, compliance is generally expected, and there tends to be little margin for alternative behavior on the part of the physician.[58] Similarly, in private law firms the partners typically develop an elaborate menu of standardized forms and documents (known as boilerplate) that the attorneys use to organize deals and business matters. Interestingly enough, however, according to Eve Spangler,[59] associates tend to be more enamored of boilerplate than senior partners, who fear that any standardization of work may interfere with the firm's ability to market itself successfully by providing custom-crafted service to its clients.

Professionals are likely to differ in their reaction to technical regulations, depending on the work setting in which they find themselves. A CPA working in an auditing capacity, for example, may abide by certain restrictions and regulations governing his conduct in order to comply with SEC regulations, the standards of his own Financial Accounting Standards Board (FASB), or even the ethics of his profession. If transferred to the tax department, however, outside the restrictions imposed by the IRS Code, the CPA may prefer and push for a more flexible work environment.

Some professionals in highly specialized work environments will resist all forms of standard procedure, regardless of their intent or type. Todd La Porte[60] found this to be the case in his study of an industrial research laboratory. Scientists not only complained about such procedures as budgeting and funding, equipment control and procurement, personnel evaluation, scheduling, forecasting, proposal requirements, and project evaluation, but declared that they accounted for or increased friction between themselves and their managers. Electronic data-processing professionals almost automatically react against traditional auditing procedures and internal security measures.[61] Nursing professionals find it difficult to put up with the reams of legal, financial, and insurance forms they have to fill out for each patient admitted, not to mention the pages of detailed charts and reports required.[62]

Faced with what appear to them to be unacceptable incursions into the work for which they have been trained, some of these professionals strike out against the system, usually by attempting to elude the procedures in some way. Although they may be able to carry off their bureaucratic subterfuge for a time, especially if the infractions are minor or perhaps even tolerated by an understanding boss, the system will eventually catch up with them. Procedures are invoked in the first place to assure continuity and predictability, and breaks in the procedures are bound to be picked up. Unless professionals are given a platform to make known their displeasure with irresponsible procedures, situations in which professionals are found to be disregarding essential policies are likely to result in considerable conflict and ill will throughout the organization. In a project development group I studied, the project needed a part, and to meet the schedules, the group cut a deal with a familiar vendor. Eventually, purchasing found out about this short cut and sent the project manager a stiff note saying they would have to qualify three vendors; otherwise, the company would be incurring severe liability. The project manager responded that it was too late, the project was already in its next stage, and no one would ever find out anyway. The purchasing director could not, for obvious reasons, accept this response; so he sent the problem up to his boss. A conflict subsequently ensued several levels above the original participants, between two vice presidents. To my knowledge, it was never resolved to the satisfaction of the original foes.

Lack of Interest in Real-World Practice

Problems with the real world stem mainly from the difficulty of making the transition from school to work. The conditions of professional education are simply not often replicated in the working world and consequently cause predictable strain during early socialization within the organization. Unfortunately, young professionals are inadequately prepared for bureaucratic life. The clean conditions for pursuing knowledge in their discipline are typically unavailable in messy bureaucratic establishments. Indeed, the best students, those who have excelled in acquiring the norms, skills, and values of the profession, are often those who have the most difficulty adjusting during their initial employment experiences.

Walter Orlow, employee relations manager at Honeywell Information Systems, disclosed that the company has not met its retention goals in its Advanced Engineering Program (AEP). Four to five AEPs are hired each year to take on six-month rotating assignments within the company and are given wide latitude in their choice of assignments as well as in their ultimate permanent job selection. AEPs are also given the opportunity to earn a master's degree during their internship. Unfortunately, in spite of the excellent opportunity afforded by the program, plus the fact that the AEPs are drawn from the highest achievers in their college classes, program participants experience a higher attrition rate than normal hires. The problem, Orlow concluded, is not that these gifted young professionals have failed in the organization. Indeed, it may be that they have done exceedingly well. Having had exposure in a multitude of technical settings, they continue to perceive themselves (and in fact are perceived by the market) as highly talented, leading-edge professionals. This tends to reinforce a cosmopolitan orientation that curbs loyalty toward the original organization.

Although making the adjustment to organizational life is especially difficult for young professionals fresh out of school, some professionals, especially those who sustain a cosmopolitan orientation, never achieve complete socialization. Their strong need for autonomy may forever conflict with the organization's need for control. During the latter phases of the cosmopolitan's career, the resistance, characterized often by antagonistic behavior, may have subsided. However, the cosmopolitan professional by this time may simply have chosen another mechanism to express lack of interest in real-world practice, namely, apathy and withdrawal.

Management, of course, is not guiltless in its involvement in conflicts over the real-world practice of professionals. Accusations of real-world naiveté are often expressions of inferiority or trepidation in the face of the young professional whose skills are likely to be sharper and more up-to-date than those of the supervisor or of veteran colleagues. Yet some professionals do little to dispel fears that they cannot adjust to the real world.

The principal issue behind real-world adjustment problems is that some professionals are unwilling to compromise on the elegant procedures specified by the profession and consider organizational requirements an intrusion into their practice. This issue has been played out, perhaps more than anywhere else, between scientists doing basic research in industrial organizations and managers of user departments. Time and time again, I have heard the complaint from management that the scientists care only about their research and have little interest in how their work will be used or in any way benefit the firm. When questioned about this form of isolationism, the scientists seem to respond in one of three ways: (1) it is not their job to convert scientific breakthroughs into profit-making ventures, (2) no one would listen to them anyway, or (3) when they do communicate their findings, nine times out of ten, production or marketing will distort or misunderstand the information it has been given. These responses may represent exaggerations, but are often quite real to the complainant and need to be addressed in an open forum with management. Occasionally, third parties can resolve the disputes between scientists and managers. In fact, engineers, as professionals trained to convert scientific discoveries into practical applications, are prime candidates to take on this role. This, in fact, occurs in many firms, but engineers are not automatically suitable to serve in mediating capacities. Some simply do not have the social skills to resolve disputes between people; others may be more oriented to one of the basic functions, i.e., R&D or manufacturing, making them unable to assume an impartial role.[63]

Certain professionals, regardless of discipline, occasionally emerge to serve internal liaison roles. They take it on themselves to link their group, whether it be research, development, auditing, legal, or software development, to other internal units within the organization that need and would make use of results from the group. The liaison role, though not always formally sanctioned by management, can be instrumental in preventing conflicts surrounding the use and dissemination of professional services within the firm.

Part of the knowledge-use problem arises out of language barriers between professionals and nonprofessionals. Professionals, having been trained to write in the technical jargon used in their field, often make little attempt to convert their reports into everyday language that can be understood by users. They may have little patience with those who have not done sufficient study to understand the most basic concepts. They may also claim that a watered-down version of their technical reports will miss the significance of their findings.

Management may not help matters by relegating the contributions of some professionals to the proverbial dead-letter file. In an interview conducted by Don Lebell[64] with a CPA in a corporate accounting office, the young auditor displayed severe disillusionment when he was transferred from the field to corporate headquarters. He found that all those "terrific" reports he had cranked out in the field had been rewritten to smooth out the cash flow. Beyond that, they were not really read. Finally, his boss reported to him, "All the action in our business is how well we price and keep our distributors happy and on the team. Who cares whether you think inventory costs are out of line? If they are, that gets cranked into the next pricing exercise. Do you know why you are really here? Because the government makes us fill out all those forms you conscientiously generate . . . ." It is difficult to imagine how this young auditor could sustain any enthusiasm for the technical aspects of his profession while in this firm. All that was required of him was to maintain a minimum level of expertise. His real love of the technical side of accounting would simply not be sustained.

Although this example is admittedly extreme, it does illustrate the pressures on professionals to adapt to the real world of management, which entails much more general problem solving, interpersonal, intergroup, and interorganizational development, and conflict resolution than what was presented to the professional in graduate school. Management practice also tends to go against the grain of the prototypical professional working style even after it has adjusted to organizational conditions. The most familiar complaint seems to be that professionals take too long. They are also accused of needing to reinvent the wheel every time they are faced with a new problem. Part of this is because professionals resist standardization of practice. Reducing the procedures professionals follow to simplified and repetitive tasks is viewed as a sure pathway to deprofessionalization. Professionals, therefore, will insist that "things be done right," i.e., through processes that demand their special skills.

Professionals may also find it easier to be in tune with the real world when they perceive their work as entailing considerable challenge, requiring perhaps an entrepreneurial solution. The formal connection between challenging and entrepreneurial work and the real-world problems of professionals, however, must await the applied discussion of the last chapter.

The Social Culture   4

Much conflict between managers and professionals stems from the character of their respective cultures, as I have been pointing out. Yet both managers and professionals affect and are affected by the wider social culture as well. It is beyond the scope of this book to explore all the social values that influence professional-management relations. The tumultuous period loosely called the 60s, however, both is distinctive enough to examine and had a major impact on the young people who now constitute a disproportionate share of today's salaried professionals. This is roughly the group that the National Opinion Research Center defines as having reached age 20 between 1964 and 1972.[1]

I propose that the value system that distinguishes professionals today from other organizational employees was significantly influenced by the 60s. I view the managers raised within the period as individuals who either did not experience it sufficiently to undergo a value change, who experienced it but eventually purged themselves of its effects in order to prosper in the corporate culture, or who experienced it and, as a result, became particularly receptive to humanistic values.

In what follows I first discuss the 60s period, its effect on what I call the 60s cohort, and the transformation yet persistence of 60s values in modern enterprise. I then show how the professions were particularly affected by the period. Conversely, I provide figures to demonstrate the relative attraction of the professions as a viable career outlet for many adherents to and sympathizers with the 60s culture. Professionals influenced by the 60s are shown as the principal constituents of the "New Class," which has received considerable attention in social theory in recent years. After contrasting the New Class professionals and their working middle class brethren, I concentrate on the difficulties the New Class professionals pose to management. In particular, the basic values absorbed by the New Class professionals will be described and explicitly contrasted with 80s managerial values, which are reasonably consistent with American values influenced by the 50s generation. In the final chapter, the strategies for change will address methods for integrating these two opposing cultures.

The 60s Kids: Why They Were Different

To start, let us consider the argument that the children raised in the 60s were different from other youth cohorts. Intellectual ferment and protest characterizing that period had occurred in prior generations. Even the 50s had its beatniks. What, then, made the 60s so different? Two reasons are primarily sociological and can be covered quickly. First, as a result of the baby boom and the tremendous expansion of opportunities in higher education after World War II, there were simply more people in our society who by the 1960s either belonged to or were affected by the intellectual community. Second, in a slightly more subtle vein, educational, intellectual, artistic, and professional groups enjoyed great respect during the 60s. Jobs and services provided by this community proliferated. Money was available in the form of grants and donations for intellectual products, and the public was disposed to listen to its intellectual leaders.

The third reason explaining why the 60s were different is more philosophical but perhaps most compelling. The baby boomers not only had more educational opportunities than previous generations, but many of them were also raised permissively by parents who had survived the Depression and World War II and who were entranced by Dr. Spock. This permissiveness was not simply behavioral; it was cognitive as well.[2] Children were encouraged not only to think on their own but to think about a wide range of heretofore suppressed thoughts. The enlightened education received by the mass of youngsters attending college during the 60s period included secular teachings that promoted alternatives to divine interpretations of reality. For the first time in history, a significant segment of the population of a major society began to believe individually it controlled its own destiny. This lesson taught the students not only to appreciate their own power but to recognize the power of the group, based on intellectual, rather than physical, prowess. Another consequence of the period, which became combustible when combined with the secular consciousness, was the guilt experienced by many baby boomers over their relative material wealth. As the formerly stable institutions of Western society began to break down—the church, the family, the local community—and as the middle- and upper-class youth of the day began to move out into widely divergent sociocultural milieus, they saw many people whose circumstances were far less fortunate than theirs. Their guilt was expressed in two forms: moral and political. Morally, they began to identify with the victims of social injustice and pleaded with what appeared to them to be massive and callous institutions to reverse their indifference and offer relief. Politically, they began to recognize that these institutions, the so-called establishment, would not heed their moral call, and so they took it upon themselves to organize as a political movement.

Without an overriding issue or purpose, much of the energy and social consciousness of the 60s would have dissipated. In fact, many of the 60s kids rejected political action and dropped out, although their rejection of middle-class values was in its own way a political statement. Indeed, this was the time of the counter-culture. Yet two burning issues mobilized enormous segments of the youth population, as well as growing numbers of their parents, professors, and patrons in the upper middle class: the Civil Rights movement whose champion, Dr. Martin Luther King, Jr., magnificently translated the struggle as not only a minority issue. And then, there was the Vietnam war. The "war," was the real turning point. There was not a sufficient critical mass of protesters who could have converted society on the basis of the Civil Rights movement alone. It was the war which funneled the moral outrage of the youthful secularists of the period into a consciousness which, some argue, has persisted to the present day. After the war ended, the strength of purpose of subsequent cohorts gradually eroded, countercultural expression became less symbolic, secular awareness became too cumbersome to support in the face of revivalist movements, declining economic opportunity reduced the material differences between the classes, and intellectual polemics was considered a meaningless spinning of wheels. The 60s were over.

Diffusion of the 60s Culture

While the 60s period ended around 1973 (one could point to any number of symbolic events, but perhaps one of the most telling was the murder of the Oakland Public Schools' black superintendent by the Symbionese Liberation Army), the cohort, of course, did not disappear. Although some commentators have argued that its spirit and values died with the end of the period, others have found that its values not only persisted but became diffused throughout the wider culture. Members of the cohort have joined the established work force, taken up careers, bought material goods, and even sat home during subsequent civil demonstrations. Yet, as was popularly revealed in a notable 1983 film, *The Big Chill*, in spite of lost ideals and connections, a sense of caring and awareness has persisted. Further, as was detected in a country wide interview,[3] viewers of the film who grew up in the 60s insisted they were still concerned about interpersonal responsibility and social justice; it was just that they had tempered their goals in the face of personal responsibilities. In the words of one respondent: "I just try to have an impact in my own sphere of influence."

What values have made their way into contemporary social culture and become relatively commonplace in corporate society? Some are the humanistic values promulgated in earlier decades, which the culture of the 60s simply reinforced. The concern that work be dignified, personal, and challenging, for example, echoed a prior interest in intrinsic values, specifically, a drive for greater involvement, responsibility, and a sense of achievement.

Numerous studies, ironically of job *dis*satisfaction conducted by survey research organizations in the 70s and early 80s, began to home in on a transformation of American work values. The University of Michigan Survey Research Center,[4] the federal then-named Department of Health, Education, and Welfare,[5] and others began to report a rather steep and pervasive decline in job satisfaction among the nation's workers. By 1979, the Opinion Research Corporation[6] had gathered twenty-five years of survey data and was able to demonstrate that the decline in worker satisfaction had not been abrupt but rather steady and continuous. What was particularly interesting about most of the studies was that pay and security concerned the workers surveyed less than such intrinsic factors as autonomy, opportunity for personal growth, and interesting work. The authors of the ORC study[7] concluded that much of the dissatisfaction expressed stemmed from demands for "tolerance of self-expression, self-fulfillment, and personal growth," values that very much characterized the ethos of the 1960s. They went on to point out, however, that these values came to the fore in industry only in the late 70s, when many men and women from the 60s cohort became permanent employees. By the end of the 70s, these demands, according to the authors, had become "ubiquitous, pervasive, and nontransient."

In addition to demanding more intrinsic satisfaction from their work, employees rebelled against the extrinsic orientation of the Protestant ethic, which asserts that success is tied directly to one's own efforts and any material wealth a person accumulates is a function of how much effort he has expended.[8] Opposition to the restrictions on leisure imposed by the Protestant ethic led to a consumption orientation: American workers determined that the sacrifices they made to earn their paychecks gave them the right to spend their earnings as they saw fit.

As one recent survey reported, however, the consumption ethic is now being replaced by a conservation ethic.[9] Fifty-four percent of Americans believe that maintaining a high rate of economic growth should no longer be given high priority. Further, over two-thirds believe that more emphasis should be placed on teaching people to live with basic essentials than on reaching a high standard of living. These findings suggest that the American social culture is gradually moving away from a purely extrinsic, materialistic orientation. As Barbara Marx Hubbard said at the 1982 assembly of the World Future Society, "we have been there." Replacing materialism will be this conservationist, ecological emphasis, which makes man the steward of the planet. Since people are assuming responsibility for themselves as well as for the earth and its inhabitants, they are seeking work that is purposeful and self-fulfilling.

Evidence of this growing trend toward inner-directed motives may be found in SRI International's Values and Life Styles profile.[10] SRI identified three principal value-driven groups in our society: the money restricteds, the outer directeds, and the inner directeds. Each group is composed of subgroups; for example, the outer directeds are divided into the belongers, the emulators, and the achievers. Only 12 percent of the population was found to be in the money-restricted group. The predominant group (71 percent) is outer directed. These people behave according to how others see them. What is most interesting, however, is that the fastest-growing group is the inner directeds, those people who are motivated by their own inner wants and desires instead of responding primarily to the norms of others. This inner-directed group, at 17 percent at the time of the survey, is expected to grow to 27 percent by 1988.

Although Americans who are willing to act on their inner needs may not be in the majority, clearly most Americans are beginning to focus on their inner lives. Daniel Yankelovich reports that by the late 70s, 72 percent of all Americans were spending a great deal of time thinking about themselves.[11] In work terms, this converts to a focus on jobs that emphasizes personal creativity, self-expression, adventure, and enjoyment. Yankelovich's "self-fulfillment seekers" of the 70s got a false start, however, on two accounts. One, they presumed that the self-fulfillment strategy coincided with economic well-being, and hence pursued affluence as the single route to the better life. Second, the search for self became a preoccupation that Daniel Bell terms a "psychology of entitlement."[12] Extending to all groups in society, not just the claims of the poor or disadvantaged for a basic minimum family income and equality of employment opportunity and *results*, entitlement applied to the management class as a right to rise to the top of the corporation. This was any employee's right as long as he exhibited the appropriate managerial traits. If he did not make it in one company, he would simply try another. Admittedly, the preoccupation with self-advancement recalled the "organization man" phenomenon of the 50s, when outer directedness was at its height.[13] In this period, work was not so much an end in itself as a means valued for how well it served the organization. Individual success was gauged by how well one conformed and adapted to group norms. An employee's or manager's success depended more on how he or she played the game than on individual productivity.

The interpretation of self-fulfillment as the critical value of the 70s is fundamental if we are to analyze the question of diffusion correctly. If self-fulfillment equals self-absorption or narcissism, the experiment of the 60s might have to be considered merely a development stage that the spoiled brats born in the postwar permissive era had to go through on their way to ultimate maturity. If, on the other hand, self-fulfillment translates into the right of every citizen to use his or her intellectual and affective capacities fully, it would have to be considered a cultural change having a potentially profound effect on the modern view of social justice. The key to this distinction may depend on whether the 60s were experienced as ordinary by those living through the period, or as a unique, never-to-be-repeated moment of history, representing a sharp break with the normal patterns of individual and institutional relations within the society. Assuming the period did have a major impact, a potentially dangerous reaction may have occurred if, as *The Big Chill* lamented, the subsequent era brought a loss of hope and, with it, selfishness and anomie. This is the form of the analysis used in Christopher Lasch's notorious condemnation of modern society, in his *The Culture of Narcissism*.[14] Given a loss of faith in America today, the narcissist seeks to live for the moment, to "get every ounce of gusto he can," in other words, to be self-fulfilled. Yet, this ethic is really one of self-preservation which obscures a lack of personal intimacy and social commitment. According to Lasch, the 60s were not much better. The 70s were not a reaction to the promise of the 60s; rather, the radicalism of the 60s merely initiated the process of using disguises to fill up empty lives.

At the other end of the spectrum, one might place Daniel Yankelovich[15] and Peter Clecak,[16] both of whom argue that the quest for personal fulfillment, which called for discarding conventional signs of success in favor of a more satisfying sense of personal achievement, as well as closer and deeper relationships, began in the 60s and has not slackened since. Yankelovich finds the new era enlightening in its diversity of life style, adventure, leisure, opportunity for self-expression, and regard for the mystery and sacredness of life. Clecak, using the concept of "democratization of personhood," finds the unique feature of the 70s to be its extension of the notion of personal fulfillment to a significant number of citizens within every social category. Hence, all the less privileged classes in society have found opportunity to move against the "prevailing structure of advantage to claim their piece of social justice and to seize their cultural space."[17]

In the 80s, which has witnessed the ultimate demise of the New Left as well as the New Deal in the 1984 presidental election and the resurgence of materialism and status-consciousness in the form of the yuppies, one is hard pressed to claim large-scale diffusion of the 60s culture. Yet there is evidence, albeit loose in the form of "Big Chill" catharses and even more subtle transformations of deeply held national values, that some of the 60s cohort are making a difference within organization life and even within the broader society. Among this cohort, one finds a disproportionate number of professionals. Although the consumption habits of the yuppies have gotten the bulk of media attention, their virtues of imagination, daring, and entrepreneurship are more telling in shaping modern American culture.[18] Further, most census counts of yuppies tend to include more 70s kids than those from the 60s protest generation. Those who still demand participation in shaping their own destiny, who would be willing to defy illegitimate authority, or who are as concerned about social justice as their own personal needs are most likely to be individuals heavily influenced by the 60s.

The 60s Cohort in Professional Life

The values discussed above do not expressly identify an occupational preference among the 60s cohort. Yet when one considers that many of these individuals had high levels of education, that many were exposed to a radical analysis of society highlighting the potential for abuse of power, and that many were not aggressively career-oriented, the professions emerge as a likely occupational outlet, especially in comparison with management. This presumption was borne out dramatically by the so-called Woodstock Census,[19] a wide-ranging, nationwide survey of 1,005 self-selected respondents from the so-called Woodstock generation, i.e., people born between 1940 and 1952 who professed strong identification with the 60s era. A full 42 percent of the respondents fell into the category of professional workers. This was followed by 13 percent who were in clerical or sales jobs. Down the list, at 6 percent, were those identified as officials, managers, and proprietors.

Having observed a pattern of significant professional participation in a self-selected sample, I consulted census figures to determine national, professional participation by the 60s cohort. For this analysis, the following assumptions were made:

1. The 60s cohort was defined as those persons who reached the age of 20 between 1963 and 1971. This distribution is similar to the National Opinion Research Center definition, but favors older youth by a year. It thus represents a restricted estimate of those individuals who were most susceptible to the value system inculcated during the 60s period.

2. Data were analyzed for three census years: 1960, 1970, and 1980. Professionals were defined according to the census category labeled "professional, technical, and kindred workers." Any changes in this definition across these three decades were judged not to affect the comparison.

3. Since age groupings had to be analyzed that were occasionally different from census age categories, the pattern of professional participation for any one group within an age cluster was assumed to follow the pattern of the general population.

Accordingly, professional participation rates were organized for the three census years by age category and are displayed in Table 4-1. Rates are per 100,000 general population. The 60s cohort, highlighted as the 19–27-year-olds in 1970 and the 29–37-year-olds in 1980, does represent the largest component of professional participation in those years. It is interesting that trends have usually shown professional participation to be greatest among the 29–37-year-olds, yet in 1970, the

Table 4-1   Professional Participation Rates*

	Year		
Age Group	1960	1970	1980
19–27	752.6	1,333.1[a]	1,101.
29–37	993.2	1,281.8	1,578.0
39–47	848.0	1,123.0	953.1
49–57	633.3	829.7	756.6
Total professionals	4,033.3	5,385.8	5,304.8

*Rates are per 100,000 general population. The 60s cohort is displayed in the boxes.
Source: *1960 Census of the Population*, Vol. 1, Part 1, Tables 155 and 204; *Characteristics of the Population – 1973*, Vol. 1, Part 1, Section 2, Tables 50 and 226; and *General Population Characteristics, United States Summary – 1984*, Vol. 1, Part 1, Tables 41 and 280, U.S. Government Printing Office, Washington, D.C.

19–27-year-olds (the 60s cohort) were participating the most. It is also noteworthy that the overall rate of professional participation decreased by 1.5 percent from 1970 to 1980, while the participation rate for the 60s cohort increased by 18.4 percent. Also, between 1970 and 1980 the 60s cohort increased its participation in the legal profession by a full 50.6 percent above the average increase in that profession, and in the teaching profession, 36 percent above the average.

Clearly, the professions were an acceptable, even preferred, occupational choice for the 60s cohort. This preference was certainly affected by an increasing demand for professional services, an increase in the number of professional schools, and greater availability of financial aid. Staying in graduate school may have also been a convenient way for some from the cohort to avoid military service in Vietnam. Yet those factors seem insufficient to account fully for the rise in participation rates. Another avenue to consider is a cultural explanation.

Cultural Explanations for Professional Participation by the 60s Cohort

A Radical Analysis

For those within the progressive to radical wing of the 60s protest movement, the professions offered the best institutional opportunity to promote social change. This can be demonstrated by citing four cultural values widely embraced during the period that could easily have been converted into occupational activity.

Defiance of Authority.

Through civil demonstrations against racial discrimination and the Vietnam war and the relative success of these efforts, represented, for example, by the passage of the Civil Rights Act and the alleged abdication of President Lyndon B. Johnson, the 60s youth learned they could defy illegitimate authority. Since many of these youth wanted to be "part of the solution" rather than "part of the problem," a job within the power structure, i.e., within management, would have been intolerable. Given their relatively high level of education, they would consider a professional job acceptable and further a base for challenging the status quo. In journalism, as one example, it was reported that young editors began to clash with older editors and to challenge the very policies of their news organizations. Staffs were reported to have bought advertising space for editorials counter to their own paper's position.[20]

Participation in Decision Making.

The 60s youth saw a real opportunity to end the impersonality and distance of bureaucracy by invoking the familiar humanistic theme of participation in decision making. By entering the professional ranks, they would first demystify the technical expertise the professions had used to separate themselves from other groups. Then, through citizen participation movements in the public sector and client advocacy in the private, they would push for accountability on the part of the professionals and for full involvement by citizens and clients in the decisions that affected them.

Service Ethic.

Related to the ethic of participation, the 60s youth saw in joining the professions an opportunity to renew the service ethic that historically had served as the moral pivot of professionalism.[21] According to 60s rhetoric, professionals had relinquished their commitment to service. As city planners, attorneys, social workers, and community practitioners of all kinds, the 60s youth would place themselves at the service of the disadvantaged, and they would be willing to listen, to be criticized, and to be humble in the exercise of judgment.[22]

Anticareerism.

Particularly among the New Left, there was deep suspicion of a sellout, a failure to support community interests in favor of the selfish pursuit of a career. Those who initially chose to pursue graduate or professional education were subject to deep personal guilt.[23] One way to avoid this was to redefine the professional role as a liberating force;

hence radical caucuses were organized in a wide variety of professional and academic fields.

A *Mainstream Analysis: The* "*New Class*"

The preceding analysis excludes the mainstream of the 60s cohort, which even the Woodstock Census[24] characterized as having a liberal rather than a radical agenda—the environment, nuclear weapons, corporate power, feminism. To that extent, the 60s cohort may be considered part (albeit the vanguard) of a much wider sociological phenomenon that has come to be known simply as the "New Class." The New Class constitutes the modern-day equivalent of Trotsky's intelligentsia, i.e., the educated class.[25] Since 1945, the West has concurrently witnessed the emergence of a postindustrial society, characterized by a shift from a goods-producing to a service economy.[26] Associated changes have included the strategic dominance of information and knowledge, especially theoretical knowledge as a basis for research and development and for policy decisions; the growing importance of science-based industries; and the rise of information technology. Hence, postindustrialism has created many kinds of jobs that appeal to the New Class. Indeed, by 1974, there were 21 million professional, technical, and managerial workers, representing one-fourth of the U.S. labor force, compared with 14.8 percent for these groups in 1940. In the mid-1980s, these workers numbered 27 million. By the 1990s, professionals alone will make up 20 percent of the labor force.[27]

Although there has been continuous debate over the membership of the New Class (let alone whether it exists), most definitions point to education (college level or above) and occupation (professional) as principal criteria. New Class individuals also tend to be economically comfortable though not necessarily wealthy, to be politically and socially liberal, and, though not in ruling positions, to exert considerable influence. This influence derives from their growing number, from their knowledge as well as use, of this knowledge to raise their economic standard, and from their services orientation, which, though it does not produce anything tangible, does enhance the quality of life for most of us. Teachers, for example, make us more knowledgeable; lawyers, more civil; newscasters, better informed; and psychiatrists, saner! Finally, beyond the services orientation, New Class members are distinguished by their use of symbols, words, numbers, concepts, and theories which impose order on a complicated world.

This last characteristic recalls the positivist orientation of professionals discussed in Chapter 3. Again, we observe the correspondence between New Class members and professionals. Beyond their occupational preference, however, New Class members are also for the most part employees beholden to their organizations. They are salaried professionals.

Although the ranks of the New Class have swelled, its status has not risen commensurately. The incompetence revealed by military, social, and corporate planners among the New Class in a whole series of nationally publicized disasters has lessened the influence of professionals everywhere. Militarily, we had the Bay of Pigs, Vietnam, and more recently, Beirut, where military officials, though displaying aplomb with computers, could not summon the skills to outmaneuver the enemy in the field, let alone defend themselves against attack. Social planning has been depreciated ever since the generally accepted demise of the Great Society program. Corporate planning was involved in Love Canal, Three-Mile Island, and the near- or full-fledged bankruptcies of New York City, Continental Illinois, Braniff, and Chrysler. Although the last has come back, its revival is seen as owing more to aggressive entrepreneurialism than to analytical planning. Not mentioned above is economic planning, but the nation's inability to resolve the problem of the federal deficit is enough to raise the eyebrows of most Americans regarding New Class contributions in this realm.

New Class Professionals Versus the Working Middle Class

What makes a New Class analysis interesting in contrast to a radical 60s analysis is the view that New Class professionals, if not quite a class, are nevertheless different from their middle-class working brethren *as well as* from their managerial-class counterparts. This offers a partial explanation of why the 60s activists, although supporting measures to relieve workers from the oppression of corporate power, could not engender support among the working middle class. According to Everett Ladd,[28] New Class professionals as an intelligentsia have split off from the traditional New Deal working class, who as a group have become "embourgeoised." Further, as the liberal contingent of the educated segment of our society, perhaps even trained in or nurtured by the mores of the 60s counterculture, they have in many instances rejected traditional bourgeois values such as emphasis on work, thrift, and the importance of material well-being. The embourgeoised working class, on the other hand, affirms these values, and hence tends to support such conservative institutions as business, a strong military, the Republican party, and, in an interesting historical twist, labor unions—once the font of American liberalism during the New Deal. The New Class is less concerned about public spending and, in fact, tends to be progovernment, since many of its members depend on either government or the service economy for their livelihood. Finally, the New Class is prototypically secular, whereas the embourgoised working class tends to support such groups as the Moral Majority in their affirmation of traditional family values and fundamentalist religion.

New Class Professionals Versus the Managerial Class

What the 60s revealed more than at any other time in recent American history was the persistent division between salaried professionals and their management. Not all New Class commentators have excluded managers in their enumerations.[29] Yet early exponents of the New Class idea were careful to distinguish managers, or the "business class," from the intellectual community. John Kenneth Galbraith[30] referred to both as elite groups but suggested an uneasy truce between scientists and academics and the "technostructure" of corporate managers and government officials. The technostructure supplies the jobs for the New Class, but the inherent tasks are essential for corporate achievement. Irving Kristol[31] was less dispassionate in his depiction of New Class/managerial cleavage. Indeed, he saw the New Class as engaged in a class struggle with the business community for status and power. New Class professionals resisted the market as the sole judge of its ideas, and hence attempted to supercede economics with politics— an activity in which it was skilled because of its facility in using the media.

Who are the occupants of the business class, referred to throughout the 60s as the power structure? Although there is common agreement that corporate executives belong, consensus breaks down when one starts to include owners, administrators in public and nonprofit organizations, and lower-level management. G. William Domhoff in his classic *Who Rules America?*[32] argued that the owners still wielded enormous power in America, along with their managers. It was the Marxist revisionist James Burnham,[33] however, who more correctly foresaw a transition of control from proprietor to manager. In his *The Managerial Revolution*, he foreshadowed such subsequent scholars as C. Wright Mills and John Kenneth Galbraith by identifying a coherent group that would gain power through "control of the access to the instruments of production and a preferential treatment in the distribution of the products of those instruments." Mills[34] later incorporated some of the other management categories suggested above, although he expressly excluded labor leaders and politicians, since their institutions are by structure responsive to popular constituencies.

The division between the manager and the New Class professional receives further substantiation from a structural point of view when it becomes clear that the manager's home base is his corporation (to which he would be likely to return even after a stint in politics), whereas the cosmopolitan professional's home base could be the university or a professional referent organization.[35] This structural distinction has been shown in recent years to have cultural parallels. Managers have been depicted as adopting a career ethic, which implies an other-directed, ambitious, marketing character.[36] These people are interested in getting ahead, in raising their worth in the market, and even in subordinating their learning or suppressing their curiosity to advance in their careers. Professionals, however, representing more of a craft ethic, are oriented to self-sufficiency, independence, and autonomy. Craftsmen are most satisfied when they control their own work—when they set their own pace and standards. Managers, as careerists, and professionals, as craftsmen, come into natural conflict as managers threaten the professional's autonomy, while professionals impede the manager's progress toward his or her goals.[37]

Ideological preference is another compelling distinction, except that it is here complications begin to arise. First, intellectual attacks on business require intellectual apologetics.[38] Hence, New Class salaried lawyers, accountants, and scientists, with pro-business (conservative) values, need to be added to the payroll to defend their enterprise. Further, although managers and professionals may differ on economic values, such as the respective merits of state planning and free enterprise, they may espouse similar moral values. Daniel Bell[39] has observed that both groups support the modernist view that the individual, rather than any institution be it government or church, should be the source of moral judgment, and that experience, not tradition, should be the source of understanding. A thawing of ideological barriers between intellectuals and managers is further supported by the well-known fact that the American intellectual community is far less radical than it was in the 60s or than even European intellectuals are today; moreover, it is far from united. And, as Joseph Schumpeter[40] once predicted, there is surprising tolerance of intellectual criticism among business people.

Future managers lived through the 60s, just as professionals did; and although they may not have acted on the values enculturated during the period, many did learn to appreciate them. This was demonstrated in a notable study by Rogene Buchholz that compared five belief systems across different categories of workers.[41] All categories—union officials, hourly, clerical, and professional, as well as management—rated the humanistic belief system highest. By the mid-70s, management clearly understood, and in many cases had adopted, humanistic approaches. What distinguished managers from professionals was not any clear difference on humanistic beliefs. Rather, professionals showed the least adherence to the organizational belief system, whereas management scored very high on this system. The organization-man pattern of the 50s, which valued status and ascension within the organizational hierarchy, persists. Work, according to this belief system, is not an end in itself, as the humanists believe, but a means valued for how well it serves group interests and contributes to one's success in the organization. Notice that this corresponds to the managerial career ethic. Management was also lowest in the Marxist belief system, which finds that most work in the United States does not provide creative and social fulfillment and is predominantly organized to benefit the ownership of the firm. Employees, in this view, should have more control over their working conditions. Managers obviously believe that Marxist conditions no longer exist. Yet the question posed by the Buchholz study is whether today's managers, still very much influenced by a 50s organizational belief system, can relate effectively to their professional staffs, who seem to have been more consistently influenced by a 60s humanistic belief system.

The 50s Manager Versus the 60s Professional

Let us turn now to explicit value differences between managers and professionals arising from their separate sociocultural traditions. These differences are presented as diametrical, although it is not unusual to find a manager with a 60s cultural predisposition or a professional with a 50s predisposition. Basically, the value dimensions, of which there are five, form continua, as shown in Table 4-2, and the most one can say is that the left-hand side corresponds more to the common traits of management, and the right-hand side to those of professionals. The disparity between managers and professionals on these social values is sufficient, however, to merit their consideration as expressions of different cultures, which can be reconciled only through unique managerial approaches.

Hierarchy Versus Participation

Management in the United States, especially in corporate enterprises, is committed to a hierarchical structure of operation. Some organizations, in response to turbulent environmental pressures, have considerably flattened their hierarchies and have even implemented ad hoc, flexible organizational structures. Yet there has been little deviation from the classic principles of unity of command and span of control—that each subordinate should have one manager and that each manager should supervise a relatively fixed number of subordinates. It is widely believed that this system is the most efficient, speeds up decision making, is the optimal communication structure, and yet offers opportunity to decentralize authority rationally.

As I pointed out in the last chapter, salaried professionals have never been entirely comfortable with this structure, but have nevertheless managed to establish an uneasy truce with their managers, provided they have been granted reasonable autonomy regarding work processes. The 60s professionals, however, may have broken this truce. In the 60s, in reaction to what was seen as the impersonal and arbitrary nature of bureaucratic institutions, participation in decision making was promoted as the definitive democratic act.[43] New Left dispatches called for citizen participation through direct popular assemblies instead of the standard representational approach. There could be no backing off from a strong grass-roots citizen role, for this embodied the heart of the democratic experience.[42] Yet this populist philosophy

Table 4-2 The Basic Social Values of Managers and Professionals

Managers (50s-driven)	Professionals (60s-driven)
hierarchy	participation
respect for authority	defiance of authority
corporate efficiency	social justice
team player	individual initiative
career	quality of life

came back to haunt those 60s activists who thereafter joined the professions, for the mistrust of institutions applied equally well to technical expertise. No amount of prior study or training gave an individual the right to intellectual dominance. This was nowhere better illustrated than in education. Courses at the secondary level, as well as in the universities, had to demonstrate "relevance" to the issues and concerns of the day, for example, the plight of women and minorities. Elective offerings burgeoned while the teaching of basic skills was sacrificed. Grades were abolished in favor of pass-fail. Students were given equal say in the design of the curriculum.

The excesses of the participation movement resulted from a misconception about the separate roles of consumer, client, and employee. Of these three, the consumer has the most choice in determining the nature and scope of the contract with the opposing party. Specifically, the consumer can choose whether or not to buy a particular product or service and also whether to reopen the relationship at a later date. The seller can influence the relationship with a consumer but typically cannot control it; rather, he must induce consumer behavior through such devices as price, reliability, service, and so forth. A client, on the hand, such as a student or patient, has less choice in the relationship, since the professional providing the service does so precisely because he or she has superior knowledge or skills. Indeed, the professional is typically granted the right to sanction qualification. Hence, the client is more reliant on the professional. New Left ideology, however, attempted to deny any citizen authority on the basis of technical expertise or intellectual status of any kind. Hence, the client classification was essentially reduced to the customer role. If one did not care for the professional services rendered, one simply severed the relationship. This logic was extended to the role of employee. If one felt one's dignity was being abused in any way by an employer, one should immediately leave the premises.

Although 60s egalitarianism may have gone too far, the 60s did raise standards of accountability for both professionals and managers. Calls for second opinions in medical cases, for informed consent in research undertakings, and for management by objectives in organizational planning, represent the more positive derivatives of the 60s egalitarian movement. What makes the role of the salaried professional so difficult, even in spite of a more participative ethic, is that the professional is at the same time a professional and an employee. There is thus an inclination to view the employer as a client, but this view extends professional participation beyond what is feasible for the manager with bottom-line responsibility for the mission of the organization.

In a study of this very issue,[44] my colleagues and I found that professionals who were encouraged to use their own absolute initiative in performing their jobs, and who were given free rein to challenge management decisions were very likely to adhere more strongly to professional than managerial standards and to sustain professional over managerial allegiance. In certain instances where, for example, the status of the organization depends heavily on professional accomplishment, such as in research universities and laboratories or in professional service organizations, this professional focus may be not only tolerated but encouraged. Some universities, for example, may support the ethic of publish or perish. Recognizing that reputation and consequent marketability may, and should, depend on the production of new knowledge, these institutions may emphasize research and publications. In these circumstances, full participation by professionals in organizational decision making may be appreciated. However, managers, i.e., deans, would probably still resist an exclusive focus by their staff on professional development, particularly if it took them away from their bread and butter functions, especially teaching.

For the most part, particularly in industrial organizations and where management requires employee loyalty and conformity to organizational goals, participation may be a counter productive strategy. Even in the research laboratory, for example, although the scientist may be given carte blanche in developing new ideas, ultimately management must make the final decision about which type of product to support and how, consequently, to allocate the company's resources. In these instances, allegiance to one's profession cannot take precedence over corporate loyalty. The boundary of the organization, particularly in a market economy where resources are finite, matters; as a result, management cannot compromise on loyalty. One cannot be an employee of the profession. Therefore, participation needs to be viewed not as an inherent right of the professional who chooses to base his or her decisions on the standards set by the profession, but as a dialogue that recognizes the constraints of organizational practice. One way of viewing this imperative is to distinguish, as I have previously, between the means and ends of the professional's work. Professionals need to control the methods and procedures they use in practicing their craft. Managers, meanwhile, by setting the goals and overall mission of the organization, actually establish the structure within which participation can proceed. Although seemingly a paradox of power, strong leadership and participation in fact go hand-in-hand. Erich Fromm, in his classic *Escape From Freedom*[45] wrote:

> . . . true freedom is not the absence of structure—letting the employees go off and do whatever they want—but rather a clear structure that enables people to work within established boundaries in an autonomous and creative way.

Thus the role of management should be to empower the professional staff to decide how they will implement the tasks assigned. Indeed, in the absence of managerial structure, participation could be harmful. Research experiments have found, for example, that in a more open atmosphere, individuals are vulnerable to being coopted by more powerful members and can actually lose power if not given adequate information and expert power.[46] Further, Rosabeth Moss Kanter[47] has added that a manager's close monitoring of the participatory process is a signal to professionals that he or she cares about what they are doing. Finally, some professionals do not want to spend much time building a participative climate. They may be perfectly happy being left alone to work on an invention, an innovative process, or an entrepreneurial venture without having to submit to constant group discussions. Hence, it is possible that overparticipation, that is, needing to participate in more decisions than desired, may become as much of a problem for some professionals as underparticipation.

Management's operational role in this scenario should be developmental and coordinative. It provides resources and support for the professional's work and ensures integration among the various operational units functioning in the organization.[48] It controls results, but not the means used to achieve them.

This view of participation is not inconsistent with humanistic approaches to management, such as McGregor's Theory Y. Previous scholars have pointed out that the original Theory Y assumptions were not meant to be entirely consistent with participative management practices.[49] In its operational form, Theory Y calls for establishing a work environment that will appeal to the employee's self-centered drive for esteem and self-fulfillment. Allowing the professional complete freedom to pursue the practice of his or her craft without procedural constraints is consistent with this approach. Participation, however, need not extend to discretion over the goals of the enterprise. That is management's purview and will be accepted by the professional as long as the organization's mission does not compromise professional and ethical standards. When working with professionals, it is quite possible that allowing them discretion over means will encourage their conformity to organizational purpose. Of course, there can be no assurances on this account. This, in fact, is the inherent logic of Theory Y.

Although this discussion has supported modified participation by salaried professionals in the running of their organizations, it should also serve as a warning that professionals cannot be fooled on participation, especially those whose social and political consciousness was developed in the 60s. They know when their judgment or opinion on a decision is being considered seriously and when it is being solicited as lip service. Just being asked is not enough to satisfy professionals. In one company I consulted with, a personnel director acknowledged that this very point may have made a critical difference in reducing turnover among some of the individual contributors in his division. The company, as a matter of course, conducted an annual attitude survey. In past years, however, where results were not considered particularly positive, feedback to the survey participants was either delayed or partially withheld. This time around, the personnel director saw to it that all results were not only fed back immediately, but were acted on. The professionals in the subsequent attitude survey noted that "the company was finally making an effort to listen to them."

Respect for Versus Defiance of Authority

The successes of the protests of the 60s, especially those against the Vietnam war, created confidence that illegitimate authority could be defied. Not everyone protested, but many did experience a resurgence in the call to the self. Whereas the 50s had been other directed, the 60s became much more inner directed. People began to discard the material symbols of success in favor of a search for identity and interpersonal community. Naturally, some substitution of authority did occur. The New Left, for example, substituted the authority of Marx for that of the philosophers of the Enlightenment or of Adam Smith. Those in search of deep personal fulfillment may have substituted Fritz Perls, father of Gestalt therapy, for Sigmund Freud. Yet, in general, there was less reliance on higher support systems to pave the way to salvation. Individuals believed they were the captains of their souls.

The secular consciousness of the period worried the traditionalists in society. Having had little training in self-expression, many saw the youth's defiance of authority as evidence that our institutions were crumbling. Many in the Movement, less confident of their ability to seek fulfillment and salvation on their own or with a few friends, developed their own self-doubts. By the mid-70s, people were ready to seek refuge from the insecurity of self-reliance in other-directed norms of thought and behavior. Madison Avenue came back with a vengeance designer jeans were in, and for those unfortified by the comfort of the latest fashions, there was no short supply of evangelists to save the day.

The defiance of authority characterizing the 60s was not unqualified. What was opposed was authority that was no longer deemed legitimate. According to Robert Solo,[50] the roots of authority lie in beliefs, ideological commitment, a sense of identity, interest, or fear. In the 60s it appeared that the legitimacy of the first two, especially, could no longer be taken for granted. Americans were brought up believing, for example, that sovereign authority rested with the people. The nation's growing involvement in Vietnam against popular will, however, and other manifestations of government bureaucracy out of control challenged this belief. Americans were also brought up to believe in a land for all the people, yet prominent cleavages between the classes and between the powerful and the disenfranchised mobilized protest against rather than commitment to a lowered form of authority—one based on fear. Yet authority based on fear rather than on loyalty and commitment can only persevere in a police state, and Mayor Daley's official response to the demonstrators at the 1968 National Democratic Convention in Chicago notwithstanding, America was not willing to go that far. Further, 60s protesters gathered momentum as their numbers increased. Together, the themes "We Shall Overcome" and "We'll Walk Hand in Hand" articulated the conviction of many from that period, from all walks of life, that people were willing to join together and fight for a greater justice.

For professionals working in large organizations, the locus of authority becomes the CEO, and both the processes and the products of the corporate organization may be objects of protest. Paradoxically, in the 60s, the protest came from the outside, mostly in the form of youths marching and picketing in front of selected corporate targets. Today, many of these same youths are ensconced within these organizations. Some have "successfully" socialized themselves or have modified their convictions to accommodate the corporate setting. Many, however, are still active. Their protest against organizational processes takes the form of the demand for increased participation in decisions that affect them. Further, they are willing to take a stand, even against the wishes of the CEO, on most corporate cultural factors. In particular, they tend to resist overspecialization in their practice, formalization of control, close supervision, and impersonal treatment.

Professionals with 60s-type values can be expected to pay attention to the social uses of the products or services delivered by the organization. For example, accountants from this tradition may look askance at the manipulation of corporate assets when it involves the wholesale upheaval or removal of jobs, as in a nonintegrated acquisition or a callous plant closing. Similarly, scientists and engineers may ask questions about the defense-related applications of a particular technology or compound. Indeed, in a recent survey the Institute of Electrical and Electronic Engineers (IEEE) found that 25 percent of more than 10,000 of its members considered assignment to non-Department of Defense work important when changing employers.

During an interview with a human resource vice president, when I presented very briefly the generational thesis offered in this chapter, the vice president was taken aback at first. He then thought for a minute and made an insightful observation. The company's executive committee held an open meeting twice a year in an auditorium. Anyone from the company could attend. During the meeting, there were opportunities for questions from the audience about the company's direction. The vice president, upon reflection, pointed out that most of the questions came from people in their thirties or early forties. Could this be an indication of the generational phenomenon, he wondered. Many of these individuals were professionals, and apparently they were unawed by the stature of the individuals on the podium. The younger employees, the vice president added, were either too inexperienced or too concerned about presenting the proper face to ask questions; the older ones just did not seem to care that much.

This anecdote suggests that it was not lack of respect that underlay the 60s' response to authority. It was, rather, a belief that authority need not be embraced simply for its own sake. Unfortunately, onlookers found some of the challenges to traditional authority figures and symbols, such as the presidency, the flag, even God, to be so excessive as to undermine the spiritual fabric of the country. Conservative critic Kevin Phillips,[51] bemoaning the loss of national spirit and common purpose, blamed the 60s for "balkanizing" America. A once proud nation, unequaled in economic and military might, was being brought to its knees by division within its own ranks. Equality of opportunity was superseded by equality of result, wherein everyone could make a claim on the government for a large piece of American pie. Tolerance of everyone and everything became the fashion. The rights of disenfranchised blacks were superseded by demands for public bathhouses for homosexuals, immediate corporate boardroom positions for women, guaranteed jobs for the infirm regardless of disability, bilingual texts for Spanish-Americans, and ramp access to every public building for the handicapped.

Facing growing alienation from what once were treasured American family values, some Americans in the 70s turned to charismatic authority figures, particularly those who could offer spiritual solace. These leaders offered security to those whose identity had been shattered under the array of choices, many of which opened up territory formerly considered off limits. Nothing brought more emotional upheaval than the continuing secular rejection of a higher being as the ultimate authority. The way was thus paved for a broad-based Christian revival, led in some instances by would-be spiritual healers who were largely self-anointed. Since such former criteria of leadership as achievement or scholarship were now debased, it was relatively easy for novices to seize the moment and, guided by an inner spirit or a nose for the market, attract hordes of followers. Even a novice politician, at least by national standards, Jimmy Carter, was able to win the presidency on a promise not to lie. When he failed to live up to his own standards, another evangelist, Ronald Reagan, who was better than anyone else at articulating the founding values of America, won the White House.

Those 60s activists who became professionals in the 70s and 80s have had to take a stand, even at times an uncharacteristically self-righteous one, against a movement of defiance that they started but that has gotten out of hand. The professions themselves are no longer sacrosanct. A doctor's first opinion is no longer taken for granted. Para- and antilegal organizations goad citizens to dispense with legal advice and handle the paperwork on their own. Teachers are abused by their students and chastised by their school committees if they do not succeed in raising test scores. Salaried professionals find themselves in a particularly difficult situation. They are urged to defer to the goals of their management at the same time they are facing attenuation of their expert authority. The chemist may prescribe an elaborate testing process to screen a new drug for toxic effects but may have to compromise his professional standards if his management tells him that the process will take too long and doom the drug in the market. Consequently, 60s professionals in particular expect management to defend its decisions and actions, especially those that are contrary to professional standards. The request for a defense of the managerial position is not technically a defiance of authority as much as a challenge to bureaucratic authorities to ensure that they have done their homework. This search for legitimacy by people who are concerned about the welfare of others is consistent with the social culture of the 60s.

Corporate Efficiency Versus Social Justice

It is commonly assumed that most corporations are primarily interested in being as efficient as possible in providing goods or services to the markets they serve. If they can lower their costs while maintaining service or production, profits and value to the stockholders will generally increase. Many salaried professionals, however, take an alternative view of their corporation's performance by showing more interest in effectiveness than in efficiency.[52] Effectiveness focuses more on doing well what one is supposed to be doing than on doing more with less. A second criterion is that the corporation and its management should not only do things well, they should also do them right. Indeed, the code of the National Society of Professional Engineers states that the engineer "will use his knowledge and skill for the advancement of human welfare." When this duty brings the engineer into conflict with the demands of an employer, the code instructs him to "regard his duty to the public welfare as paramount."

The notion of a corporation holding itself accountable for its social actions has turned into a field of management study in its own right. Its origin, however, dates back to the 60s, when not only business but all institutions came under increasing attack. Protest against the Vietnam war and against racial discrimination led the way. The period also saw increasing concern, however, over the plight of the poor, the infirm, and the elderly, and it was during this time that the consumer and environmental movements, more identified now with the 70s, got their start. Among the principal agenda items of the protest movements of the 60s was a fundamental questioning of the desirability of economic growth for its own sake.[53] Caught up in the wave of such protests, corporate organizations were being pressed by legislative and regulatory action as well as public sentiment to respond to issues beyond their traditional task of producing goods and services at a profit. The nature of the pressure ranged from laws backed by enforcement agencies, through the vocal urgings of special interest groups, to the concerns of more general segments of the population and the idiosyncratic consciences of corporate executives. Although all institutions were affected, the movement toward social responsibility by business was particularly dramatic because the historical criteria for evaluating commercial enterprises had been so relatively simple and clear-cut.[54]

By the 1970s, notwithstanding the conservative economic attack on the notion of social responsibility by such scholars as Milton Friedman, most corporate executives were acknowledging that business had a responsibility to contribute to the overall well-being of the community in which it operated, as well as to the overall quality of American life. As a result, managing the corporation became more than a technical exercise. At a conference on business environment and public policy, George Steiner reported that top managers were spending a preponderant part of their day dealing with social and political questions. This included "addressing social concerns of society, complying with new social legislation, communicating with legislators and government executives concerning new proposed laws and regulations, meeting with various self-interest groups concerning their demands and/or grievances, and administering their organizations in such a way as to respond to the new attitudes of people working in the organization."[55] Further, operating managers were being held accountable for their social and political actions as well. Finally, many exponents of the so-called social responsibility movement were suggesting that it was no longer enough for business to respond to social concerns; rather, as one of many vital institutions in society, it had a responsibility to anticipate the social, political, and ethical consequences of its actions.

Although most of the writing in the social responsibility literature focused on private corporations, the movement, as a pluralist conception, affected all major institutions, including not-for-profit and public organizations. Moreover, although management was singled out as among the key decision makers to be held accountable, professionals did not remain unscathed. In the domain of private practice, clients were challenging the heretofore unassailable technical expertise of professional practitioners. Surgical decisions were being contested not only by patients but by third-party payers, client organizations like H.A.L.T. were openly questioning the need for legal counsel, and the fundamental value of psychotherapy was subject to increasing debate.

Salaried professional practice was scrutinized even more closely than private practice, since performance was reviewed not only by external societal agents but also by management. Malpractice suits forced hospital administrators to exert greater control over drug dispensing by their health-care professionals; accounting staff were told to heed approved financial accounting standards more carefully so as not to incur more SEC regulation; pharmacists were given less discretion over the dispensing of exempt drugs. Technical professionals were perhaps subjected to the greatest scrutiny during this period. The Vietnam war challenged the belief that technology means progress and the technological imperative that if you can do it, you should do it. The fight against and ultimate defeat of the supersonic transport (SST) beginning in the mid-60s aptly illustrated how views of technology were changing. Concern over the ultimate disposition of a technological advance, known as technology assessment, would henceforth appear as one of the criteria in investment decisions involving new technology.

What the 60s brought out in professional practice, perhaps more than during any other proximate period, was a need for professionals to be as concerned about social justice as about their clients and the methods of analysis used in solving the clients' problems. In medicine, for example, the prevailing issue was less the technical quality of care offered by physicians than the extent to which medical services could be organized to extend care to all segments of society. Containment of medical costs and physicians' views on the great moral dilemmas of abortion, euthanasia, and artificial insemination were similarly compelling. In law, concern was voiced over access by the poor to basic legal services.

During the 60s, many professionals responded to this cry for social justice by volunteering their services in behalf of the socially related concerns of their profession. The case of internal auditing is illustrative. The work of internal auditors is fraught with conflicting pressures. The auditor must, of course, maintain his or her independence from the activities subject to the audit. However, as former SEC Chairman Harold Williams[56] once pointed out, the realities of corporate operations also dictate that the internal auditor serve management in fulfilling its particular responsibilities. What should the auditor do, for example, when told by management to overlook a bribe to a foreign official, because that it is the customary method of gaining business in the country in which the company is operating? Although the accounting profession generally has a good record of establishing standards of acceptable practice in instances of this kind, government officials did not feel it was doing enough and, consequently, in 1977 the unpopular Foreign Corrupt Practices Act was passed, which imposes stiff fines for making illegal foreign payments.

Outside auditors working for public accounting firms have also come under greater scrutiny in recent years. Arthur Andersen, for example, is facing no less than seven lawsuits because of its failure to detect at Frigitemp such abuses as chronically overstating earnings, concealing losses, bribing officials of major defense contractors, and flagrantly misusing federal funds.[57] The question raised by these suits is whether independent outside auditors sometimes become too close to their corporate clients and in that way fail to protect public investors. As a result of some of these outside auditing abuses, at the time of this writing the House Energy and Commerce Committee was planning to undertake a major review of problems encountered in the accounting profession.

To head off regulatory oversight or to avoid costly liability suits, many companies are taking concerted action to respond to the warnings of their more conscientious professional employees, especially those likely to initiate reformist, or whistle-blowing, actions.[58] In reformism, employees operate on the inside to change a corporate practice that might be damaging to the wider community. For example, a scientist working for an environmental compliance agency might react to an overextended caseload by advocating the hiring of additional scientists, by pushing for increased computerization, or by asking for the creation of a new unit to perform prescreening reviews. In law, the American Bar Association has established a Code of Professional Responsibility which invokes an obligatory hierarchy of actions for a corporate counsel who discovers an illegal corporate action or one likely to result in significant harm to the corporation. The code advises internal review as a first step in this process but sanctions public disclosure as a last resort.[59]

Whistle-blowing, in contrast to reformism, constitutes this last resort of external action to inform the government or the public about an undesirable activity. It normally places the whistle blower at great risk, although statutes are beginning to be enacted at the state level to protect whistle blowers against automatic firing. For example, in New Jersey, Mobil Oil Corporation settled for $425,000 in compensatory and punitive damages when it fired a research biologist who had pressed the company to report two toxic chemical accidents at one of the company's labs. An engineer in California is pursuing a court case against Raymond Kaiser Engineers, Inc., which fired him because he had filed reports indicating the company was using unqualified suppliers in the construction of a nuclear power plant.[61]

Companies can do more than simply open communications channels for their more socially conscious employees or respond case by case to allegations of impropriety. In an effort to balance their pursuit of corporate efficiency with an acknowledgment of the value of ethical consciousness, some companies are beginning to see benefits to formulating a corporate social policy. Although there are many variations on such a policy, (as I shall demonstrate in the next chapter), Robert Ackerman and Raymond Bauer's social response process[61] proposes a three-step approach. First, the chief executive promulgates a formal policy recognizing the social responsibility of the organization in its diverse product-market segments. Second, technical specialists are assigned to design a data system to analyze the firm's social environment and actions. Third, a social policy becomes institutionalized as operating units gradually are held accountable for the social implications of their day-to-day activities.

Although few organizations have adopted a social response process, it is unlikely that the demand for social justice will die out. Indeed, as 60s professionals occupy positions of greater influence in their organizations, their deep sense of humanism is likely to induce increased awareness and response to social issues.

Team Player Versus Individual Initiative

Much of the tradition of professionalism rests on an assumption of individual initiative. The modern research university of the late nineteenth century fostered increased specialization by professionals to respond to the needs of advancing civilization. The days of the cowboys opening up spatial frontiers were over. The new cowboys would be the professionals who would open up technological frontiers. But in so doing, one wonders if they might have gone too far, as Alexis de Tocqueville had warned a half-century earlier. He feared that the inherent individualism of specialization could result in usurpation of the needs of the wider American community, causing Americans to become isolated from one another. Indeed, it is arguable in their drive toward increasing specialization and individual initiative, professionals in this century have neglected an equally critical obligation to speak to the ethical questions of the society as a whole.

In the 1960s, the spirit of individualism reached new heights in America, as the notion of self-sufficiency was superseded by the rights of self-fulfillment and self-expression, especially in the realm of morals and personal relations. The ethic of self-fulfillment, however, had a new ideological twist. It would apply only to individuals, not to institutions, and especially not to economic enterprises. Indeed, during the 60s many citizens turned to the government to protect individual freedoms from business encroachment. Environmental quality would have to be preserved at the expense of economic growth, equal opportunity would have to supersede short-term productivity, and safety would have to come before proficiency.

Observers of the New Class phenomenon could not fail to notice, however, that the gradual government encroachment on private enterprise caused a redistribution of power from the businessman to the professional and technical intelligentsia.[62] The task of controlling individual rights required an infusion of professional expertise, be it engineering in environmental control or law in equality of opportunity. Hence it could be argued that the support of individual initiative was appropriate as long as the initiative was taken by a professional and not a manager, especially a business manager.

The release of the professional from institutional constraints to pursue good works was seen by some as excessive. No one should be given an unbounded contract, lest the preoccupation with one's expertise no longer permit an objective appraisal of one's worth. Some 60s professionals were quite willing to submit their work to review, not only by their peers and superiors but also by their clients. Yet others confused their right of individual initiative with unbridled autonomy.

No data show with any accuracy what percentage of professionals during the 60s crossed the line from individualism to selfishness. In individualism, the professional grants himself the privilege of pursuing individual interests and behaviors without the contaminating control of institutional forces, be they economic, religious, or bureaucratic. In Daniel Bell's terms, the individual can operate within a climate of "liberation" as opposed to "liberty."[63] Liberation releases the professional from bureaucratic role requirements that are inherently depersonalizing and destructive of the whole man. Nevertheless, within this realm of personal freedom, the professional is still controlled, not only by his peers, but by the strength of his own convictions. The reaction of most Americans to this quest for and, in some cases, achievement of, personal liberation was fear that such individual initiative might go unchecked. It was assumed that most professionals or anyone else granted the privilege of unrestrained individual initiative would abuse that privilege. They would become preoccupied with their own self-interest and display an absolute disregard for the concerns and interests of others. This outcome is what I refer to as selfishness.

The wide reports of a growing narcissism in the 70s, especially among American youth and young adults, leading to what critics began labeling the Me generation, lent some credence to this fear. In what many considered the premier social criticism of the 70s, Christopher Lasch in his *The Culture of Narcissism*,[64] essentially depicted the American of the period as bereft of any communitarian impulses, as an automaton of selfish action. Lasch's thesis is that the blind pursuit of individualistic activity was basically an attempt to escape the emptiness of most lives. Even the radicalism of the 60s, according to Lasch, was therapeutic, not political, in that its chief purpose was a search for meaning in a world devoid of social intimacy. He acknowledged, however, that the cultural criticism of the 60s did entail an element of self-examination and individual consciousness. To Lasch, the 70s represented the nadir. Individuals from all walks of life committed themselves to live for the moment in an attempt to avoid the boredom that suffused their lives. Owing to the breakdown in major social institutions, especially the family, individuals during the 70s lost the art of interpersonal relations. Friendships became sources of manipulation; it was nearly impossible to find individuals of character. To Lasch, people were no longer interested in overcoming their difficulties; they were just interested in surviving them.

Even the more conservative Daniel Bell complained that modern man lacked sufficient intellectual, moral, and spiritual resources to fashion a mature identity.[65] Selfish excess had reduced his capacity for what Bell termed self-transcendence, the ability continually to stand outside and judge oneself.

Although there can be no doubt about a growing tendency during the 70s toward selfish pursuits, the narcissistic label for the period may have carried the argument too far. A more balanced perspective might find that the attribution of selfishness resulted from dismay over the decline in familiar bourgeois standards, be they social roles, sexual mores, religious values, or authority relations. Meanwhile, on the left, critics bemoaned the degeneration of the best energy of the protest movement and the decreasing influence of New Left cultural and political perspectives.[66] Further, America by the 1980s was perhaps a culture in the midst of a redistribution in its rights, entitlements, responsibilities, and obligations. Millions of individuals joined the quest for self-fulfillment. Many were, of course, novices in this quest, so it is natural that abuses occurred. The hopefuls among the American critics assumed that this cultural adolescence would pass, leading to an adulthood of greater caring and less selfishness.[67]

Although writing a decade or two earlier, Abraham Maslow spoke convincingly to the professionals of the late 60s and 70s about the appropriate interpretation and implementation of the selfishness concept. In his notion of the self-actualizing person, Maslow depicted the individual as already having met the selfish needs for acquisition, security, affection, or prestige. Indeed, in self-actualization, the self becomes enlarged to include all aspects of the world. Self-actualizing people are interested in "seeing justice done, doing a more perfect job, advancing the truth, rewarding virtue and punishing evil."[68] For the self-actualizing professional, intrinsic, transpersonal values are paramount. Since one has already developed a healthy sense of self, attention can be refocused on activities outside the self, particularly within one's profession and within the wider community. A persevering interest in social justice might be one rather convincing clue that the professional has moved beyond narcissism through selfishness to a more healthy quest for self-actualization.

Professionals in this category are capable of working outside themselves. They are sufficiently confident to become devoted to their craft. Some are even capable of looking beyond the processes of the craft to the effects of the profession on society. These attributes would seem to ease the integration of professionals into work teams. Yet it is precisely this concentration on the craft that distinguishes the professional's approach to teamwork from the manager's. Professionals are certainly capable of teamwork, but they are uncomfortable relying on groups to perform individual assignments. They prefer the challenge of solving a problem by themselves, using the group as a resource. They might readily consult with the group regarding a problem and even take direction from it, but ultimately they want to work on their own.

Managers tend to be opposite. They see the group as the unit that performs the work. Especially at upper levels in the corporation, the group is assembled to resolve fundamental strategic issues, with individuals being used as resources. Direction comes usually from the top, but the chief executive expects information to flow back after having been processed by a group of individuals, unless it is a response to a special request of one person.

It is an interesting paradox that although managers expect to function in a team, according to Michael Maccoby,[69] they also expect through individual initiative to rise to the top of the group. They are not so much concerned about using initiative to discover a new application within their craft, however, as with working with the team to solve a problem to impress the boss. Hence the team player is really a game player matching wits against his or her peers to see who can survive the corporate battlefield. Lasch finds this game playing to filter down malevolently to subordinates, who become pawns in the battle of wills. Occasionally, they are given a bone of participation, but this is more likely to occur when things are going well in the company. When things turn sour, the subordinate may not be as readily consulted and may not want to participate for fear of contributing to further bad decisions. Whatever the outcome, the game conveys to the subordinate that the boss can be a winner and that the team that supports the right candidate can reap ample rewards.[70]

The depiction of managerial teamwork as a game is admittedly extreme, and if it does apply, it may occur less at middle and lower managerial levels, where most salaried professionals can also be found. Further, recent depictions of the superior American companies suggest a genuine concern by managers for others, whether that concern is for the firm's human resources (expressed through benefits and rewards such as stock options and profit-sharing, through honest performance appraisals and legitimate promotions, or through creative incentives such as pay for learning new skills) or for the firm's external community (expressed through attention to social responsibilities and responsiveness to affected community groups, such as underprivileged citizens, users, consumers, or even creditors).[71] Yet even in the acclaimed *In Search of Excellence*, by Thomas Peters and Robert Waterman, although the individual is seen "as a source of ideas, not just acting as a pair of hands," the manager is depicted as someone willing to train the subordinate and to "state reasonable and clear expectations" of him.[72] The underlying logic of the principles of excellence is a responsibility of the manager to shape the values of the subordinate in the direction of increased commitment to productivity and organizational excellence, all for the good of the team.

If there is a gradual blurring of the lines between professionals and managers on the distinction between teamwork and individual initiative, the message conveyed above demarcates the lines more clearly, at least for the 60s professionals. There is a subtle hint of manipulation in the work of management as depicted by Peters and Waterman. In their view, managers, through stories, myths, and other cultural artifacts, set about shaping the values of their organizations. Once these values are formulated, they work to ensure commitment to them through these organizational symbols. Unconditional loyalty is expected of subordinates, who by this time are so convinced of the moral rightness of their leaders that they willingly accept responsibility to work as hard as they can to succeed. Meanwhile, the managers become the guardians of the culture. This includes not only reinforcing its beliefs, but "deciding who belongs and who doesn't."[73] This kind of teamwork probably goes too far for the 60s professional. Certainly, the manager has the right to set the strategic course of the enterprise. To develop a rich accompaniment of symbols that are used to reinforce the mission, however, and which may be further used to exclude those who do not conform, is antagonistic to the values of egalitarianism and social justice proclaimed in the 60s. So, it may be a question of where one draws the line. Professionals are quite willing to pursue their work for the good of the team but not as an exclusive end. They look to a higher authority to negotiate those problems that, although within the cultural norms, are not clean enough to pass professional scrutiny. In some instances, professional scrutiny becomes synonymous with moral scrutiny. Hence moral power ultimately rests within the individual who is sustained by the group. The group is as likely to be a professional referent organization as a work group. The manager does not have the backing of a comparable referent organization and so may rely more on internal cultural forces, sustained by the managerial team. In this sense, and again it is a matter of degree, the professional is more individualistic.

Career Versus Quality of Life

Of the five dichotomies presented contrasting managerial and professional values, this last one has seemingly eroded most since the 60s period. As economic and social forces have created greater occupational uncertainty, the 80s have witnessed a virtual fascination with the concept of career. In particular, economic recessions and separate declines in certain sectors of the economy have forced people out of jobs heretofore believed secure. Demographic shifts, such as the movement of the baby boomers themselves, have caused dislocations in particular occupations. For example, buoyed by increasing federal support for education, many 60s professionals went into teaching, only to discover that the subsequent withdrawal of federal monies along with declining enrollments obviated the need for teachers.

Nevertheless, I believe that when challenged to choose between career and quality of life, although career has surely become important, professionals, especially those with 60s values, will still end up on the side of quality of life. Although quality of life has many facets, to the salaried professional it typically means having an opportunity to explore all aspects of the self and the world and the interconnections between the two. It also suggests an opportunity to communicate about oneself within an unconditionally accepting community. Thus, within the work environment, it requires being treated as a person, not as a number, and being accepted for one's dignity rather than for one's connections. Although quality of life entails "doing your own thing," it does not exclude community and interpersonal relationships. Autonomy and discretion are treasured, but so is the opportunity to make a contribution to one's loved ones as well as to the wider community.

These values are inconsistent with the blind pursuit of a career.

Rather, the career is viewed at best as a vehicle to help one achieve the best possible quality of life. The professional is likely to consider a job, organizational, or even career transition whenever his or her work no longer supports the most treasured pursuits of identity and community.

The original impetus for an anticareer ethic came from fears by 60s protestors (collectively, the Movement) that any formal career pursuit could lead to a sellout. Ask anyone from the 60s period and it will seem amazing how widespread this anticareer ethic was. Anyone choosing graduate or professional training who had shown sympathies with the Movement was subject to extraordinary guilt. The professions themselves were placed on the defensive unless they willingly solicited participation from their client base. Pursuit of the profession for its own sake or according to standards established by some elite professional body was soundly condemned. Those who continued their professional training in spite of the guilt attempted to justify their vocation, usually by citing its service ethic. They claimed humility before the "people's will" and demonstrated how professional skills could be used to contribute to the general welfare of the oppressed in society.[74] For example, architects could extend their skills to the design of commercial dwellings and low-cost housing complexes; management professors could educate their students in business ethics; policy analysts could diagnose the causes of blight and propose innovative social solutions; physicians could offer their services to indigent populations; and computer scientists could design information systems to be used in furthering community networking.

Although the social consciousness aspect of the professional's work has waned since the 60s, the interest in quality of life has not, and professionals have still not wholeheartedly embraced the career ethic. Quality of life may now be more narrowly interpreted as the opportunity to fulfill oneself professionally, but even that narrow definition precludes adherence to a determinate career track. Professionals want to keep their options open and avoid obsolescence resulting from taking specialized roles within the same organization. Career development for a professional may mean developing oneself as a human being able to assume greater responsibility for one's own work rather than moving up the corporate ladder. The former may be possible only through corporate advancement, but believing that the professional is therefore no different from the manager misses the point.

The career ethic is essentially a managerial property. Today's organizations are extremely large, requiring much division of labor and complex hierarchies. As capital has steadily replaced labor and technology has permitted greater control of output, spans of control have also been enlarged. Hence, there is more need for trained management technicians who can coordinate the diverse elements of the organization. These managers do not have to engage in a craft as much as administer the craft or the operating performance of others. The key to motivating them is to provide opportunities to obtain greater status, salary, and authority by rising through the hierarchy. These people are most satisfied by work that gives them a chance to get ahead and to become more attractive to the market.[75] They demand unreserved loyalty from their subordinates and in return reward and protect them. They expect fair play in their assigned roles and want simply to know the rules of the game established by their executives. The side effects of this ethic include anxiety about falling behind. Some are even depressed about the competitiveness and unfriendliness of organizational life.

As I have pointed out, some managers act like 60s professionals and thus will resist the career ethic described above in favor of a better quality of life. They are less driven by promises of power, promotion, and status and more interested in challenging work and satisfying interpersonal relationships. They strive to find fulfillment in other life pursuits (their family, another vocational interest, a community service organization) rather than succumb to a life of anxiety, driven by a desire to prove their worth by symbols of success. These are the managers who can most appreciate the message of this chapter and influence their associates to behave toward their professional staff in ways commensurate with quality of life rather than strictly career values.

Toward Professional/ Management Understanding   5

To this point, I have focused on the differences between salaried professionals and their managers that arise from the differences in their cultural backgrounds. Although I have necessarily overstated the case, I believe the differences are clear enough to be classified generically. Figure 5-1 presents professionals' complaints about management and management's complaints about professionals as opposing pairs. All of the cultural factors and values discussed in the preceding chapters are represented. The table intentionally casts the complaints as dichotomous extremes. Yet the values representing the professionals' complaints are consistent with what we commonly think of as the values of the management culture. Likewise, the values representing management's complaints are elements of the professional culture.

The direction the book now takes is to look directly at the integration of these polarized values. Each of the six pairs is treated separately, and the six sections of the chapter are named for the inherent problem in each value set: (the problem of) overspecialization, autonomy, supervision, formalization, real-world practice, and ethical responsibility. Thus my treatment of organizational strategies for managing professionals will be logically grounded in an understanding of the cultural differences that have potentially caused the parties to clash. It is my expectation, therefore, that the mediation strategies I describe are significant because they respond to the specific needs of professional accomplishment *and* managerial proficiency. Because management is in a better position than professionals to foster organizational change that accommodates professional interests, most of the mediation strategies are management-based. Occasionally, however, I point out per-

Figure 5-1   The Polarized Values of Professionals and Management

Professionals' Complaints	Mediation Strategies	Management's Complaints
Managers who require over-specialization	⟶ ⟵	Professionals who wish to remain overprofessionalized
Managers who underspecify ends but overspecify the means of practice and who expect adherence to the organizational hierarchy	⟶ ⟵	Professionals who demand autonomy over and participation in ends as well as means
Managers who maintain close supervision	⟶ ⟵	Professionals who resist close supervision by insisting on professional standards of evaluation
Managers who show respect for authority and who believe in formalizing control of professional practice	⟶ ⟵	Professionals who might defy authority or disregard organizational procedures
Managers who in the interest of career and teamwork condone jobs lacking challenge, entrepreneurship, personalness, and stability	⟶ ⟵	Professionals who, in the interest of quality of life and individual initiative, display little regard for real-world practice
Managers who strive for corporate efficiency	⟶ ⟵	Professionals who retain an overriding interest in ethical responsibility

sonal strategies individual professionals can adopt to improve their
own work environments.

The Problem of Overspecialization

| Managers who re-quire overspecialization | → | *Mediation Strategies*
1. Linkage Devices
2. Open Internal Labor Market Policy
3. Organizational Socialization
4. Mentorship | ← | Professionals who wish to remain over-professionalized |

Specialization becomes a problem under two conditions. The first
is overspecialization, depicted in Figure 5-1 under "Professionals'
Complaints," and signifies the organizational compartmentalization of
professionals who are required to perform fixed and standardized tasks
apart from other professionals or managers. The second is overprofessionalization, which is a management complaint and signifies the
professional's inclination to practice his or her specialized competencies and to serve professional interests without consideration of corporate goals.

Otherwise, specialization is not automatically a problem. To begin
with, professionals are hired to perform specific tasks because they
have specialized skills. Early in their careers, especially, young professionals want to practice the skills in which they were diligently trained.
There is little point in making a generalist out of a confirmed specialist. Most salaried professionals realize, however, that the choice of an

organizational career requires at a minimum a need to care about the organization's mission. Professionals generally want to help the organization they serve as long as it doesn't contravene personal or professional values. As experience accumulates, the professional is expected to devote more and more energy to the resolution of organizational problems.

Linkage Devices

Management, through linkage devices, tries to increase the professional's corporate identification and to help him or her see where his or her contribution fits into the entire organization's structure and purpose. Meetings between professional groups and between professionals and line management constitute the most simple linkage devices. Although such meetings can be informal, they need to be efficiently run, with agendas aimed at furthering understanding of the respective parties' goals and operations. The meetings should be short and infrequent. They should occur on a regular basis (unless special needs arise) and should be made as lively and engaging as possible.

Professional employees are curious about their organization's financial and contractual matters as well as the marketing plans for its products and services. Essential, strategic information such as this can be covered during a corporate-wide meeting, perhaps held annually. This meeting would provide a platform for the organization's executives to describe the problems and opportunities facing the firm. During this meeting, questions could be entertained from the entire staff regarding professional as well as nonprofessional concerns.

There are many other means of initiating communication across professional groups or between professionals and management. Periodic seminars can be instituted in which professionals are invited to present a paper or an idea informally. These seminars can be made accessible to nonprofessionals. Memos, electronic media, suggestion boxes, and bulletin boards represent just a few of the possible linkage devices, each of which will appeal to particular organizations, depending on their tastes and history. Recently, industrial architects have made great strides in designing physical spaces that promote informal exchanges. Finally, social activities that strip away the facades of role and responsibility can be an exciting way to mix people across boundaries. Social events, of course, may occur without planning on an ad hoc basis, but may require managerial instigation if their purpose is to mix groups. The Silicon Valley beer busts have become famous for achieving this precise goal. Being able to talk to someone from another group or stratum in the organization without role requirements is likely to appeal especially to 60s professionals, who were raised to shed the baggage of background, status, and appearance in their relations with others.

Although meetings and informal linkage devices may benefit individual organizations wishing to reduce overspecialization and overprofessionalization, they may not go far enough to implement coordination between professionals and management. Some companies, Bechtel for example, simply demand that their technical people be exposed to their line operations early in employment. Some kind of structural mechanism needs to be inserted to ensure that the professional staff is made aware of the organization's ultimate objectives. In manufacturing, for example, where low cost and producibility have become essential criteria for success, it is simply unacceptable to separate R&D from the operating divisions.[1] Consequently, someone has to be named to coordinate the respective functions. It is often preferable to have a manufacturing engineer participate in a R&D project team. Some companies also include marketing personnel in their R&D projects. It may also help to have an interdepartmental committee organized on an ad hoc or permanent basis (depending on such strategic and structural considerations as the life cycle of the company's product line, its product turnover, whether it operates in a matrix format, and so forth) to review progress toward operational goals.

The problem of overspecialization arises in part out of traditional management principles, such as division of labor, that some managers subscribe to but that have become obsolete in many dynamic product and service environments. American management education has also overpromoted another potentially misguided principle, namely, the manager as generalist. Young managers are often trained to believe they can operate in any kind of environment. Regardless of the industry, the principles of general management remain the same. A by-product of this approach, however, is real shortage of technical managers. The CEOs of U.S. companies, for example, have far fewer qualifications in engineering and science than their counterparts in Western Europe.[2] The net effect of this concentration on general management is that U.S. managers do not know how to communicate with their professional staffs, leading to the latter's further isolation and solidarity. American management will not become technically proficient overnight, but greater attention to professional and technical concerns in both classroom and on-the-job management training is mandatory. Such disciplines as social work, education, health care, and political science have done a reasonably good job on this account, mainly because administration was added to technical courses in response to an institutional need for more trained managers. Unfortunately, industrial and commercial management has not followed suit. As an aside, one wonders whether the recent resurgence of corporate takeovers resulting in diversification beyond core business areas has resulted from this overemphasis on generalist training. There is some evidence that professional satisfaction as well as corporate performance is higher when managers attempt to "stick to the knitting."[3]

Advocating changes in the system of management training may be a bit far-fetched for the typical manager, although the message of becoming technically conversant still obtains. There is no substitute, however, for building worksites within one's organization that promote cross-disciplinary communication among the various professionals contributing to the work unit's goals. Compatibility among professionals, and between professionals and management at the work-unit or team level, can be increased with sensitive staffing practices. Specifically, it helps to recruit individuals who are interested in sharing their work with others outside their discipline. A recent study of health-care professionals discovered that within any one organizational unit members of different professions may have more in common than they do with members of the same profession.[4] This results in part from the way management structures the project team or work unit. If the manager sees to it that there is open collaboration among all the members of the team, then barriers between disciplines can be torn down. For example, at Du Pont, where scientists were once allowed to operate largely in a vacuum, researchers are now expected to get cost analyses on competing products from marketing. In turn, the scientists are expected to estimate how much customers are willing to pay for their new products. James M. Hutchinson, research supervisor of the agricultural-chemicals department, was quoted as saying, "We aren't just researchers any more. We are businessmen."[5] In spite of this cross-disciplinary collaboration, top management needs to keep in mind that as Thomas Watson, Jr., once recounted, "all our ducks are flying in formation." Hence, there also needs to be coordination between the interdisciplinary teams and the strategic goals of the enterprise.

Open Internal Labor Market Policy

Among the most self-interested of strategies for management to consider in promoting positive professional relations is an open internal labor market policy. Overspecialization and ensuing obsolescence are scourges of salaried professional practice. Faced with either, a professional will probably first attempt to move elsewhere. If nothing is available or other life preferences take precedence over work, he or she may choose to remain in the organization and become unproductive or even maladapted. The most effective means to ward off these results is an internal mobility policy that promotes freedom to try new skills and jobs.

The critical components of an open internal labor market are shown in Table 5-1. Management cannot expect to create all these conditions at once, but all should be feasible eventually. For illustrative purposes, the table contrasts an open policy with a closed one. These are extremes, however, and the arena of change is the middle zone. Managers should make efforts to move to the right for each component.

The first component captures the essential difference between the open and closed internal labor market policies. The real question is how much flexibility the organization will give employees to move within the firm. The closed organization allows movement only within the confines of a narrow field of specialization. Hence, it basically relies on the external labor market to supply labor for open job slots; the one exception is intradepartmental promotions. The open organization, in contrast, permits employees with the aid of extensive training to consider new horizons not only within their own disciplines but in others. This type of organization is principally interested in making a long-term investment in its professional work force. It views its professionals as individuals, not merely as job incumbents. It is interested in seeing its employees develop, not only for their own well-being but for the organization's well-being, since it recognizes that satisfied employees can more easily commit themselves to the organization's mission. Whether through job posting or some other vehicle, the internal mobility-oriented company provides an opportunity for any qualified applicant from any place in the organization to bid on

Table 5-1   Open Versus Closed Internal Labor Market Policies

CLOSED	OPEN
Promotion along traditional lines, usually within department.	Promotion widely dispersed throughout the organization.
Training normally provided only in own discipline.	Training available in all areas to prepare for future open jobs.
Dependence on supervisor for career development.	Dependence on self for own career development; can negotiate career plans with supervisor.
Little information on jobs in other areas.	Abundant information on all job openings.
Little information on career paths flowing from particular jobs.	Abundant information on multiple career paths within the organization.
Little feedback on why turned down for any job.	Open feedback regarding job applications.
Need to play politics to get ahead.	Role of politics in career development minimized.

Source: Adapted from Joseph A. Raelin, *The Salaried Professional* (New York: Praeger, 1984).

open slots. An exception may be made when a very specific set of qualifications is required or when a potential candidate is sorely needed in his or her current department. Not only are jobs open to all; employees affected by the above exception as well as those whose bids are turned down are told why they were not selected. This open feedback allows applicants to make up for any deficiencies in their skills or other aspects of their record so that they can be potentially more successful in subsequent applications.

According to one of the original exponents of the open internal labor market policy, Theodore Alfred,[6] a common criticism is that the policy detracts from management's ability to plan, since one never knows when one will lose some very valuable contributors in a particular department. Although this may surely happen, Alfred points out that management in the affected department is also looking to attract qualified candidates from other departments. Rather than detracting from planning, therefore, the policy requires it. Managers need to think continually about developing their people, which means they must also think about their successors.

Where comprehensive job posting is premature, management can take a number of creative steps in anticipation of this practice. The organization might begin with a job-rotation plan wherein professionals are allowed to try out new positions on a temporary basis. If someone's interest in the temporary assignment persists, he or she is given permission to bid on a job in the new department. Some companies, aware that middle managers and supervisors sometimes become the greatest roadblocks to personal career development, have called for the issuance of "hunting licenses," usually through personnel, which grant the employee the right to talk to other managers and supervisors about alternative job opportunities. Other companies might go to the next step of creating "transfer boards" to ease the transition between jobs of internally mobile employees.

An open-door promotion policy essentially establishes multiple career lines for the professional staff, which both symbolically and in a real sense militate against overspecialization and potential obsolescence. Few professionals ever leave their original discipline, but many wish to try out different facets or subspecialties within it. In many cases, the only way to do this while staying in one's own organization is to make some kind of lateral transfer. Few practices can promote organizational loyalty more than giving the professional this kind of opportunity. Most professionals consider staying on their current jobs indefinitely to be quite limiting. They want to try something new. Moreover, given the hierarchical nature of most of our organizations, the reality that few can afford unlimited vertical opportunities, plus the indifference of some professionals to managerial responsibilities, lateral transfers offer the best vehicle to promote professional growth and development.

Especially during times of economic stress, management might also promote downward transfers. Properly planned downward moves can "unstick" professional employees caught in dead-end career paths, make a cross-functional move less risky (since the new job may be at a lower level of responsibility), or move a poor performer back to a level where he or she previously experienced success.[7] In my consulting work, I have seen older yet emotionally secure professionals, in particular, benefit enormously from downward moves that allow them not only to get off the fast track but also to act as mentors to younger, less astute professionals.

Besides lateral and downward transfers, there are many other vehicles to consider in adopting an open internal labor market policy. Project work, wherein professionals might give up their formal positions to work on a task with a predetermined end point, might be an attractive alternative. Given their high level of expertise, select professionals can also be occasionally assigned to work in an internal consulting or troubleshooting capacity. Finally, some companies, Ford being one example, are experimenting with employee "swaps," where two professionals may trade jobs for a specified period.

I agree with Tim Hall that especially for professionals who mistakenly assume that overspecialization can be avoided by rapid and upward career advancement, a managerial strategy of slow promotion through skill broadening is a preferable internal labor market policy.[8] What this suggests is that professionals might adopt career paths based on skill rather than on position. Growth is thus interpreted as further development of the skills of one's profession rather than accomplishment in a multitude of vertically linked jobs. Implementing such a policy requires the uncoupling of pay and position, so that skills and their use are rewarded, rather than passage through a succession of positions. The inherent logic of a skill-based career system is also sustained in the dual ladder, which I shall address in the next section.

A flexible, internal labor market policy also requires eliminating what has been referred to as the tournament mobility model of career development, in which an individual must keep winning promotions at each level or risk being out of the game.[9] We have to allow professionals to get back in the game even when they have stayed out for many years as a result of any number of life or career circumstances. I have seen some professionals who have been outside the game for many years suddenly reinvigorate themselves with additional training or just a change of attitude and take on the most challenging of assignments. We have to learn to accept that people confront the various stages of life and family development in very different ways, so there may be times when professionals need to pause and reassess their commitment to work. At such times, it may be better in the long run to allow the professional to let up a little, or even to take a leave of absence or a sabbatical, than to push him or her to higher and higher levels of responsibility and potential stress.

A related offshoot of the problem of excessive specialization is the pressure some organizations exert on professionals eventually to consider the managerial track. For some professionals who have become redundant as a result of overspecialization, this may be the only outlet. The danger of redundancy can be minimized, however, by personal and professional development, which is fostered by open-door promotion practices. As I shall discuss at length when considering the dual-career ladder, many professionals prefer not to see their contribution undermined by organizational pressure to embark on a managerial career. Management relies on its technical staff to meet the needs of the organization. Not all professionals are interested in the administration; those who are not should be encouraged to advance in their professional careers where they can continue to flourish while simultaneously making important contributions to their organizations. One way to ensure the loyalty of professionals is simply to recognize their professional contributions. Since major professional achievements can also be expected to win the esteem of one's peer group (both within and outside the organization), corporate recognition can only solidify feelings of belonging and contentedness.

A basic theme emerges when the open and closed approaches to the other components in Table 5-1 are compared. Essentially, the open policy trades off information for politics. There is an inherent wisdom in this trade-off, in that the substitute for widely shared information is informal communication, such as might be expressed through rumor or politics. Since information is largely unavailable in a closed internal labor market system, employees need to seek other, more implicit ways to find out where they stand. The best place to start is with one's supervisor. The professional as a staff member is by and large out of the mainstream of critical management information to which a supervisor may be privy. If a constructive relationship with the supervisor can be developed, the professional can more effectively plan his or her next career moves. Of course, there is much uncertainty in this tack, since it is not always easy to cement a close personal relationship (the professional may ask, for example, "At what cost?"), and the supervisor may not be an effective counselor. If the supervisor cannot be counted on, the professional needs to solicit career information through other informal sources such as a mentor or another recognized professional sponsor, a gatekeeper, an influential colleague, an "in" in personnel and so forth.

Most professionals, committed to their profession and not necessarily to the process of organizational politics, are not interested in the gamesmanship needed to advance in the closed internal labor market. Some simply refuse to "play" and since little information is available on other opportunities or on their potential for vertical or lateral transfers, they remain on the sidelines. Some become sufficiently disenchanted that they leave their organizations without a fathom of information about promising internal opportunities.

Organizational Socialization

As we know from Chapter 3, professionals typically face a conflict in expectations when they arrive at their first job, because the clean conditions of specialized study and research at a university are not commonly replicated in the organizational environment, which presents messy, indeterminate problems and decisions. Management needs not only to understand this potential conflict but to defuse it with strategies that ease the transition to organizational life. Otherwise, the professional may react by becoming further isolated from the organizational mainstream. This could take the form of exclusive concentration on the skills for which he or she has been trained, though other maladaptive reactions, and even resignation, are possible.

Two broad types of managerial action are applicable in promoting organizational socialization. The first takes place before the professional enters the organization; the second, immediately thereafter. Beforehand, management can provide information about the culture in the organization by going directly to the professional schools. Student exposure to organizational life varies considerably among the professions. Doctors, of course, are automatically exposed through their residency requirements. Lawyers, however, are typically given little exposure, especially to corporate work. Unfortunately, those schools that spend little time on questions of organizational transition may not be receptive to business or public involvement in their curricula. Management should try to establish contact with the professional schools, however, and to work with university administrators to prepare students to make the transition to organizational life. If time cannot be found in the regular curriculum, perhaps career seminars can be held. The types of jobs available to professionals in a particular field can be outlined, including their typical content throughout the first year or so. This would also be a good time to discuss future career opportunities. Evidence from successful preorientation programs with which I am familiar suggests that students prefer dealing with an experienced professional from their field, rather than a company representative from either personnel or even management. They tend to relate most easily to someone who knows their language and yet can discuss the ins and outs of real-world experience.

It is also important that the company representative provide a realistic picture of what the graduates are likely to encounter within the organization. Management has begun to realize that it is of little value to raise expectations or engender false hopes about corporate life, only to find a dissatisfied novice professional on its hands after some initial work experience.[10]

In certain professions socialization is furthered by a professional culture bred by alumni who report back on their work experiences. Thus expectations about life in the working world are established firmly before graduation. Law firms, for example, knowingly recruit those law students preprogrammed to work hard and compete with one another. Once these people are hired, the firms do everything to encourage their proclivities by alluding to the potential rewards of high salary, a partnership, and collegial support.[11]

Once entering the organization, the new professional employee should continue to receive an honest portrayal of life there. Personnel may choose to start off with an orientation program, which could provide an overview of the organization, familiarize the new employee with rules and procedures as well as benefits and opportunities, and offer insights into the new hire's first job.[12] It is not a bad idea to invite senior managers to introduce the company to the new employee so as to give the professional a sense of the organization's history and culture. This begins the process of identification, which is a first step in experiencing positive corporate socialization. Both the supervisor and the novice's peers should be asked to take time out to familiarize the new hire with the work environment and answer questions. In sum, it is critical that the orientation make the professional aware of how his or her expected contribution fits into the overall organizational structure and mission.

Once on the job, the new professional should continue to receive support during the breaking-in phase. For some professionals, adjustment to organizational life is just not easy, and they will need someone or some kind of group to answer their questions. Basically, they need social support to help them overcome their conflicting expectations.[13] This support can also help prevent the professional from becoming too isolated. Social support consists of a network whose members are friendly, approachable, trustworthy, cooperative, and warm. Much of this socialization is expected to occur on its own through the hire's new peer group. Management can further the process, however, by ensuring that there is both a time and a place for social interaction to occur. This interaction, in turn, may be supplemented by a more formal buddy system, in which management designates two or more hires to act as junior mentors to one other.[14]

Both professional peers and managers should be aware that the new hire may be perplexed about and at times disenchanted with particular organizational policies and even with professional practices as interpreted by the particular department or full organization. Rather than attempt to disabuse the young professional of his or her ideas, the veteran should listen to the suggestions and explore with the individual the reasons for certain policies and practices. If the listener is willing to keep an open mind, the novice may even come up with innovative and practical suggestions, which, if implemented, may benefit not only the esteem of the new hire but the productivity of the unit.

It is especially helpful to the new hire to receive honest and constructive appraisals of his or her progress on particular assignments. Although professionals are accustomed to working on lengthy assignments and monitoring their own progress, it does not hurt to provide periodic feedback at critical milestones. Professionals like to be challenged, but they also desire to know how they are doing.

Mentorship

Although mentorship is a proven strategy for socializing the young professional, who in mentorship is referred to as "the protégé," it is also useful in helping the experienced professional avoid the dangers of overspecialization. Indeed, mentorship may be viewed as a critical stage of professional development that comes as an outgrowth of one's success as a technical specialist.[15] While performing the mentor function, mature professionals tend to broaden their area of expertise. They develop contacts and clients outside the organization. As they begin to carry out more responsible work and be of greater service to their clients, they need the assistance of junior-level people who can help do the detail work and develop the mentor's ideas. The mentorship stage of professional development is associated with less direct experience, but it simultaneously requires keeping one's skills and knowledge up to date.

The mentor is typically accorded respect by both professional colleagues and management, and is seen as important in the organization. The commitment to counsel younger colleagues, especially to teach them the organizational ropes, may constitute a signal to management that the professional has arrived—that he or she is now "one of us." Of course, mentorship can focus on professional concerns to the exclusion of organizational problems; but that is not usually the case. It normally consists of the mentor's translating professional developments into organizational processes and outcomes. Hence, the mentor tends to be viewed as an important member of the organizational team who has developed a base of technical support, respect, and power.

If the mentor has earned an influential position within the organization, his or her guidance and assistance can be critical in the protégé's development. Through their mentors, protégés can obtain otherwise unavailable opportunities and privileges. Thus the mentor relationship can greatly simplify integration of protégés into the organization and prevent overprofessionalization.

Few organizations have formal mentorship programs.[16] Most managers of professionals simply let the process take care of itself. A variety of organizational circumstances, however, be they the stability of the internal labor force, the nature of the organizational hierarchy, or the peculiar characteristics of the promotion system, may impede practical development of the mentorship strategy. It may be useful, therefore, at least to promulgate a mentorship policy and provide time for relationships between potential mentors and protégés to form, even if the organization does not designate mentors formally. The grassroots approach tends to work better, since it provides the necessary step of feeling each other out. It is critical that both parties agree on the boundaries of their relationship and spend time outside their professional discussions monitoring its development.

Although there can be tremendous benefits to both parties in mentoring, there are risks as well. The mentor's reputation and effectiveness can be seriously harmed if he or she is seen as carrying the role beyond the bounds of the organization. Both parties are at risk if jealousy or resentment emerges among peers or other managers.

A specific organizational implication for the protégé relates to both the timeliness and the accuracy of the mentor's perceptions and advice. It is critical, for example, that the mentor have adjusted to the present conditions of the organization, be aware of the future outlook of management, and have the authority to affect certain decisions that may involve the protégé. Out of enthusiasm to support their protégés, mentors may overstep their bounds, thereby impeding rather than furthering the protégés' career progress. For example, a mentor might attempt to advance the cause of his or her protégé at a succession meeting. If the norms of the organization dictate that the department head perform this function, the mentor may be seen as meddling, which could damage the protégé's reputation.

Mentorship entails personal risks as well. Foremost is the emotional involvement demanded of both parties. This is, in turn, associated with substantial time demands, both on the job and away from it. Although the emotional attachment between protégé and mentor can be positive, it can also compete with other important relationships in one's life, even with a spouse. Moreover, the protégé (and the mentor, too, in some cases) is susceptible to becoming overdependent. The emotional involvement between the two parties may also lead to some blind spots when dealing with third parties, as objective, rational points of view are overlooked. Finally, female mentorship and across-sex mentor/protégé relationships are particularly fraught with risks because women, although reportedly benefiting greatly from mentorship, typically face greater obstacles in trying to enter the power structure of an organization.

The risks and rewards of mentorship suggest three steps management might recommend to the parties to ensure that the relationship works to their mutual advantage.[17] First, regardless of who initiates the relationship, both parties should use their information resources to evaluate the other. The protégé wants to be sure that the mentor is respected by the organization and is personally compatible. The mentor wants to be sure that the protégé is a capable individual with the personal qualities to achieve his or her career goals and is willing to listen while not surrendering his or her independence.

Second, the parties must be willing to share their mutual expectations. Each must be willing to invest time and commitment and to accept criticism from the other. Finally, the parties need to monitor their relationship, not only to ensure that it serve their own needs but to see that it is viewed as constructive by others in the organization. Mentorship has become a very acceptable relationship in the professional environment, but petty jealousies do emerge and have to be handled. Each organization sets particular boundaries on the relationship, and these must be correctly diagnosed by the parties. For example, there may be an implicit standard regarding the appropriate time for termination. The parties will not want to carry the relationship beyond the acceptable threshold.

The Problem of Autonomy

| Managers who underspecify the ends but overspecify the means of practice and who expect adherence to the organizational hierarchy | → | *Mediation Strategies*

1. The Dual Ladder
2. Transition to Management
3. Managing Ends Not Means
4. Professional Participation | ← | Professionals who demand autonomy over ends as well as means |

Many scholars of professionals and bureaucracy believe autonomy is the most critical issue in the field. Indeed, a recent full issue (Vol. 24, No. 2) of *Human Resource Management* was devoted to this issue, casting the problem as a dilemma between the control of the manager and the autonomy of the professional.

As I have defined it throughout this book, autonomy refers to the discretion on the part of professionals to determine the problems which they will examine as well as the means to be used in confronting these problems. What makes autonomy such a difficult issue in salaried as opposed to private practice is that it has to be compromised when the professional can virtually be hired, promoted, and fired at the will of the manager whose job it is to control the resources of the organization.

As I established in the earlier chapters, managers tend to overcontrol the means of professional practice but are lax when it comes to telling the professionals what the company stands for. Meanwhile, some professionals demand autonomy over both means and ends; they expect to participate fully in all decisions that affect them. It is my position that it is management's job to establish the strategic goals of the enterprise and to communicate the values that guide behavior within the organizational community. Once an assignment has been formulated with a potential target date, however, the professional should be left alone with his or her peer group to solve the problem or provide the necessary service.

The mediation strategies addressed in this section have been developed to disentangle the dilemma over how much autonomy or participation to allow any professional or professional group. Much depends on the type of organization, the individual professional, and his or her position in the organization. Nevertheless, some guidelines and specific programs can work to achieve a manageable balance between autonomy and control.

The Dual Ladder

The dual ladder has the greatest potential of any structural accommodation we know of to resolve the classic need of the professional for autonomy, discretion, and participation in professionally based organizational activities. It is unique in providing a way for the professional to advance in the profession without having to adopt a nonprofessional career track.

This approach, which has been in use for over thirty-five years, comprises the usual managerial ladder of hierarchial positions leading to increased managerial authority and another ladder of professional positions that carries comparable prestige in terms of salary, status, and (often) autonomy and responsibility. The principal intent of the dual ladder is to reward professional accomplishment and managerial proficiency comparably. It was initially based on evidence that young professionals in organizations that placed less emphasis on the desire to manage contributed more and were more loyal to their organizations than those in organizations that highly valued managerial aspirations.[18] The dual ladder, then, was introduced as the perfect answer to the dilemma of professionals who wanted to advance in their careers without becoming managers. Some professionals, given their dispositions and value systems, even personalities, simply cannot adjust to a managerial life style characterized by general problem solving, decision making under uncertainty, and interpersonal, intergroup, and interorganizational conflict. Those who do make the adjustment tend to fall into one of four categories. Those in the largest category simply see the transition to management as a natural progression of responsibility. Indeed, many engineers see managing as the ultimate accomplishment of their career. Another group goes into management as a replacement for an unrewarding professional life, which, ironically, could result from dissonance with managerial expectations. A third group chooses management rather than having to find a new job in the profession, and members of a fourth group consider management when they fear their professional skills are becoming weakened or that are obsolete.

Professionals outside these four categories, including many of the company's most productive individual contributors, prefer to stay in their professional domain. They are not particularly enthralled by engagement in such managerial practices as working with diverse individuals, coordinating group efforts, configuring the organizational system and its subsystems, acting on subjective judgment, using political expediency as a factor in a decision, and dealing with uncertainty.[19] Unfortunately, what they may in fact be interested in is also largely identified in American enterprise with managerial work. In fact, as a variant of the second category of professionals listed above, some seek managerial status to obtain recognition within the workplace, especially to receive credit for their achievements.[20] They also seek decision-making autonomy in their research to affect the direction in which their projects will go. Finally, they seek the resources of management, namely, the large staffs, generous budgets, and costly hardware needed to make outstanding contributions in their fields. The essence of the argument in favor of dual ladders is that these characteristics of the work environment, which confer considerable autonomy on the practitioner, need not be made available exclusively through the managerial track.

The structure and operation of the dual ladder, although varying from company to company, typically call for a branching into the two tracks about midway up the organizational hierarchy. Most dual tracks today can be found within R&D laboratories or new-product engineering departments, especially in the pharmaceutical, chemical, and electronics industries. Nothing prevents management from developing dual ladders in nonscientific professions, however, or from having several ladders corresponding to separate disciplines. At Aetna Life and Casualty, in Hartford, Connecticut, the law department of nearly 100 attorneys has a professional and a management path, both of which are about equally chosen.

Crossovers between the professional and managerial ladders can be allowed but typically do not occur at the upper levels, where incumbents have normally made lifelong commitments to their fields. A recent innovation has been the establishment of three career ladders: the managerial, technical, and a third ladder for project management. Initiated almost exclusively for engineering professionals, the third ladder entails some technical work but also requires a great deal of coordination characteristic of matrix management.

Although there are arguments for considering project management a distinct career orientation,[21] its performance requirements, growth potential, and psychological attributes, especially at later career stages, approximate those of the managerial ladder.[22] By allowing professionals to take responsibility for increasingly difficult and challenging assignments, project management removes one aspect of the traditional ladder mentality that troubles some professionals, namely, its hierarchical character as expressed in formal titles and positions.

Figure 5-2 displays a prototypical dual-ladder format for a general engineering career path. Although equal numbers of levels are shown here, some organizations may have fewer levels within the professional track. Each title requires an increasing degree of recognized expertise

Figure 5-2   Prototypical Dual Ladder For Engineering

Levels

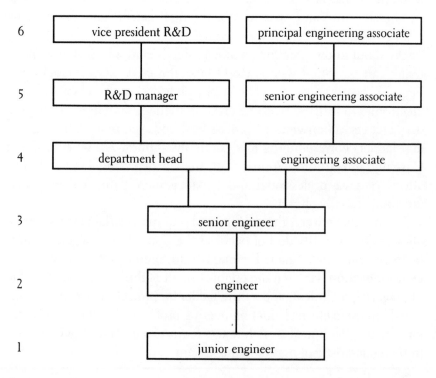

and technical contribution. As is shown, the highest title on the professional side is considered equivalent in status, authority, compensation, and benefits to that of vice president. It is typically reserved for a very select group of outstanding performers who have acquired national or international reputations.[23] Selection and evaluations are usually done by a committee of professionals who hold higher ranks. For the highest levels, committee members may even be drawn from a distinguished list of professionals who do not necessarily belong to the organization. Promotion up the professional ladder should be based on very carefully defined criteria generally recognized as representing excellence in the discipline. Whereas movement up the managerial ladder is normally associated with increasing power and decision-making authority, movement up the professional ladder normally is indicative of the attainment of greater professional autonomy.

Some architects of the dual ladder also believe that advancement up the professional track should be contingent on contribution to organizational goals.[24] Although this may at first seem inconsistent with the professional culture, it is nevertheless consistent with the position of autonomy over means. By the time one achieves senior status, typically one has meshed one's professional agenda with the organization's overall mission. Disputes at this level focus more on the means toward the organization's goals (i.e., the technology to employ) than on the goals themselves. Contribution to organizational goals should never, however, take the place of professional standards of excellence among the criteria for advancement.

Although dual ladders have not received a great deal of support in the literature, the barriers to successful implementation have more to do with loopholes in their actual operation than with the integrity of the concept itself. The most common complaint is that the dual ladder does not in fact reward professional and managerial accomplishments equally. When this complaint occurs, one wonders whether the dual-ladder system has really been implemented at all. The whole notion is to provide equivalent salary and status. The professional ladder may need fewer rungs than the managerial ladder, but whatever job evaluation system the company uses, salaries should be pegged to equivalent requirements in terms of such criteria as knowledge, problem solving, and accountability. As far as status goes, there can be no substitute for wide promotion of the dual-ladder concept internally in creating an organizational culture that values technical contributions. Some companies may believe they have such a culture when in fact employees, professional or otherwise, get the message that success means becoming a manager. Unfortunately, many of these same companies propagate the myth that technical creativity is limited to one's early years in the profession. Yet we know that some of our outstanding researchers and scholars have made their mark at varying periods throughout their careers. Companies need to publicize that permanent professional careers are not only available to their talented individual contributors but are also encouraged and rewarded. In a recent study by Karen Epstein,[25] in only one of three organizations examined was there satisfaction with the technical ladder. In that organization, individuals were given full information about the salary and career potential in both tracks.

The issue of equivalent influence is much more complicated and serious. It centers around the view that professionals are no different from other employees in desiring the power to allocate limited resources and to pursue diverse goals.[26] Not all salaried professionals are interested in managing operations, but they can still acquire influence through the professional culture. For example, some may act as gatekeepers for communications within their department and between it and the outside world. Although these gatekeepers have considerable influence, their control is informal. The professional track within the dual ladder may constitute an ideal arrangement to stimulate the gatekeeper's growth and development.

One of the most often cited complaints against the dual-ladder is that it serves as a dumping ground for failed managers. This illustrates the precise instance in which the fault lies not in the concept but in its operation. Although management may see it as humane to transfer an ineffective manager to the professional track to keep up his salary and status, this is one sure way to devalue the whole dual ladder system. The criteria for admission and advancement throughout the various rungs of the professional ladder need to be as rigorous as those for the managerial ladder. Indeed, one author suggested that the professional track should be kept exclusive, although exclusivity in its own right can destroy the expectation of reward for concerted effort and valuable performance.[27] My view is that as long as the criteria for promotion remain consistent, the system can survive and exclusivity will not become a central issue.

Some complaints lodged against the dual ladder are essentially design problems. For example, there may be a shortage of rungs on the professional ladder or a ceiling for advancement well below the top position on the managerial ladder. Further, managers may find professionals reporting to them who have higher status or rank in the organization. These design problems require the obvious: a more careful design or redesign of the system. One reported strategy entailed convening a task force made up of managers, professionals, and human resource staff that began by defining the rungs in the professional ladder through an analysis of job levels within the department.[28] The group then defined titles, job responsibilities, qualification criteria, and accountability standards for all rungs within the dual-ladder structure.

Another relatively common complaint centers around the symbolic significance of the titles in the professional track. In short, they are not always held up as worthy of esteem. I have already discussed the importance of establishing a culture of professional excellence within the organization that exists apart from the criteria for managerial excellence. Two other strategies for ensuring that the professional ladder confers status are, first, to give professionals at the top levels of their ladder access to key executive decision makers and corresponding influence in executive decisions involving professional work; and, second, to have professionals predominate in decisions on promotions within the professional track.

In summary, the dual ladder represents an excellent vehicle to provide professionals with sufficient autonomy to carry out their craft yet ensure their integration into the organization. For those professionals truly devoted to their profession, the dual ladder represents a system of rewards and potential career advancement that permits wholehearted contribution to the organization and at the same time a commitment to the discipline.

Transition to Management

It is perhaps ironic that after singing the praises of the dual-ladder approach, I include managerial transition as a mediation strategy to resolve the interest of professionals in autonomy. Yet the hierarchial pattern of control is a fixture of modern American management and is unlikely to be replaced permanently by dual hierarchies for professionals and management. Further, some professionals indeed not only want to become managers, but have all the necessary skills and attitudes to be successful in this role. The caveat is that only interested and qualified professional candidates should be considered for the job. The candidate needs to be approached in a serious manner by a supervisor or personnel representative who can inquire about the individual's true intentions. There should be an attempt to determine whether the interest is genuine or the result of pressure to advance so as to acquire money or social status within the organization. If it turns out to be the latter, every effort should be made to allow the professional, if qualified, to meet his or her social and esteem needs while remaining within the professional ranks. Transition to management should be considered only where there is a real commitment to this alternative career track. Further, since time away from one's profession can damage one's confidence and outdate one's knowledge, it is advisable to allow the professional to take a provisional managerial assignment, to test and demystify management as an ultimate career objective.

Professionals who commit themselves to a managerial career face a skills hurdle, since successful performance as a manager requires different competencies and aptitudes from those required of a professional. In particular, managers need to be skilled in interpersonal relations. They typically do not have the luxury of dealing with a single problem or working with a single group of colleagues. Not only do they have their own subordinates to worry about, but they spend inordinate time talking with managers in other functional areas as well as people outside the organization. They also must be counted on to make objective judgments, to act under uncertainty, to delegate considerable responsibility, and to use political expediency as a factor in their decisions, all of which go against the grain of professional behavior.[29]

On the other hand, professionals find that some of their professional skills are quite useful in managerial work. Their analytical skills, for example, can normally be applied to the financial and systems analysis needed to control operations. Further, they typically know a good deal about the technology employed in their organizations.

Some professionals also enjoy the greater influence available to them in managerial roles, especially when it gives them a chance to see a project through to completion. Their activities are broader in scope, and they can afford, at times, to take a longer-range perspective on their projects. They also may be given more opportunity to assist other professionals in their development.

The essential difference between professionals and management is that professionals desire independence of action and intellectually compatible colleagues, whereas managers derive satisfaction from directing others and working with diverse individuals. Professionals interested in giving up sole concentration on the field for which they have been trained in order to direct others are prime candidates for transition. They need to be made aware, however, that assumption of managerial duties may result in gradual obsolescence of their professional skills. In some disciplines, it may be a very short time before they find they can no longer solve a problem by themselves. For a professional, therefore, the urge to lead has to be strong, since it may eventually undermine the very roots of professionalism.

Besides the soul searching suggested above, professionals need additional time and training to adjust to a transition to management. As was recommended earlier, a temporary assignment might provide a good internship in management. Professional candidates should also consult with their supervisors and other managerial personnel, to get a sense of the job. Basically, professionals may require an orientation or a reorientation to the organization, including its officers, policies, and procedures. They also need to learn about the informal structure and processes. This may entail finding out what is appropriate and expected in the new setting, charting the relevant players and where one fits in, uncovering sources of resistance perhaps even to oneself, learning the local language, and assessing how well the job is currently being done. A new manager also will want to ensure that there is an adequate support group of both like professionals and managers who appreciate the difficulties of transition.[30] Although some learning about how to manage can be derived from in-house training or academic programs (an MBA program, for example), ultimately there is no substitute either for observation or for experience. Professionals committed to the managerial role can become very successful managers with the right mix of talent, previously acquired skills, and development.

Managing Ends Not Means

The art of managing professionals requires special talent, regardless of the manager's background. One might think professionals would make very good managers, since they know from whence they came. Yet the skills of management may be antagonistic to professional training. Further, professional-administrators are known to forget their past, and, out of a new loyalty to their organization or in conformity with senior management's expectations, sometimes to be even more overbearing than nonprofessional administrators. They may even demand programmed, generalized solutions to problems they know require more sophisticated treatment.

The manager ought to let the professional control his or her own work processes. The professional has been expressly trained to deal with specialized organizational problems. There is little point in meddling with the means used to attack these problems. Indeed, the best administrator frees the professional to do his or her work and minimizes the routine reports and forms that are admittedly necessary in the organization. Pelz and Andrews[31] long ago concluded, and there has been little to dispute their findings, that the ideal professional-administrator knows how to balance autonomy and control, frequently interacts with the staff, permitting staff members to make many of their own decisions.

Since it is apparent that professionals have the maturity to carry out their tasks somewhat independently, the managerial role is much less directive than it might be when supervising nonprofessionals. Many of the traditional managerial functions (e.g., interacting with clients, determining work methods) have been transferred to the employee.[32] The manager becomes more a buffer between the operation, of which the professionals are a part, and the upper administration of the enterprise. The manager also coordinates tasks among the various operating units and provides resources to the professional work groups. Finally, the manager should be prepared to resolve conflicts between operating units or between a particular professional team and external groups, such as customers or clients, government agencies, and vendors.

A familiar theme of this book is that managerial control should be exerted only at the end point. Unfortunately, believing that professionals insist on freedom to establish their own research goals, managers tend to leave them alone, which results in a lack of integration between technology development and overall corporate planning. Yet management also tends to place constraints on professionals' operational autonomy (purchase of equipment, personnel requisitions, budget limits, etc.). Lotte Bailyn believes these control functions are totally misplaced.[33] Since professionals' work is highly complex and skilled, it makes little sense to control the procedures they use to achieve results. Further, many aspects of the professional's performance defy measurement.

I believe that control of results is nevertheless problematic, since, in some settings, it is nearly impossible to determine whether professional behavior has induced a desired change. Yet along with peer control, control of results is really the only effective means to control professional behavior.

An example is in order to illustrate this point. In a discharge arbitration case reported in the *Industrial Relations* journal,[34] a seemingly very competent PhD computer scientist was hired to work on a problem both he and his management felt was well within his capacity. Upon review by his supervisor as well as an outside consultant, however, his progress was deemed inadequate, mainly because he could offer no concrete plan for implementing his ideas. He was repeatedly informed of his shortcomings. Two years later, management judged his performance to be unsatisfactory because he had still not made progress in providing a practical solution to the assigned problem. At the arbitration hearing, the discharged employee contended that neither his supervisors nor the other reviewers were competent to understand his ideas, that they were innovative ideas that would eventually contribute to solving the problem, and that the company's resources were too meager to develop a fast and proper solution.

Although the discharge was upheld in this case, it does demonstrate how the complexity of professional jobs and the extreme variety in professional work environments make control difficult. Moreover, it shows how tempting it is for management to try to control the means of practice to hold the professional to a given product and timetable. Nevertheless, once the manager and professional agree on a finite goal, the manager should focus attention on compliance or on a legitimate reason why the goal cannot be reached. Of course, recognized progress toward goal attainment should be taken into consideration.

The complexity of professional work might cause management to despair that there are no available methods of evaluating their professional staffs. On the contrary. Staying with the notion of controlling ends and not means, it is possible to devise a performance-appraisal system based on behavioral outcomes. Given the variety in the professional's work as well as its organization-specific character, it is nearly pointless to use an appraisal scale developed for nonprofessionals, or even for professionals in another organization. The focus of any intrinsic instrument should also be on outcomes rather than procedures, since the latter are hopelessly variable. One method of deriving appropriate behavioral outcome scales is to interview a sample of professionals, using critical incidents. Respondents could be asked to think of a colleague whose performance they consider superior. The interviews would create a data base of behavioral items describing successful performance. A peer group of professionals along with management could then decide which items to retain from the interviews. One study that used this method identified a number of behavioral outcomes that were subsequently used to evaluate engineers.[35] Among these were product cost-cutting or profit generation, creativity and originality, implementation of new ideas, high work quality, visibility and leadership in the profession, and publication of innovations in professional journals. Another excellent vehicle to appraise professional performance, management by objectives (MBO), will be discussed in the next section of this chapter on the problem of supervision.

Most of what has been said so far about managing ends is related to operating management, those managers in supervisory or middle positions charged with carrying out organizational policy. The operating managers transmit this corporate policy throughout the organization and serve as links between the various organizational units. It is the express role of the top management, however, to set not only broad corporate policy but to articulate the values that guide behavior throughout the enterprise. This is really where the management of ends starts. There should be no dispute that as people expressly hired to serve the contractual purpose for which the company or agency was organized, top management has not only a right but a responsibility to communicate those ends to all personnel. There are style differences across organizations, of course, that allow lower-level staff more or less to shape the values and objectives of the organization. Thus, at times, corporate policy is something that emerges rather than is formulated. But with a clear articulation of corporate objectives from the top, professional employees are able to evaluate their own ideas within a definite context, allowing them to reconcile their professional and personal goals with the corporate goals.

Basic research provides one of the best examples of managing ends at the top. Many technical professionals are convinced that you cannot plan basic research. How can you predict what you are going to discover? Well, Guy Suits, former director of research of GE,[36] believes that in fact a good deal can be said in advance about expected discoveries. One can anticipate their probable outlines and timing and their probable impact on industrial technology. In addition, it is top management's job to plan the organization and the operation of its scientific research program so as to have the desired impact on important technology. Since the professional is faced with many alternative choices and directions, why not, according to Suits, make the research objective clear? Then the professional can commit himself to reach it and can make choices that favor this objective.

Successful researchers do not typically plod through their scientific careers stumbling on things accidentally. Powerful innate curiosity combined with many other exceptional aptitudes is surely involved; but one cannot avoid the conclusion that the careful sorting out of trivia and the selection of important objectives play critical roles in influencing the results of a successful basic research program.[37] Hence, top management does not have to be shy about telling all its employees what it is about. The professional staff will for the most part be grateful that these organizational objectives and values are placed out in the open. It gives them something to shoot for—as long as they can control the means of getting there.

Professional Participation

By participation, I refer to the managerial strategy of giving subordinates an increasing role in helping determine the policies and methods used in the organization. It is derived from a fundamental humanistic belief that people are more contented and committed to an objective when they are involved in decisions that affect them. Organizationally, it is more commonly translated as a belief that management holds no monopoly on good ideas; hence, productivity benefits if employees are allowed to suggest ways to improve their jobs in particular and the organization in general.

The chief concern is how much participation to allow. My own research has revealed that when professionals are allowed maximum participation (i.e., over procedures, decisions, and performance), they tend to value their professional colleagues outside their organization much more than their managers.[38] In certain settings, where, for example, the status of the organization depends heavily on professional accomplishment, such as in research universities and laboratories, or where the clients of the organization are entirely dependent on the professional staff, such as in professional service organizations like law or accounting firms, this may not represent a terrible state of affairs. Professionals in these settings need to subscribe to basic managerial controls, but otherwise, their productivity depends more on professional accomplishment than organizational allegiance.

In most industrial organizations, however, there has to be a limit on absolute participation. The boundary of the organization places a limit on external collegiality. One cannot be an employee of the profession. Hence, participation needs to be viewed not as the inherent right of the professional who chooses to base his or her decisions on the standards set by the profession, but as a dialogue that recognizes the constraints of corporate obligation. Most professionals will not object to these constraints surrounding the ends or direction of their work. In fact, they often need a sense that they are working within an acceptable framework so that their knowledge and creative talents can be used effectively.[39]

Professional participation should be primarily over means. The professional's job is never clearly defined, since the inherent tasks are complicated and often uncertain. Hence, management needs to allow the professional the right to determine what is to be done on the job and how it should be done. The outcome of any professional's effort depends on the ability to control working conditions.[40] Management's role in this scenario is developmental and coordinative. It provides resources and support for the professional's work and ensures integration among the various operational units in the organization. It is also charged with communicating to external groups and organizations about the company's objectives, products, and services. Depending on management style as well as the organization's culture, the professional staff may also be invited to participate in setting the organization's policies and goals. Professional control over the means of practice should be constrained by the criterion of accountability. Those professionals imbued with 60s-type values would have it no other way.

One source of accountability that limits professional participation is the profession itself. Aside from legitimate corporate needs to protect trade secrets, management should allow ample opportunity for the professional to be judged by peers within the professional community. In addition, the professional's own working group can provide peer control. The individual professional, meanwhile, under the strategy of output control, operates under rigorous performance standards. If the professional has missed a deadline, the principle of accountability demands an honest and straightforward explanation. Thereafter, together, management and the professional mutually plan the next milestone for review. It is reasonable for management to expect this subsequent review to occur sooner or with more periodic consultation.

In summary, up to this point I am calling for professional participation over means but with accountability. Professionals are by nature fascinated with performance; it is what turns them on. Their colleagues and their managers, occupying different roles, are available to keep them on track. Participation may also extend to the goals of the enterprise.

In the remaining pages of this section, I would like to consider specific approaches that induce responsible professional participation in means and, to a more limited extent, ends. First, it is axiomatic that managerial strategies that involve professionals in corporate decision making and that at the same time draw on the professional's technical expertise are likely to induce corporate loyalty. Management needs not only to articulate its corporate values and policies but also to illustrate the link between the professional's work and particular corporate objectives. Professionals, in turn, should be asked to comment on these links and hence be involved in critical committee assignments, interdepartmental task forces, technical project or proposal reviews, and policy boards considering such items as awards, patents, benefits, and special assignments. Another approach is the designation of qualified professionals to represent the company at meetings. With proper orientation and practice in presentation skills, the professional can be a valuable resource in external relations.

So much has been written about organization development (OD) techniques designed to extend participation throughout an organization that it would be pointless to attempt an exposition of all those methods.[41] Basically, OD attempts to improve an organization's problem-solving and renewal processes by using collaborative techniques; i.e., involving employees in decisions and allowing them to contribute to the limits of their potential. One such technique that can be very successful with professionals is the attitude survey. This method provides two-way communication between managers and the professional staff by soliciting professional attitudes on a wide array of company practices. The results of the survey are typically fed back to the employees for immediate review and subsequent action planning. Professionals should be involved in all aspects of the attitude survey, including question design and analysis, to make it a meaningful process that involves the professional staff in organizational policy. It should be understood that management is not being asked to accede to any set of suggestions through this process, but to listen and consider all points carefully.

Another common OD technique that is often associated with the concept of participation is team-building. Professionals who work in groups or who might form a group undergo a variety of clinical strategies designed to help them improve their group process skills, which, in turn, betters their decision making and upgrades their performance. Often, the team is given considerable authority to make and implement specific decisions. Groups do not appeal to all professionals, and there are circumstances in which groups are not appropriate decision-making vehicles, such as when one professional clearly has greater expertise on a subject than others or when there is time pressure. Teams work best when management assigns them a meaningful, well-bounded set of tasks to be completed by a specific time, when there are standards of accountability and performance the team must meet, when there are persistent efforts to train the participants in group dynamics, when there is a mechanism for all those who have a stake in the team's mission to get involved, when there is recognition and reward for the team's efforts, and when there are clearly understood processes for the team's formation, termination, and transfer of learning.[42]

Two other clusters of approaches deserve mention, although I take a dim view of their ability to induce genuine professional participation. On the one hand, management can attempt to buy professional involvement through lucrative benefit packages. On the other, professionals can attempt to mandate participation through the legal or bargaining route. The first method normally contains an incentive for renewed loyal and productive behavior or a reinforcement for existing beneficial behavior. For example, after the organization has experienced a particularly productive financial year or quarter, professionals may be given some kind of bonus or allowed to share in profits, regardless of whether it can be determined that individual professionals actually changed their behavior during the affected period. An employee stock ownership plan (ESOP) may also be set up, wherein professionals can purchase company stock, normally in conjunction with contributions from their employer. Although such a plan might give the professional more interest in the success of the organization or, with sufficient build-up of funds, even give professional representatives a voice in managerial decision making, it is my view that these outcomes will occur only among managements already sympathetic to genuine professional participation. Hence, although I wholeheartedly support professional benefits and incentives, I think they are far more effective in responding to the problem of supervision of professionals than to the problem of participation.

Legal or bargaining approaches that mandate professional participation are no more likely to induce a spirit of genuine professional participation than the carrot approach just discussed. One device that is popular in Europe, called codetermination, allows professional and other employees to serve on their companies' boards of directors. Although codetermination might appear to provide more leverage to professional personnel when it comes to corporate policy decisions, it is not clear that the professional board members would have sufficient impact to make a difference in management practice, nor would they necessarily be viewed as faithful representatives of professionalism.

Another, more forceful tack is for professionals to push for greater participation through their representative bodies, such as their professional associations and societies. Although these associations generally do an adequate job of establishing standards, of promoting the profession within society, of assessing and recognizing professional contributions, and of furthering communication among professional members, their impact in advancing the autonomy and participation of their salaried members has been very limited.

Professional unionism represents a logical alternative in the face of the inadequacy and, perhaps more accurately, the lack of interest on the part of professional associations in representing salaried employees in their own organizations. However, the more militant tactics of unions, their predominant agenda of bread-and-butter items— namely, wages and working conditions—their standardized methods, and their seemingly callous disregard of the public interest dishearten even the most alienated salaried professionals. Few see unionism as a means of encouraging management to allow them greater autonomy over their practice and greater participation in managerial policy making. My own observation of professional unions, especially in nursing and teaching, suggests that once a union makes significant inroads into a profession, that profession has already been seriously deprofessionalized by institutional, regulatory, or bureaucratic means.[43]

The Problem of Supervision

| Managers who maintain close supervision | → | *Mediation Strategies*

1. Self-management and Peer Control
2. Professional-Administration
3. Management by Objectives (MBO)
4. Gatekeeping
5. Professional Incentives | ← | Professionals who resist close supervision by insisting on professional standards of evaluation |

The culture of management requires results. Ultimately, if managers are to make their mark in the organization, they have to show a measurable impact on the bottom line. Unfortunately, there is also pressure on management to show results in the short run. Public reactions to the organization sometimes require immediate results. Moreover, internally, it is not uncommon to find managers who plan to stay on their jobs only a short time before they advance. Hence they need to demonstrate performance as quickly as they can.

Professionals, meanwhile, are more comfortable with longer-range results, since most of their work entails protracted thought and action. Chemists, for example, need to organize innumerable trials on a given compound before they consider it ready for public consumption. This rather significant difference in time orientation between professionals and managers can create enormous strain in the organization. Management tends to get very nervous when it does not see the results it is looking for within the time it has established. As a result, there is a natural tendency to maintain close supervision over the professional staff to try to induce it to perform on time.

Professionals, on the other hand, find close supervision a nuisance that, if nothing else, impedes their progress, since they need constantly to explain their every action to the largely uninformed manager. They would much rather simply rely on their peers for help and suggestions to get the job done. Their own professional standards are far superior when it comes to evaluating their progress than any kind of managerial oversight. The strategies I shall discuss in this section carry this argument further.

Self-Management and Peer Control

Perhaps more than any other occupational group, professionals devote most of their working life to control. It is part of the ethos of their socialization. It is fundamental to the scientific method. Professionals learn to proceed one step at a time in their tasks, and at each step, they stop to inquire about their own progress. This is the essence of self-management. Groups of repetitive tasks can be performed all at once, but even then there is a fundamental need to get feedback on performance. With this kind of devotion, it is difficult to conceive why management must preoccupy itself with close supervision.

The answer, of course, is that the manager wants the organization's goals to somehow fit into this devotion to task. The trick, then, is to discover how to demonstrate to the professional compatibility between professional and organizational goals. The chance of this occurring is increased enormously when the manager has established a trusting relationship with the professional. Although this is more likely to occur where the manager can demonstrate some technical competence, any manager will be better able to take advantage of the professional's self-management when he or she can establish a nearly collegial relationship with the professional. In this way, the professional, acknowledging the role of and pressures placed on the manager, will try to cooperate and serve the organization. It is even conceivable that formal supervision will be dispensed with altogether, since the professional, feeling himself or herself part of a team, will want to inform a superior of the progress being made on the tasks at hand.

Close supervision can also be waived where there is sufficient peer control to evaluate the quantity and quality of the professional's output. Often, this form of control arises out of a consensus among one's colleagues at the same level or even among those of superior rank. The rationale for peer control is obvious. Peers are in a position to observe the individual professional, and beyond that, they are more likely to have the necessary qualifications to make an objective assessment. The reliability of peer review, however, depends on a number of conditions. First, not all of one's professional colleagues are competent in the same area. Subspecialties have proliferated to a point where each individual becomes a technical empire unto himself. Hence, one's colleagues may not be in a position to evaluate one's work adequately. A consensus has to be arrived at, then, regarding which colleagues are best able to evaluate a given outcome. Even if colleagues are technically up-to-date in the field, they may hold preconceptions about their colleague's work, or they may simply not be receptive to different or unconventional ideas or methods. Further, they may lose their objectivity if their colleague's success affects them personally. Finally, personal acquaintance itself has always been feared as a contaminant of objective peer evaluations. Nevertheless, where evaluations are conducted anonymously, and where there is genuine respect for the advancement of professional knowledge and contribution, peer evaluations can be very specific and quite objective. They can also free management to spend more time on tasks other than close supervision.

One company with which I am familiar takes the notion of peer control to another level by submitting the technical work of some leading members of the technical staff to outside review. If the reviewing parties are disinterested and there are no outstanding security problems, this is an excellent method of soliciting critical comments on a professional's contributions. Academicians do this as a matter of course, but the practice has yet to take hold in the other salaried professions. Professional associations are best equipped to facilitate outside peer review, but corporate management needs to support it if it is to gain any popularity. The competitive pressures of the American free enterprise system will probably impede its spread, however.

Professional-Administration

The professional-administrator could be the key link between the professional's need to observe professional standards of evaluation and the manager's need to control operations. Since self-management and peer control have been established as critical elements of professional review, administrative control will be easier if the professional staff see the supervisor as one of their own.

Some professional-administrators may forget their past and begin to act "like a manager," which has fallaciously been equated with bossing. Unfortunately, this style of supervision by professional-administrators holds no advantage over control by purely administrative types; in fact, it may even bring on deeper-seated resentment characterized by feelings of betrayal. Nevertheless, once exposed to the pressures of the management role, professional-administrators will undoubtedly assume some managerial characteristics, such as using nonprofessional (political) considerations in setting policy, adopting nonmerit criteria in reviewing performance, or simply assuming a more detached or objective stance when it comes to heeding professional advice.

If professional-administrators are to be effective in their dealings with professional staff, according to Robert Davidson,[44] they need to frame their requests in terms that capture professional commitment and values. They need to remember where they came from but also not hide from their new responsibilities. Professional-administrators who use their good instincts in this way, who are allowed a natural transition to management, and who are explicitly trained for their new responsibilities can become very good supervisors. Some organizations, in fact, use only professional-administrators, believing that a business administrator simply cannot understand the technical work at hand well enough to be effective. There tends to be more reliance on professional-administrators at the supervisory level, however, than at higher management levels.

The greatest advantage of a professional-administrator at the supervisory level is technical knowledge. Subordinates are more likely to support the administrative solutions proposed by supervisors who not only show an interest but also participate in technical solutions to the professionals' problems. Where the supervisor is competent technically, that individual can be viewed more as a colleague than as an administrative hack and, hence, can participate in peer control.

It is perhaps too utopian to expect the professional-administrator at the supervisory level to retain state-of-the-art knowledge when supervisory duties require less and less exposure to technical matters. In this event, the professional still has an advantage over the purely business administrator, in that he or she still has the necessary technical background to understand the professional's needs. What is key in this situation is that the supervisor not forget the conditions under which professionals work best. The only change in the relationship between professional and supervisor that needs to take place when the supervisor's skills become outdated is that the supervisor must then refer technical questions to others. This may shake the supervisor's confidence. Perhaps the supervisor will be viewed with less esteem by the subordinate. But if the professional-administrator has learned the task of management well, the needs of the professional staff can still be met. In the critical coordinative role of management, for instance, the supervisor can ensure that technical resources are provided to those professionals in need of assistance. Thus an effective professional-administrator can keep the relationship with his or her staff intact by substituting managerial skills for technical shortcomings. As was discussed in the section on transition to management, interpersonal skills are particularly critical in furthering the performance of any professional team. Yet, beyond skills, professional-administration is also a matter of leadership style.

The style of participative management is at its best when the supervisor can draw out the best in his people, allow decisions to be made at the point of influence and contribution, and create a spirit that everyone is in it together and that if something is unknown, they'll learn it together. There are also times when the appropriate style is one of laissez-faire management, which permits the staff to work on its own without interference. Finally, there are also times, though infrequent, when the supervisor must be very directive about goals and purpose. Participative management has been shown to be by far the most effective leadership style, particularly in building motivation and stimulating progress toward organizational goals. Laissez-faire management tends to be a recourse when the administrator has little or no technical competence in the area in which the professional staff are working.

In support of a situational approach to managing professionals, I prefer to see some flexibility among professional-administrators in adapting their style to local supervisory circumstances, although the participative style tends to work well in most situations. Further, any supervisor must also be true to himself, and not try to behave in a way that is inconsistent with basic personality. Although the traits of good supervision depicted here seem subtle and complex, most professionals have the sophistication not only to understand but to practice them effectively.

At upper administrative levels in the organizational hierarchy, the impact of professional-administrators is less than at the supervisory level, for a number of reasons. First, there is much more opportunity to employ business types because technical competence is less of a factor. Further, some professionals at the supervisory level refuse to go much higher for fear of separating themselves altogether from professional endeavors. Those who do, tend to adopt a more managerial personality and thus are not necessarily considered different from business administrators by the professional staff. It is clear that the higher the administrator's position in the organizational hierarchy, the more the concern for problems of coordination for the whole organization. In other words, the higher the position, the greater the use of superordinate control, that is, control that is bureaucratic and thus arising from the goals of the organization and impacting all organizational units and personnel.[45] The lower positions among professional-administrators depend more on colleague or peer control.

Concentrating professional-administrators at the supervisory level and relying on them less at the upper management levels makes good sense on a number of accounts. At the supervisory level there tends to be more time for technical decision making, and this appeals to professionals who do not wish to give up their professional interests entirely. It also in some ways takes them off the hook regarding high-level policy problems that may plague the professional staff. Of course this can also work in reverse, since as the person in the middle, the supervisor has to account for organizational rules and regulations. The greatest advantage to the organization in using professional-administrators is that it provides an opportunity for those who command respect to bring a managerial perspective to the professional environment. There is still a chance for the supervisor with a professional background to be viewed as a colleague; therefore, this individual can become an important conduit for information originating both from the top and from below. Professional staff members are likely to accept some of the managerial responsibilities carried by these professional-administrators as long as they preserve operational autonomy for the staff. Meanwhile, with a base of power in the organization centered on the professional-administrator, the professional staff may also tolerate the bureaucratic control of the top administrators.

The position of project manager holds a unique role in the context of professional-administration, since a project manager tends to be by definition a professional-administrator as well as a professional generalist. The position is typically created in technical organizations that, in response to nonroutine market circumstances, like to emphasize loose or ad hoc organizational structures such as the matrix. The project manager is often in charge of a team of professionals and paraprofessionals assigned to complete a specified project. After the project is concluded, the team disbands or moves on to another project.

What is most interesting from the point of view of supervision is that project management gives individuals the opportunity to assume responsibility for others without losing the opportunity to engage in meaningful technical work. From the point of view of career development, it has further been found that project managers tend to have an advantageous external labor market for their skills and services. Hence, they tend to be highly involved in their jobs and to consider themselves relatively successful, since they perceive opportunities to grow in their professional work, either inside or outside their organizations. Data show, however, that project managers as a whole assume attitudes much more commensurate with managerial than professional work.[46] Thus, project managers drawn from the professions, like all professional-administrators, need continually to remind themselves that they were once plain professionals.

Management by Objectives (MBO)

Management by objectives (MBO) can be an extremely important tool in supervising salaried professionals. In the prior two strategies, I stressed the value of the manager being viewed by the professional as a colleague with administrative responsibilities. No developmental technique better induces this spirit of managerial/professional cooperation than MBO. It also has uses in planning and coordination and is a popular performance-evaluation method. Its evaluative function is very secondary, however, to its primary purpose—the development of employees in connection with their work responsibilities.

MBO consists in having professionals decide with their managers what the objectives for their jobs are, how long it will take to meet the objectives, and what criteria should be used in evaluating progress toward or achievement of the objectives. By its very nature, then, it is mutual in its purpose and process. It operates on a foundation of trust. It solicits the advice and review of the manager but in a way that avoids the necessity for close supervision. In fact, since the parties agree on the time and criteria for evaluating progress, close supervision would defeat both the spirit and the operability of MBO.

MBO is particularly suited to professional environments because it recognizes the dignity and maturity of subordinates in taking responsibility for their work goals. Professionals have been depicted throughout this book as mature by definition. They demand a degree of control over their own work. I have also characterized their tasks as highly complex and hence difficult to measure. Proxies of professional contribution; whether they be number of problems solved; number of clients served; savings or sales resulting from projects; number of publications, patents, or papers presented, have seldom been viewed in themselves as worthwhile indicators of professional performance.

MBO recognizes the complexity and variety in the professional's work by allowing each person in conjunction with his or her management to articulate what is critical in the job and how the greatest possible contribution can be made to the organization. The criteria for performance evaluation may include some standard ratings, but they are tailored to the specific job and to the individual. Since the evaluation is person-specific, creative professionals and managers can attempt to measure some of the more intangible or idiosyncratic aspects of professional work, such as generation of new ideas, development of ideas, assistance to colleagues, or favorable impact on clients. Further, since professionals actually participate in setting their own job goals and thus are able to include their personal values, skills, interests, and priorities, there is great potential for MBO to reduce some of the stress inherent in professional work, which typically consists of multiple tasks with multiple contacts in multiple settings.

We know, of course, that some professionals do not display enough interest in organizational goals, preferring to concentrate on their own work goals. MBO remedies this problem by its requirement that both professional and manager work out a set of performance objectives. The professional is drawn into the environment of management and forced to acknowledge its responsibilities and pressures as the manager presents the department's or organization's perspective on the problems the professional is working on.

The review of the objectives, set by the professional and manager and conducted at the conclusion of a specified period, almost always entails a meeting. This feedback session brings the parties together to review the extent to which the objectives were met or unmet, the barriers that had to be overcome, unforeseen circumstances, and, finally, the next set of objectives, time period, and criteria. The feedback session is really the heart of the MBO program. It is at this time that the collegial character of the manager is put to the test. Using such critical interpersonal skills as listening, information seeking, clarifying, and summarizing, the manager must try to bring out the professional's honest feelings about his or her efforts and performance during the period. Although some managers may not be able to understand all the technicalities of the professional's work, they should be able to determine whether a genuine effort has been made; more important, they can learn about and later remove some of the blockages preventing the professional from registering a top performance. Although the feedback session may go into some detail on the processes of the professional's work, it still represents the best of output control, since the initiating focus is on how well the professional did. Work processes are reviewed only to clarify the route taken in arriving at the final outcome.

The manager, then, basically pursues a problem-solving approach in discussing the outcomes of the professional's work, but is by no means a passive observer. In fact, I argue for three principles to be heeded when conducting the feedback session:

1. Don't be wishy-washy
The manager and professional need to focus on particular behaviors and standards.

2. Don't be goody-goody
The manager should feel free to discriminate between good and bad points.

3. Don't be bum-headed
All behavior needs to be considered, not just the favorite ones of the parties.

Turning to the mechanics of a successful MBO program, it must be acknowledged that empirical evidence on the effectiveness of MBO has been mixed.[47] As with many managerial initiatives of this kind, the success of a MBO program seems to ride on its careful implementation. In addition, MBO seems to work better in some situations than in others. I have made the case here that it is ideal in a professional setting. But a number of conditions can affect its ultimate disposition.

1. MBO is consistent with a humanistic, Theory Y management philosophy. It is as much bottom-up as top-down in its approach. Employees are empowered to decide for themselves their critical goals and the means they will use to meet these goals and measure their achievement. Hence, MBO can be successful only in an organizational climate of trust, openness, and respect for the individual. It needs full support and participation from the top, and this commitment needs to be transmitted throughout the entire line operation. All organizational goals are subject to review in MBO, so no goal should be viewed as sacrosanct and hence unmeasurable. Further, the data on MBO results should be considered in earnest. This means that the top managers need to be willing to examine their corporate goals where they may be inconsistent with actual personnel practices, professional values, work conditions, or environmental responses. A genuine humanistic climate cannot be created overnight. If management has operated with a closed, top-down philosophy, it should not use MBO as an agent for change. Rather, the climate should first be gradually opened up and made receptive to such humanistic practices as MBO. Depending on management's responsiveness, this can take from two to eight years.

2. The ultimate MBO plan worked out between professional and manager should be a simple one; it is better to formulate a limited set of challenging and attainable objectives than dozens of insignificant procedural objectives. I have found that setting five or six objectives beyond normal responsibilities is reasonable. Although it is difficult in the first attempt to be precise about the necessary rigor desired for the objectives, the subsequent review should reveal whether the professional over- or underplanned. Adjustments can then be made for the next round of objectives. Since the objectives are self-initiated, it is not necessary to develop overcomplicated formats for recording them. There is no question that MBO requires some paperwork, but the extent of detail is left up to the parties. The best forms tend to leave considerable blank space for personal development of objectives.

3. The parties should use their creativity in designing a set of objectives that truly captures the essence of the professional's job. The objectives should also fit the person. No two objective sets among professionals should be absolutely alike. Further, the measurement of objective achievement does not have to adhere to any standard method, whether it be a ranking versus a rating, a scale versus an absolute index, or a quantitative versus a qualitative measure.

4. No MBO plan should be cast in concrete. By its very nature, MBO demands open communication between professional and manager. Any number of circumstances could distort or outdate a planned objective. Professional work is by nature ambiguous and unpredictable, so adjustments need to be considered. Further, there may be a change in management, or market conditions may have changed, causing a project to be reformulated. In these instances, either party should have a right to call for a revision.

5. The objective-setting process should not occur in a vacuum, as if the professional's job had no impact on the respective department or on the organization as a whole. The manager has a perfect right to insist that the professional's objectives be consistent with corporate planning. I earlier cited the benefits of permitting some bootlegging of professional practice, but this normally ensues after the professional's organizational responsibilities have been met. In a fully integrated

MBO program, middle management is also meeting objectives consistent with top management plans, so it is expected that these top-level plans will filter down to professional-staff levels. The process also works, of course, in the opposite direction as plans are developed by individuals at the lower levels of the organization. The process, when functioning effectively, can be very responsive to both external market needs and internal personnel requirements.

Gatekeeping

Although gatekeeping is normally associated with professional communication, it can also be a powerful, if indirect, tool for promoting the maintenance of professional standards and the improvement of performance. It is consistent with peer control; hence, it can also reduce bureaucratic control and close supervision of professionals.

The gatekeeping role essentially provides an information channel between the professional staff within any one organizational department and other departments as well as the outside environment. The former role is sometimes called internal liaison. Both internal and external gatekeeping occur at the boundary between the professional staff and other professionals or users of professional services. Although many professionals, especially cosmopolitans, keep up their professional contacts, many others become too busy with their own work to stay abreast of state-of-the-art developments in their field. Further, research on engineering professionals in particular has demonstrated that interpersonal communications are the primary means by which professionals acquire and disseminate important ideas and information.[48] Thus it is through informal contacts and personal affiliations rather than through written technical reports, publications, or other formal methods that those professionals who are sincerely interested can keep up with professional developments. Without the assistance of a gatekeeper, many professionals might simply lose sight of the latest uses of particular professional technologies. This can have far-reaching performance consequences within the firms that employ them. Some work may be getting done less efficiently and effectively than is currently possible. There may be user departments within the same organization that could benefit enormously from professional developments in other departments but that, without the gatekeeping function, might be unaware of these developments.

Another aspect of the gatekeeping role with implications for performance is its association with professional-administration, particularly at the supervisory level. Many gatekeepers are also supervisors and are among the most effective individuals in the organization in helping young professionals make the transition to organizational life. One study has found gatekeeping supervisors to be responsible for significantly reduced turnover rates and higher rates of promotion among their professional subordinates than nongatekeeping supervisors.[49] Thus gatekeeping supervisors not only gather and disseminate external information, they also help interpret internal communications for their professional subordinates and take an active role in shaping their personal growth and development.

Management can view the performance of the gatekeeping role like mentorship. It can create a work environment that encourages this role, or it can formally appoint individual professionals to serve as gatekeepers. There are few formal programs to my knowledge, so most gatekeeping seems to proceed on an ad hoc basis. Since gatekeepers can be instrumental in advancing the work of the organization, management should learn to identify the traits of effective gatekeepers. By definition, they are good communicators, whether with sources inside or outside the organization. They also seem able to inspire improved communications on the part of others. They tend to be personable and helpful, and are typically high performers. They possess a high level of technical competence and are widely read and even known. They make it their business to stay informed about developments in their field by reading professional journals, attending conferences, and maintaining a wide network of outside professional contacts. Gatekeepers have also been characterized as psychologically mature professionals, meaning they have the ability to communicate with anyone, regardless of background or discipline, and to see beyond the details to the unifying concept behind any professional initiative.[50]

Although gatekeepers are usually thought of by managers as assisting in professional and technological development, some are particularly adept at identifying market opportunities. These marketing gatekeepers are similar to technical gatekeepers in personality and competence, but prefer to discuss product and service concerns with the organization's customers and clients. In the R&D environment, they can play a particularly critical role in ensuring that any innovation meets the identified market, which may change during project development.[51]

While the gatekeeper's contribution to corporate and professional development has been lauded here, it should be recognized that the role is not without personal stress. Gatekeepers typically operate without formal authority, particularly when they operate outside the boundaries of their own organizations, they do not have ready access to third-party mediators if conflicts arise. Hence, if their role is sanctioned in the organization, they need at least some informal support from management as well as from their peers. At the same time, it is natural for management to ensure that they correctly represent the department's or organization's position (depending on the locus from which they operate). Therefore, adequate communication between nonsupervisory gatekeepers and management about department and organizational policies is essential. Gatekeepers as spokespersons for a group or for an organization have a responsibility to protect the interests of the party they represent.

Professional Incentives

If professionals are able to meet both their own and their organization's expectations without close supervision, is there anything managers can do to sustain their performance other than keeping them among their peers? It is correct, in my view, to assume that professional productivity is not guaranteed among professionals without some incentive. In this way, professionals are no different from any other employee group. Some professional incentives, however, are different from nonprofessional incentives.

Professionals are just as interested in basic financial benefits, whether they be salary increases, bonuses, or profit-sharing options, as other employees. Although they have an intrinsic attachment to their work, this does not mean they do not want to be paid well for their expertise, effort, and performance. Like other employees, they also compare their pay and benefits with those of employees having similar workloads and responsibilities, whether inside their own organization or elsewhere. Not only do they compare among themselves, they compare with management too. Any evidence of significant inequities, whether in absolute compensation or relative increases, will be deleterious to both attitude and performance.

Besides pay, other basic extrinsic benefits are likely to appeal to professionals. In recognition of their status as important contributors as well as their need to work independently, it is helpful to give as many as possible a private office. Even if the space is small, it is worth it to give professionals this privacy. At TRW, where an experimental program called for converting a crowded computer room into windowless offices, each wired with state-of-the-art personal computer equipment, there was nearly a 40 percent jump in productivity among the software designers.[52] If it is simply impossible to give everyone a private office, perhaps management can arrange to build a library or some other type of quiet room for its junior professionals.

Although not necessarily interested in management, professionals do like many of the perquisites of managerial jobs. The most obvious is a private secretary. Some professionals who require limited clerical assistance can easily share a secretary, and in some cases the professional may prefer the assistance of a technician rather than a secretary. Another incentive that has been found to be particularly useful in creative environments is the freedom to keep a flexible schedule that reflects the needs of the job rather than adherence to a time clock. Another perquisite of management that Lotte Bailyn[53] believes is important among R&D professionals is the right to report directly to higher-level executives. The purpose is not to go over the head of the boss, but rather to see for oneself what the direction of the organization is and to have a chance to feel a part of and even affect the organizational mission. In some instances, as in so-called "open door" policies, it might be necessary to let professionals bypass bosses to have complaints investigated. Finally, where a dual-ladder system has not been installed, some professionals might get a boost from having official titles that capture their specialized education and responsibilities.[54]

Some incentives have a characteristic professional ring to them and may therefore be particularly attractive to professionals. Many of these are basically attempts to create an academic climate within the organization. I have already discussed the value of peer control and the use of behavioral-outcome measurement. These approaches assure the professional that the predominant basis on which he or she will be evaluated will be technical, as opposed to, say, social, political, or economic. I have also addressed the need to provide the professional with multiple career options so that the spirit of inquiry and development never expires. Related to the career notion is the need to give professionals every opportunity to continue their education. Most organizations with which I am familiar do a very good job on this account. Many have quite liberal tuition reimbursement programs and respect the value of self-improvement through formal education. The only cautionary remark I can make, then, is that management needs to ensure that the professional gets a chance to practice, to the extent possible, the newly learned skills and concepts. Continuing education suggests continuity of development not only in the classroom but on the job as well.

Other professional-specific incentives include the provision of adequate supplies and equipment so that professionals have available the tools of their trade. Professionals should also be both encouraged to make and rewarded for contributions that are recognized in the professional or academic community. For the most part, this means having papers published in leading professional journals and reviews, having patents filed in the individual's name, and making presentations at professional association meetings. Although the organization may derive only indirect benefit from these professional undertakings, (and indeed on occasion, where, for example, trade secrets are involved, they must even be prevented), it at least has the good fortune to sponsor an active and developing organizational member. The reward for professional activities does not always have a clear-cut impact on the bottom line. What it does is acknowledge that the professional's work is important, that the individual is contributing to something that is greater than mere self-gratification, and that one's peers recognize the effort.[55] Moreover, few things have as powerful an impact on professional motivation and creativity.

A final incentive to productivity is sponsorship of participation in professional associations. Most, but especially cosmopolitan, professionals find such participation a source of worthwhile personal development and a means of increasing their status and recognition. Meanwhile, the organization sponsoring the involvement stands to benefit from the additional knowledge imported into the firm. Some of the other explicit benefits for both professionals and organizations include:[56]

1. increasing the technical knowledge of the participants
2. broadening their background and viewpoint
3. providing an excellent source of new ideas
4. providing an opportunity to stay abreast of new developments in the field
5. increasing the reputation of the organization
6. providing for exchange of ideas, which prevents inbreeding
7. enabling professionals to meet the leaders in their field and receive inspiration from them

There is a natural suspicion among management that professionals who become heavily involved in professional activities are precisely the ones who will need close supervision, since they may end up spending work time on outside duties. Although this in fact occurs, most professionals are reasonably mature about it, and draw a distinction between outside and inside work. Too, some of their professionally centered work is indistinguishable from their organizational responsibilities, so one benefits from the other. The point, though, is that those who aspire to become recognized professionally are going to continue to work on their papers, inventions, and so on, regardless of the amount or nature of supervision received. Excessive supervision will simply cause them to bootleg their professional work. Management may as well get the benefit of this bootlegging energy. If a project is truly outside the mainstream of the organization's principal line of business, then perhaps the professional could earn time credits to work on it. Essentially, I believe that if the manager can win the confidence of his creative professionals, give them some free rein, and work with them to develop mutually beneficial projects and services, these same professionals will do their utmost to nourish the organization, thus eliminating the need for close supervision.

The Problem of Formalization

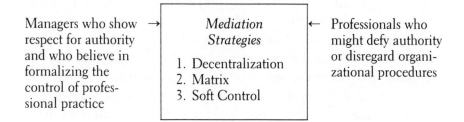

Managers who show → *Mediation Strategies* ← Professionals who
respect for authority might defy authority
and who believe in 1. Decentralization or disregard organi-
formalizing the 2. Matrix zational procedures
control of profes- 3. Soft Control
sional practice

As agents hired to carry out the objectives of the organization, managers use rules and regulations to maintain control over their respective operations. How formal this control is depends on organizational purpose, structure, and stage of development, and on individual style.

Professionals tend to resist formal rules and regulations. Formalization is presumed to reduce autonomy, contravene peer or collegial control based on expertise, and undermine professional standards—all values within the professional culture. Formalization does not always impede professional development, however. Some rules and regulations can actually further professional endeavors within the organization.[57] It has been found, for example among accountants, that formalization can be fused with professional norms, obviating the need for close supervision.[58] In some circumstances, rules and regulations can also reduce role ambiguity, cause greater adherence to organizational policies, and even induce organizational loyalty and identification. These effects depend heavily, however, on how cosmopolitan the professional is. Basic research scientists, for example, have been found to prefer less formalized work than engineers,[59] and thus might experience fewer of the side benefits of formalization if it were to be imposed on them.

Those who have argued in their research studies that formalization can induce organizational commitment have not provided practical strategies for management. Here, I present three strategies that might improve salaried professionals' receptiveness to rules and regulations.

Decentralization

This first strategy, stemming from concerns beyond mere reduction of rules and regulations, nevertheless can rationalize control procedures not only by reducing their quantity but by bringing them closer to professional employees. The thrust toward decentralization has been affected by such global changes as the rapidly changing business and business/government environments as well as astonishing advances in technology, and is also a response to the growing professionalism of the work force. Consider, for example, the dynamic nature of many product markets, especially in the high-technology industries. To compete effectively in the international arena, manufacturers have to deal with incredibly shortened product life-cycles. In one recent survey, it was estimated that 55 percent of the minicomputers and 80 percent of the general-purpose computers in the market had been introduced within the preceding four years.[60] Product life-cycles in some industries have been attenuated to such a degree that standard mass production technologies based on economies of scale have become outmoded. Competition in the industrial sector has also been intensified by government deregulation of many traditional segments, such as transportation, communications, and financial services. Such changes as these require flexible and responsive organizational structures, such as are afforded by decentralization.

The impetus toward decentralization arising from the growing professionalization of the work force is consistent with many of the values of the professional culture, including resistance to bureaucracy. In smaller units, there are fewer managers at middle levels to answer to. Professionals can rely on themselves and their own standards to control their work. They can achieve greater autonomy over their own projects and operations, even to the point of becoming in-house entrepreneurs.

The flattening of organizational structure as represented by a decentralization strategy is likely to accelerate. We are witnessing a breaking down of the classic hierarchical organization into network structures made up of smaller-scale, more adaptable units. The work of the corporation of the future will probably be done by these small, relatively autonomous units, which will be connected with each other and with a headquarters by advanced computer and telecommunications technology. For example, we are already seeing just-in-time (JIT) principles, which require precise and sophisticated coordination of deliveries from parts suppliers to lower inventories and smooth production, supersede vertical integration strategies. JIT also makes it possible to reduce the size of the organization by relying less on in-house technical assistance.[61]

Conceivably, professionals as well as other employees in the future will be allowed to carve out their own temporary, almost ad hoc, organizational units if they can prove to top management that they can operate a particular module more efficiently than can corporate bureaucracy. What makes this structural reform possible is the emergence of broad-band electronic computer technologies that permit dialogue, integration, and control of modular subentities by responsible corporate professionals. Familiar paper technologies that tend to clog the system may be replaced by these electronic technologies, which allow almost instantaneous communication of multiple lines of information. Assuming the professionals involved in the modular operations are committed to the organization's goals and know how to operate these electronic linking devices, there can be less reliance on middle management control and more direct accountability for the individual professionals and their teams. Professionals, independently or as team members, will negotiate the basis of control over their operation. Their managers' role will be to assist in coordinating the work of the multiple units into a coherent corporate strategy and to negotiate the appropriate financial arrangements to fund the separate operations.

The best size for a decentralized unit is very difficult to specify, since it depends so heavily on the technology in the operation, the actual product or service in question, requirements for capital investment, the sophistication and even discipline of the respective professionals, and so forth. Yet, when organizing professionals to work on specific project assignments, James Quinn[62] prefers to see teams composed of only six or seven key people. This number is large enough to constitute a critical mass of skills but not so large as to interfere with maximum communication and commitment among the members. When selecting a size for a total operating division, decentralized organizations like to keep their numbers below 400. This allows for no more than two layers of management to maintain a span of control over seven professionals. Johnson & Johnson already goes further than this by keeping its divisions at about $30 million apiece, which probably requires staff levels of about 100. This entails much reorganizing and assignment of considerable trust and autonomy to each operating division head.

Although professionals in some cases and, most certainly, their administrators desire greater authority in decentralized operations, this does not necessarily come at the expense of less authority for top management. Using streamlined electronic control devices, top managers can still control their organization and receive up-to-the-minute status reports on the progress of each unit. What is critical to encourage professional initiative is that these managers not overuse this new source of information by expecting immediate results or by imposing standards that may thwart individual autonomy. Each professional unit in the organization functions as a loosely coupled system, connected with other professional units by strategy, culture, and telecommunications technology, but independent in its own role. For example, the litigation practice of a large law firm may have units covering such areas as securities and finance transactions, real estate, international trade, taxation, insurance, and environmental law. All the lawyers in each unit are involved in the same area of practice.

Although they are involved intimately with a select group of partners and associates, they must also work with the firm as a whole to refer business, to negotiate for the services of another unit, or to take on new assignments and increasing responsibility.[63] The decentralized system tends to work because of the independence and entrepreneurial character of the professional work force, which sustains itself through self-management and peer control. Should top management attempt to formalize this system by imposing restrictive and standardized control devices, professionals in the autonomous units would tend to rebel.

The challenge of rationally decentralizing a large organizational operation has been more observable in corporate research and development than anywhere else. Acknowledging the proclivity of technical professionals to seek out academic-like environments, corporations have traditionally set up centralized R&D laboratories apart from the divisions so as to free their technical personnel from the short-term pressures of market needs. Corporate R&D also tends to benefit from the merger of several technologies relevant to several businesses, from its interdisciplinary focus, and from its flexibility, especially to pull together resources and move quickly when a target has been identified. There is no question that centralized R&D has produced impressive results, whether in nontargeted generic research (for example, Bell Labs' Nobel Prize-quality work on transistors, lasers, information science, and solid-state electronics) or in targeted developments (for example, GE's R&D Center's innovations in X-ray tubes, silicones, man-made diamonds, and computerized tomography).[64]

Nevertheless, as the pace of technological development has picked up and product life cycles have shortened, it has become apparent that centralized research has suffered from lack of sufficient commercial guidance. Communication links between the lab and the divisions are simply not adequate in some cases to produce desired results. Some workable developments languish until they are picked up by an interested division, and by then it may be too late. Hence, most medium-to-large companies have found it necessary to decentralize some of their research to an appropriate operating division, especially when the research in question has reached the development phase. Short-term innovations can also be initiated in divisional facilities in response to the needs of operating managers or customer requests. In actual practice, most corporations operate with both corporate and divisional R&D facilities. Linking the various research units has often been the most critical structural problem, and companies have used a wide assortment of strategies, including reports, reviews, seminars, physical location, liaison personnel, interdisciplinary committees, and even distinct departments to make the link. The advent of high-speed telecommunications and computer technology, however, has eased the problem considerably. Many groups can come together even in an ad hoc project fashion to complete an assignment, and can be disbanded before bureaucratization sets in. Professionals with different backgrounds, disciplines, and values can be merged periodically, which increases their productivity, creativity, and enthusiasm. And some units can proceed with their professional work without the burden of excessive organizational regulations, which tend to slow down the creative process.

Some companies have actually institutionalized ad hoc ventures by creating new-venture units to operate outside of the bureaucracy. These represent the extreme of decentralization and are typically organized to exploit R&D opportunities that do not fit into the conventional technical and operational processes of existing product lines. Within a traditional structure, they might erode scarce resources, disrupt profit-and-loss records, or dislocate current manufacturing or service operations. They tend to operate, therefore, as semiautonomous entrepreneurial enterprises that attract professional volunteers who enjoy taking risks and are committed to being at the leading edge of their fields. At Allied-Signal Corporation, the New Ventures Group, funded at $20 million, sponsors projects involving technologies developed in the company's R&D laboratories, which, though having great profit potential, have been left sitting on the shelf. This unit provides transition time and funds to resourceful professionals who are willing to invest themselves in nurturing a fledgling operation, who like to operate in an intense and freewheeling environment, and who may not want the added burden of starting their own company. Some companies encourage internal ventures to seek sponsorship from several divisions to expand market opportunities for their work. At 3M, professionals can seek funding for new ventures from their own division, from other divisions, from a central lab, or from the New Business Ventures Division.

Some enterprises may not be interested in decentralizing their operations to the extreme of sponsoring independent-ventures groups, but may nevertheless want to sustain an interest in an emerging technology that shows considerable commercial promise. In this case, a company may wish to spin off a venture as an independent company but attempt to maintain a relationship with it by holding a minority equity share based on the contribution of equipment, inventories, and patents, by setting it up as a vendor or buyer, or by sponsoring its marketing program. In some instances, the spin-off may be the only way the company can retain a relationship with some of its very talented professional entrepreneurs who want to go it on their own. Lotus Development Corporation, for example, recently provided $1 million in product development to Raymond Ozzie, the mastermind behind the Symphony software. In return, Ozzie's spin-off has agreed to extend to Lotus exclusive rights to license, market, and support his products.[65] Finally, a third alternative to the internal new venture is for the parent company to simply acquire, buy a controlling share in, or set up a joint venture with an independent company and support the latter's professional staff and management by contributing financial resources and market knowledge and image.[66]

Regardless of the format of any redesign introducing decentralization, professional human resource concerns need to be explicitly brought into the decision-making apparatus, since decentralization offers a unique opportunity to meet many professional needs. In particular, it can free professionals from the constraints of formal control procedures, which though well conceived, may interfere severely with professional concentration. Reducing the layers of bureaucracy on top of the salaried professional can ultimately allow for greater reliance on peer and self-control, which represent the cornerstones of account-ability in the professional culture.

Matrix

The matrix organizational structure is, in its own right, a response to increasing formalization and bureaucratization. It constitutes a structural change designed to substitute relatively flexible and interactive behavior for bureaucratic behavior. It is very consistent with decentralization as a management strategy in that it effectively decentralizes decision making down to professional units, in particular to their coordinators or leaders. These units are typically assigned professional tasks that require timely responses in the face of environmental demands, be they product market variations, technological change, acceleration in competitive pressures, or regulatory changes.

Understanding how the matrix works is really quite simple. It usually combines two organizational structure types so as to decentralize operations to the individual cells of the matrix. The cells normally contain individual contributors, in many cases professionals, who are assigned to work on a project using their particular expertise. Hence, at least two sources guide professional responsibility in a matrix structure. First is the function, discipline, or specialty in which the professional normally works. Second is the project (normally associated with a product) to which he or she is assigned. Figure 5-3 displays a typical matrix organizational structure.

The matrix design reduces control procedures imposed on professionals from many levels above them within the hierarchy. They still must submit, however, to what may be quite rigorous controls at the project level. Yet, within the relatively small group that constitutes the project, these controls often become more understandable. The matrix also allows the project leader to revise standards of operation to respond to immediate changes, whether in the project's technology or in the potential market.

Although the matrix clearly reduces formalized methods in favor of more interactive patterns of behavior, most professionals report that living in a matrix requires some adjustments:

• A project may last only for a short while. Professionals accustomed to developing long-standing friendships and familiar and secure work routines will find in some instances that they have to get used to much more temporary work conditions. They cannot rely on working with the same colleague or being at the same work station year in and year out. They need to adapt to constant changes in project configurations. Further, their assignments will tend to vary widely, which offsets any impulse to standardize professional roles, such as through formal job descriptions.

• Professionals need to adapt to dual evaluation and reporting sys-

Figure 5-3   Typical Matrix Structure

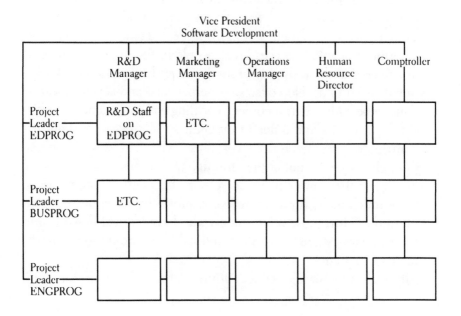

tems; on the one hand, they continue to report to their functional or technical managers, on the other, they need to heed the directives of their project or product manager. These separate middle managers may or may not collaborate in the professional evaluation process. Further, the professional will face role conflict if the requests from these different managers are not coordinated. Sometimes, the professional will feel as if his or her contribution hangs in the balance while the superiors negotiate on the disposition of the individual's time. Requests for additional work and opportunities for advancement may come from either side—functional or product—forcing the professional to take the initiative in his or her career planning.

• The matrix requires an extraordinary amount of communication and collaboration. Some pure professionals are bound to complain that they are "meetinged to death." Most of this is a function of the decentralized climate that supports the matrix structure to begin with. Project managers are normally given the right to subcontract for services outside the organization, should the corporate functional departments be incapable of supplying the necessary expertise, service, or hardware. Functional managers also acquire equivalent rights to sell their services outside.[67] Hence, an incredible amount of negotiating goes on as people in the organization come to realize that the only way to survive is to share resources. Professionals need to develop effective interpersonal and communication skills, especially when it comes to dealing with colleagues in different departments and different disciplines. The reward system in a matrix structure tends to favor those who can solve problems through consensus rather than through one-upmanship. This is not to suggest that power plays no role in the matrix. Power goes to those individuals, however, who can prove the value of their contribution. Thus those professionals who have learned how to communicate and share their values and skills will profit most from the matrix experience.

Although the matrix reduces formal procedures that can limit professional autonomy, it substitutes an informal code of conduct that promotes loyalty to the project group with which the professional is associated. Further, although the matrix in some way obscures the organizational hierarchy, it can also subject the professional to greater scrutiny by the project manager. But assuming a reasonable commitment to the project, professionals have a basis for integrating their professional skills with corporate economic interests. To that extent, the matrix is also an answer to overprofessionalization, since the goals of the project are always present, in one way or another, in the minds of the staff.

To ensure that the matrix works effectively, top management has to set a tone of coordination and cooperation between the functional and product sides of the organization. Functional managers, many of whom are former professionals, need to be willing to become more entrepreneurial, partly by viewing their function as services for sale. They should see their departments as containing valuable resources that can be loaned to product groups which, in turn, make use of these resources to produce innovative ideas, products, and services. Indeed, as potential consumers of functional services, the product groups help keep the functional organization alive. Functional managers are also known to perform best when they are allowed to concentrate on the technical details of a project.

Meanwhile, product managers, many of whom are also former professionals, trade off a certain degree of autonomy and independence for the opportunity to carry a unique product, process, or service into the marketplace. By the time they take on the job, they are typically willing to assume the leadership of product or service areas that conform to overall business objectives. Their performance hinges on their ability to coordinate the resources to make their project a success.

Soft Control

Organizational control need not be exerted exclusively in a formal way; it can be as effective using softer methods, which I define as a special manner of informal communication. What is communicated to the professional is a sense of purpose that underlies the values of the organization. The desired effect of softer methods is a balance between professionals' needs and managerial goals results in a commitment to the organization's mission. It is a people-centered form of control.

Unfortunately, most formal control processes are impersonal; they are developed to affect every one in virtually the same way, so they allow for little discretion. Further, managers at upper levels in the organizational hierarchy, by virtue of their rank and status in the organization, not only impose these rules but typically submit to fewer of them than the professionals. Since professionals do not see themselves as inferior to management (certainly when it comes to knowledge and expertise), they tend to prefer control systems allowing more discretion.

Softer control methods, then, need to take into account the relative maturity level of the professional staff. The formal control process can be made less bureaucratic, as we have seen, through decentralization and organizational design changes, such as the matrix structure. Softer methods, however, go beyond structural change. They suggest a more subtle set of approaches that allow for greater self-control among certain employees, such as the professional staff. Among the softer methods, one might consider the following:

1. Devise ways in which professionals can earn professional recognition while meeting organizational goals. If a scientist, for example, contributes actively to the development of a particular research application, he should be given the appropriate credit in the patent. As long as the professionals and management are all going in the same direction, there simply will be less need for artificial, externally imposed operating rules.

2. Break down barriers that separate professionals from managers. This might be done by loosening up the chain of command so that the professional staff is permitted access to top managers, or by breaking down physical or social status barriers, such as office spacing. It can also be done by simply opening up the lines of com-

munication, for instance, by keeping an open-door policy, conducting open question-and-answer forums pertaining to company policies, or just plain managing by walking around.

3. Maintain an open but rigorous hiring policy. By open, I am suggesting that managers be frank with potential professional hires about the mission and style of the organization, particularly of the unit being hired into. By rigorous, I refer to the need to engage in an exhaustive selection process that can single out those capable professionals who are most likely to make a contribution to the organization and to derive personal satisfaction from becoming a member. Since there can be no assurances how professionals, especially novices, will behave once they come to work, their adjustment can be eased by orientation and training programs that provide more intensive exposure to organizational practices.

4. Acknowledge the maturity and competence of the professional staff so as to shape interactions on the basis of reason and knowledge rather than authority. Professionals desire to work in an atmosphere relatively free from pressure and conducive to personal autonomy and creativity. Although they may need to be reminded from time to time about the overall objectives of the organization, direct orders or formal and impersonal controls will be no more effective in inducing commitment to the enterprise than give-and-take conversations. The ultimate aim of control interactions with professionals is to demonstrate how voluntary compliance with basic organizational procedures, accompanied by self-imposed personal and professional controls, serves their self-interest. As the professional gradually adapts to the corporate culture, the manager can rely more and more on professional self-management and peer control rather than having to resort to excessive external operating rules.

5. Further the thoughtful conversion of professionals to the organizational culture by deriving a small set of common values that appeals to the professional staff as well as to all other employees of the organization. Where professionals represent a high percentage of employees, as in professional service organizations, it is easier to formulate a set of values that represent professional interests. Al-

though professionals, then, can have a role in shaping the values of the organization in a bottom-up fashion, top management is in a better position to articulate what the company or agency really stands for. The benefit of using cultural values for control purposes is that they contribute to greater reliance on implicit, informal, and more personal methods. Of course, they cannot be used to manipulate professionals or to act as a tool to force conformity to organizational customs. As long as they are perceived as egalitarian, they can lead directly to voluntary, self-imposed control processes. A nice illustration of how this method works are the park rangers employed by the U.S. Park Service.[68] Most people who have frequented the national parks will acknowledge not only the competence of the park rangers but their dedication to their work. There have rarely been any scandals in the service, nor has there been much evidence of catering to special-interest groups in local areas. This may seem somewhat anomalous, considering how scattered the parks are and how limited is the opportunity for formal supervision over the rangers. Yet the Park Service operates with a minimum of formal controls. Rather, there is a handful of commonly accepted procedures for reporting and responding to various problems. Rangers otherwise act independently but nevertheless in seeming compliance with the Service's mission. The reason appears to be a common dedication to the values of service, ecology, and the environment. Besides these values, the culture is supported by common symbols—the uniform and badge—and by a training program that inculcates the values and mission of the Service.

I have depicted the culture of management as depending heavily on teamwork; indeed, early definitions of management would use such language as "working with and through people to accomplish organizational goals." Teamwork suggests a code of conduct in which the individual's interests are subordinated to those of the team, and team members abide by the rules of fair play. As long as the subjugation of self does not become a single-minded devotion to authority, but accommodates critical thought and analysis, this culture seems to work

The Problem of Real-World Practice

Managers who, in the interest of career and teamwork, condone jobs lacking challenge, entrepreneurship, personalness, and stability. →	*Mediation Strategies* 1. Job enrichment 2. Entrepreneurship 3. Personalness 4. Employment Stability	← Professionals who, in the interest of quality of life and individual initiative, display little regard for real-world practice.

quite well. Individual managers in this culture may flourish by advancing on the basis of earned accomplishments and raw ability.

Although this code of conduct is productive, it does not always fit with the value system of professionals. Although professionals work in teams and rely on their peers, they prefer to work alone during significant stretches of their assignments. Personal and professional controls serve as checks on their work. Further, although they want to be paid adequately for their expertise, they are not necessarily interested in making it to the top. They simply want to do better and more responsibly the work for which they have been trained and to which they are devoted. When interpreted broadly as the development of self, the concept of career converges with the value of quality of life.

Is it possible to manage professionals so that they merge their interest in professional integrity with a commitment to corporate purpose? The strategies described in this section are often alluded to as management development methods. Here, however, I show how they may be applied to respond to the individual needs of professional staff members. I shall also demonstrate how their implementation will cure the professional of the malaise of lack of interest in real-world practice.

Job Enrichment

By the 1970s, all workers, but especially professionals raised under a 60s values system, were becoming increasingly interested in intrinsic values such as autonomy, opportunity for personal growth, and challenging work. Through a strategy that builds these values into professional work, management can develop some confidence in professional commitment to the real-world practice of the organization.

Job enrichment answers the absolute need of professionals for challenge by allowing them to use their many skills fully. It allows them to stretch their intellectual abilities to the limit, to be involved in their work, to identify with what they are working on, and to see their contribution. The two components of enrichment, horizontal and vertical job enlargement, establish the parameters for job redesign incorporating challenge. In horizontal job enlargement, professionals are encouraged to work with peers to decide how the total job is to be done. The result of this continuous consultation may be the opportunity to do a variety of assignments rather than the original one only. In vertical job enlargement, professionals do not take on additional assignments; they develop greater depth and autonomy in, and take more responsibility for, the work originally assigned to them. Vertical job enlargement is the only method to satisfy the professional's intrinsic motivation, that is, motivation derived from the work content itself rather than from its context. Purists might say that only redesigns that intensify intrinsic motivation constitute true job enrichment. I prefer a more comprehensive definition that incorporates both components— horizontal and vertical job enlargement—and even some other approaches that have as their underlying purpose the personal development of the individual.

The three other strategies discussed in this section contribute to job enrichment. Entrepreneurship signifies the conferral of freedom to pursue independent professional projects, and may also involve the professional in independent client contact. Indeed, Frederick Herzberg[69] has lately referred to job enrichment redesign as allowing workers to serve clients both within and outside the organization and to have increasing responsibility for service to these clients. The theme of responsibility remains very strong in professional entrepreneurship.

Personalness, whereby employees are treated as people rather than numbers, addresses the need to provide working conditions that respect and foster personal dignity. Professionals interested in quality of life carry this one step further when they associate personal dignity with the pursuit of knowledge.

Finally, a policy of employment stability, although not necessarily guaranteeing lifetime employment, assures the professional that the organization will do everything it can to treat its people as members of a family, in return for a commitment and dedication to the overall mission of the organization. In recognizing the value of stability, management attempts to free the professional worker to pursue his or her craft in service to the enterprise without fear of unjust discharge.

The professional-participation strategy previously discussed may also be considered an enrichment vehicle, since it allows professionals full information and authority to manage their own jobs. It also connects them with the corporate decision-making structure so that they can be involved as responsible human beings in shaping the decisions that affect their daily work lives.

Each of these strategies reflects trust in the individual and recognizes that allowing people the freedom to reach their potential can serve as the most effective way to accomplish group and organizational goals. Naturally, the pursuit of individual goals has to merge with pursuit of organizational goals. This is what is called for in real-world practice. But if attention to and interest in the organization's mission are made conditions of employment and the goals of the organization are clear, professionals are unlikely to reject them, although they may criticize them. Job enrichment, then, tries to sustain a balance between individual dignity and organizational purpose.

Besides the approaches already mentioned, five other performance ment-development methods. Here, however, I show how they may be criteria need to be incorporated in a complete job enrichment strategy.[70]

1) Diversity

Professionals should be able to work on a wide range of tasks and assignments, making use of diverse skills, abilities, and creative talent.

Assignments should also differ in their scope, thus affording varying levels of complexity, challenge, and time for completion. Professionals should also have the opportunity to change jobs from time to time so as not to become stale, overspecialized, or pigeonholed in one area of competence. Not having the opportunity to try new things can be a fatal precursor of obsolescence.

2) Choice

Professionals want some say in their choice of assignments. Trying to achieve a fit between the job and the person can benefit the organization if the requirements for excellent performance on the job are commensurate with the individual's current or potential skills. It is usually helpful to both parties if the job requirements exceed the candidate's qualifications slightly, so as to offer the professional an attainable yet challenging goal. It is also in the professional's best interest to find a job in which he or she can make a significant contribution to the organization.

3) Flexibility

Consistent with a quality-of-life orientation, professionals should be allowed to balance work requirements with off-the-job commitments. To the extent feasible, professionals should have the opportunity to work under flexible schedules that permit them to meet family and community responsibilities. Allowing professionals to set their own agendas is only fitting for individuals who have proved in their early training that they are willing to do what it takes to master their craft and contribute their expertise to the advancement of knowledge or to the production of goods and services.

4) Mobility

I have already spoken about the need to maintain an open internal labor market policy so that the professional will not be confined to a particular position that may limit his or her skills. The horizons of the organization should be extended to other technical areas for professionals who want to try something new. Further, if it becomes apparent that the opportunities in the current organization are inadequate to meet the need for personal growth and development, the individual should be free to seek employment elsewhere with no fear of recrimination.

5) Responsibility

This is the essence of job enrichment. Professionals simply want to work in jobs where they are responsible for their own decisions. They desire jobs in which they can have an impact, no matter how small, on the world, and they want the right to participate in, or at least observe, this impact.

Entrepreneurship

Entrepreneurship, as I have used the term in this book, reflects a managerial policy that grants professionals an opportunity to choose and work on their own projects without constant oversight. A more familiar application of the word to external new ventures led Gifford Pinchot III to coin the term "intrapreneurship" to refer to the internal version of the concept.[71] Intrapreneurs, according to Pinchot, get an idea for a product or service their company could provide. They then take responsibility for putting their idea into action, assembling a professional team, and overseeing the enterprise until it becomes a successful business within the parent company.

Unfortunately, it is unreasonable to expect the majority of any company's professionals to start new ventures. The unlimited drive and tenacity required are reserved for only a few. A company should at least make entrepreneurship possible, however. Entrepreneurship is as much a strategy of style as of practice. What I am most interested in proposing in this section is that management create an environment that encourages entrepreneurial behavior. Some observers may see entrepreneurship as antithetical to professionalism. On the contrary, research has found that in certain settings, such as research laboratories, entrepreneurship has been equated with autonomy, a condition that frequently leads to increased professional productivity.[72] Further, the fear that entrepreneurship will cause professionals to sell out to management has not been borne out. Simply stated, some professionals will develop an interest in management after experiencing success in championing a project or series of projects. Others may simply continue to ·be interested in further project development that offers increasing challenge. Management needs to provide future opportunities for both types: management for some, professional development for the others. Data General has been successful in holding on to only some of the team members who built the Eagle, the superminicomputer whose infant development was made famous in a Pulitzer Prize-winning book, *The Soul of a New Machine*, by Tracy Kidder. Most of these loyalists went into management, lured especially by enticing salaries and stock options. The majority of the Eagle team, however, left Data General, mainly because they said they wanted to have new adventures in designing computers at technology's leading edge. Further, they wanted to remain engineers rather than become managers.

Admittedly, some entrepreneurial-minded professionals will want to move on after working on a successful venture, no matter what their original company offers them. There are some definite steps managers can initiate, however, to retain some of these extremely resourceful individuals. These form the elements of an entrepreneurial strategy.

1. Establish a climate within the regular bureaucracy for mavericks not only to survive but to succeed. Professionals should have the opportunity to try new things or to recommend new ways. There has to be constant encouragement of innovative activity, whether it be to let an individual try a totally new approach to an assignment, to try a new job, to change the location or even the group he or she might work with, or, most important, to fail. Not every entrepreneurial venture will result in a success; but if they are to try again, professionals need to know that failures are just part of the process.

2. Allow some bootlegging—work outside the mainstream of the business—but bring it to the surface rather than force it under the

table. As long as it relates in a general way to the corporate mission, it may result in a successful project one day. One way to institutionalize bootlegging is to allow professionals actually to earn time to work on personal projects. In other words, if they prove that they can be effective in their formal assignments, management can allow them to work on informal assignments, which includes granting them access to corporate resources. If the personal project grows, however, say, from an idea into an actual development, then it should be submitted to outside review, whether by peers or by management. Although the originator should be allowed to stay with a development once it assumes full project status, it will eventually have to pass through more formal review to receive continued funding.

3. Allow the entrepreneur to develop client relationships and other external contacts to ensure a valid and reliable source of feedback on his or her work. In most instances, the client is an ultimate user of a product or service and thus has a direct interest in such key criteria as quality and usefulness. While abiding by reasonable canons of organizational confidentiality, the entrepreneur should have direct access to the client. Where face-to-face contact is impossible or impractical, telephone or mail contact may suffice. The purpose of the contact is to allow the user to comment as specifically as possible on the product or service, to help the professional make the necessary improvements to perfect the innovation. Freedom to pursue client relationships has implications for some of the other components of job enrichment, especially diversity, flexibility, and responsibility.

4. Make sure that any successful entrepreneurial venture is rewarded appropriately. An inventor, especially a professional who stays with a project, should receive adequate equity participation in the project and not have to face an artificial salary cap, even if this means earning more than a manager. At Lotus Development Corporation, a system of financial awards tied to unit sales could allow the lead developer of a hit product a bonus of up to a year's salary.[74] A successful entrepreneur should also be rewarded with new career opportunities. The rewards for successful entrepreneurship should be kept out in the

open as encouragement to others who may wish to embark on innovative activity. Care should be taken, however, to identify the individuals who actually contributed to the success of a new idea or venture. Where it is difficult to distinguish actual incremental contribution, the professionals involved should be asked to discuss their respective roles and to consider a fair sharing of the rewards for their success.

5. Professionals seem to feel more comfortable trying new things when their environment is casual, especially when they have open access to one another. This does not necessarily mean breaking down walls, for professionals need their privacy, too. Yet an informal atmosphere seems to breed entrepreneurial behavior. Of course, management cannot let this informality get out of hand; basic procedures still need to be observed. Further, management cannot afford to have every worker acting in a totally independent manner. If certain professionals are identified as particularly creative, however, it may be beneficial to separate them and simply let them go at it for awhile. In a separate location, they may be able to combine their creative talents to do something unique. Further, off in their own area where the rules are temporarily suspended, they are unlikely to pose a threat to the mainstream of the organization.

6. Consistent with the last recommendation, and recalling the earlier discussion of decentralization, it may be necessary to create new-venture teams. Although these units need start-up capital and then continuity of funding if their ventures are ever to succeed, they seem to work best when kept small and lean. This forces the professional members to innovate rather than buy solutions, which is what new ventures are all about. Admittedly, only a handful of the professional staff may ever get involved in this kind of operation. Nevertheless, a new-venture unit stands as a symbol (which can be a very rich one) of the organization's commitment to entrepreneurial behavior.

Personalness

Some may see a paradox in my advancing a strategy of personalness as a method of integrating professionals into organizational life. If following this strategy means creating an atmosphere devoid of formal manner and appearance, as in the notorious Silicon Valley beer busts, at least two objections might be raised. First, if only certain professionals act in this way, they could be immediately branded as not being "real-world." Second, they might be accused of not acting professionally, which in some circles has come to mean acting with reasonable decorum.

My response to these legitimate objections is that personalness is not synonymous with wild and irresponsible behavior. To me, it means treating employees as people, not as numbers, and, especially with professionals, emphasizing knowledge over organizational politics as the way to obtain corporate rewards. Although this is consistent with creating organizational environments in which people feel close and open with one another, and where they are also approachable, trustworthy, and cooperative, it does not need to incorporate dress, for example. How people look or act depends much more on the individual organizational culture. In some companies, it may be a means to an end. At Genentech, the "Hertz" of the biotechnology industry, President Bob Swanson has done away with reserved parking spaces and executive dining rooms, has allowed his scientific staff to come to work in grubby jeans, and has organized Friday night "ho-hos" to create an egalitarian atmosphere—one in which, as he says, the young scientists "get the credit."[75] The purpose of these practices is not to let the professionals go wild and undisciplined, but wild into their discipline. The beer bust is really just a method to break down artificial barriers, especially between professionals and management. When the scientists at Genentech get to see President Swanson dressed as Tweedledee at Halloween, they know he is approachable. They know they are going to be treated as people. They are going to have to work hard, they are going to be expected to observe concrete business goals, but they will get a more than a fair shake.

In setting the overall tone of the culture at Genentech, Bob Swanson hopes that other managers will follow his style in their dealings with the firm's professionals. The key to the personalness style is to keep the door open so that anyone from the professional staff can feel free to walk in to discuss any work-related matter. C. F. Cook[76] goes further in his recommendation that, especially for young professionals, management should also be prepared to discuss non-work-related concerns, such as family, recreation, and religious issues. Although I may not go as far as Cook, I cannot overemphasize the value of approachability and friendliness in inspiring professionals to commit themselves to the real-world problems of the firm. Although this atmosphere can be felt by anyone walking into an organization, it has to be consciously nurtured. Bureaucracy has a way of depersonalizing relationships. Personalness is a strategy for reversing this traditional characteristic of size.

Personalness also has a team-building dimension. Salaried professionals often work in groups and are stimulated to increase their personal and corporate productivity by the resulting interaction with their peers. The group, as a complex social system in which individuals have to deal with each other's personal idiosyncrasies, habits, and styles, needs to be nurtured by management. Using a strategy of personalness, the manager works with the group to establish its goals and then follows up with support in the way of resources. Although the manager should insist on a climate of excellence, he or she should also set a friendly tone wherein people work together, consult with one another, and have an opportunity to achieve within the context of the group. A true team, while accomplishing a unified purpose, can still recognize the achievements of the individual. This kind of team effort does not happen overnight. It has to be founded on a climate of trust, in which individuals feel free to take risks without others suspecting hidden or illicit motives.

Management's encouragement of teamwork has to be gradual but unrelenting. There is also no better way to lead in adopting a personalness strategy than by example. An open-door policy needs to be manifested consistently, especially where there has previously been an atmosphere of mistrust. The manager needs to demonstrate that he or she is not only willing to listen to but will also heed the suggestions of the professional staff, and where appropriate, will actually join with the professionals in making the decisions over which they mutually have control.

Employment Stability

In providing employment stability for professionals, management is essentially saying that, regardless of internal or external changes, employment will be continuous as long as the professionals live up to the terms and conditions of their contractual obligations. Although an auspicious policy, employment stability need not be provided all at once. Indeed, the Work in America Institute[77] sees it as a continuum in which an absolute guarantee of lifetime employment represents the end point. For example, not all employees need to have the same degree of security; permanent employees are typically granted greater security than temporary workers. Length of service may also determine the degree of security. In addition, professionals may be assured of permanent employment but not necessarily in the current position, at the current salary, or at the same location.

There are interim strategies a company can take to prepare for an employment-stability policy. For instance, before moving to a no-layoff policy, a company might institute a hiring freeze or try to maintain lean staffing so as not to allow the work force to grow faster than the workload. If an economic decline is forecast, the company might institute buffer or anticipatory strategies such as overtime, transfers of professionals, temporary employees, and subcontracting. If labor costs simply have to be cut, the company could attempt to arrange for reduced working hours, work sharing, early retirement, product diversification, and so forth. If all else fails, the company should prepare the professional staff for dismissal while providing such outplacement services as financial bridging, retraining, pension portability, or even subcontracts for those going into private practice.

Whether the employer guarantees lifetime employment or is in the process of establishing a policy of stability, professionals are likely to respond very favorably. They will feel free to develop their professional skills but their professional pursuits will probably begin to merge with organizational pursuits. The company's commitment to employment stability will be viewed as a commitment to the individual, who will likely respond with increased loyalty to the company. Thus stability not only promotes real-world practice, but also induces a greater sense of shared responsibility for corporate outcomes. Professionals feel secure in taking the initiative in establishing the procedures governing their work. They expect to be consulted on the strategic mission of the organization but may not demand strategic autonomy. Stability promotes trust, and in a climate of trust, professionals are more willing to grant managers their presumed right of bottom-line responsibility.

Participative, entrepreneurial, and risk-taking behavior seem to flow from a sense of security. Professionals are simply most apt to contribute or to try new things when they know that their management will do everything it can to protect their jobs during both good times and bad. This is in contrast to the feeling of insecurity and mistrust bred by a straightforward employment-at-will policy. Even if they are not laid off, professionals will always be aware that they could be, and this will make any attempt by management to alter their work patterns more difficult. Professionals will be much more responsive to organizational changes and much less desirous of protecting artificial professional standards when they feel secure in their employment.

The strategy of employment stability seems to have taken hold more among blue-collar workers, especially in unionized settings, as seen in the recent contracts between the United Auto Workers (UAW) and GM and Ford. It would be a mistake to believe, however, that professionals are not interested in stability because of their relative mobility. With their growing interest in quality of life, many professionals are not as interested as some managers in changing jobs in order to advance. Committed to their family and community, some professionals are also prepared to make a long-term commitment to one employer in one location. High mobility rates among professionals in the past were usually accounted for by the low cost of job searches and the taste for mobility acquired through professional training.[78] One might also hypothesize, however, that mobility rates have been affected by corporate instability. A reversal of employment instability practices may go a long way toward inducing greater commitment to the organization and its real-world problems.

Employment stability as a managerial strategy is not just a one-way street. Professionals who feel secure may be stimulated to contribute more actively to the success of the organization. Beyond this, however, a stability policy enables an employer to move rapidly when a business slump ends, since the company may have produced for stock during the downturn. It also reduces the costs associated with turnover, such as replacement and rehiring expenses, productivity reductions due to bumping, and income security costs. Although no one is ready to claim that stability causes productivity improvement, the example of such stability-conscious companies as IBM, Eastman Kodak, 3M, Exxon, and Lincoln Electric, known for their flexibility, judgment, leadership, and foresightedness, suggests stability can be an important factor in productivity gains. Employment stability may also enhance management's image by contributing to the stability of the community.

The corporate culture in the United States has generally operated on a belief that management's basic responsibility is to maximize profits for the company's stockholders. There have been countless attacks on this principle through the years, however. A notable early criticism

The Problem of Ethical Responsibility

| Managers who strive for corporate efficiency | → | *Mediation Strategies*

1. Promoting Ethical Consciousness
2. Ethical Process and Structure
3. Institutionalization | ← | Professionals who retain an overriding interest in ethical responsibility |

was by Adolph Berle and Gardiner Means, who documented a transformation in American corporate practice that has become known as
the First Managerial Revolution.[79] According to this observation,
ownership and control had been separated in the corporation, with the
formal owners or stockholders delegating decision-making power to a
class of professional managers. The word "professional" was used to
suggest that these managers would be trained to operate across different
types of organizations. Although this practice has not come to pass,[80]
management has also seen its "professional" role as being accountable
to other groups in society beyond the stockholders. Nevertheless, regular surveys of Fortune 500 executives still find stockholder allegiance
to be paramount.

Defenders of the profit-maximization principle advocate it as the
best vehicle to manage the workings of society. If there is profit to be
made in pollution abatement, pollution will be diminished. In the
meantime, however, certain groups may escape notice by the market.
This may even include the organization's employees, who are subject
to instant dismissal—known as the "employment-at-will" doctrine.
Should not these groups have a right to challenge management
practice?

The answer to this question, of course, is yes, and professionals
from the 60s New Class tradition might tend to be the leaders of the
opposition. The salaried professional typically shares his or her loyalty
to the company with loyalty to society and to the profession.[81] The
professions have sustained a call to service from the earliest days.[82]
Through codes of conduct and other less formal structural mechanisms (such as professional review boards), they have seen fit to police
themselves. This self-regulation has intensified in recent years as client
and public groups have demanded legal action to curb publicized
abuses, such as an accountant giving a clean bill of health to a nearly
insolvent company with which he has a consulting relationship, a research scientist doctoring data in order to win grants, or a corporate
lawyer concealing a theft of corporate assets by management because
she has a presumed proprietary relationship. Self-regulation also serves
the salaried professional whose ethical standards may be compromised

by managerial directives. It is easier for a professional supported by a professional association to resist corporate malpractice than for a manager, whose standards are set almost exclusively by the employer.

Professionals, then, are not easy collaborators in corporate irresponsibility, whether the impetus for their position be personal or professional. The most accommodative position for management is to embark on a socially responsive course that modifies the pure profit maximization standard. This approach suggests that a sole focus on one group with which the corporation interacts, the stockholders, could have negative consequences on other groups in its social environment. Hence corporate management needs not only to respond to but also to anticipate the social and political consequences of its actions in society. This approach has sometimes been referred to as the "stakeholder" approach, referring to the multiple-interest groups, including professional employees and clients or customers, who are affected by corporate actions.[83] The strategies discussed in this section address how corporate management can embark on a social policy that is likely to appeal to the ethical interests of its professional staffs.[84] Fortunately, some companies have already gone a long way toward transforming themselves into socially responsive entities.

Promoting Ethical Consciousness

In considering the idea of ethical consciousness, we must once again enter the domain of culture. Since habits, customs, and attitudes vary widely among organizations and even industries, it is not surprising that some companies have evolved a culture of ethical consciousness, whereas others have not. Similarly, the strength of ethical consciousness in a particular corporate or industrial setting may vary across a range of issues. For example, although the steel industry has had a rocky history with regard to fair employment practices, its safety record is a model compared with that of the coal industry.[85]

The problem of variability in the application of ethical consciousness stems from vagueness about when to apply an ethical principle. Most managements agree to abide by the law on any given issue. Differences begin to appear, however, when observance of particular regulations impedes economic efficiency. The situation becomes even vaguer when dealing with practices that, although questionable in many eyes, may not be illegal, such as investment in South Africa, advocacy advertising in behalf of particular causes, promotions that result from exclusive networks, and so forth. The view this book takes with regard to ethical consciousness derives from a 60s view of social justice, which recognizes the dignity of the individual. Within the corporation, this view grants each employee the right to be treated with respect, equity, and impartiality. This incorporates the right of free speech, and in particular for the professional, the right to question management if corporate practices deviate from professional standards.

Although social scientists have been baffled in trying to explain differences in ethical cultures across organizations, we do know something about how to stimulate cultural change. In promoting ethical consciousness, the impetus has to come from the top. The chief executive and his or her staff represent the ethos of the corporation. The incipient corporate culture typically is shaped by the founder, who ultimately may or may not continue as chief executive. The founder, though, sets the tone of the organization, which translates into its strategic mission. Whether by personal example or through communication with others, this individual also establishes behavioral standards or processes that come to be considered the accepted norms of corporate practice. Those norms can be changed, of course, by subsequent executive officers, if they have sufficient tenure and personality to make an impact. Cultural change is slow, however, and if an ethical consciousness has not been established previously, the current executive has to move carefully.

The most critical step in raising ethical consciousness, and the one most likely to appeal to professionals, is a pronouncement from the CEO that the company is continually responsive to and interested in a free and open exchange of ideas. This position informs the professional staff that it is expected to contribute its insights, be they technical or ethical, to the decision-making processes of the firm. No suppression of ideas can be tolerated, since the organization's adaptability and creativity depend on people being free to speak their minds. The domain in which the CEO needs the broadest view, of course, is the organization's primary market or service area. From an ethical point of view, all social and political consequences of the firm's activity in this primary area are particularly subject to inquiry.

The professionals in the firm can serve as allies of the CEO in mobilizing ethical consciousness. They are characteristically more interested in doing things right than doing them expediently. Hence their first instinct is to oppose methods that might interfere with quality in manufacturing or service. Thus a design engineer is likely to resist price-fixing on heavy equipment, since the purchase criteria in this instance would not necessarily include quality and contribution. Similarly, a corporate auditor would find it difficult to face peers and other coworkers if evidence of fraud in the firm's financial dealings were revealed.

Hence, the professional staff can be a useful resource in promoting ethical consciousness when their best instincts are tapped. Because of their relatively high status in most organizations, the professionals may also represent an authoritative symbol of social responsibility. Their status often derives from the freedom to operate outside some of the standard bureaucratic procedures.[86]

This special status needs to be used in behalf of social justice for those involved in and affected by corporate actions. Not all professionals can be expected to act responsibly, and many will fail to voice their concerns when the corporate culture rewards silence. With encouragement, however, they can take a prominent role in supporting ethical standards of corporate behavior.

Regardless of any support from the professional staff, the chief executive must take the lead in promoting ethical consciousness. This person's actions can serve as a message to the rest of the corporation regarding a commitment to ethical issues. For example, he or she may speak out on a particular issue or set of issues at meetings of industry and trade associations, stockholders, and civic groups. He or she may become active in organizations and committees involved in studying ethical problems and influencing opinion about policy approaches. Seminars at all levels may be sponsored to formulate the corporate position on social and ethical issues that fall within its primary market area. Employees' opinions and suggestions could be sought and used to generate support for ethical positions. Indeed, time could be allocated during regular staff meetings for discussion about the ethical implications of particular policies and practices. The CEO and staff might even recognize past failures in responding to particular problems but provide an explanation of what is being done about them now. Finally, the CEO, once having stimulated interest in corporate ethical concerns, should consider formulating a company policy on the major social issues facing the corporation and use the appropriate forum to communicate this policy to all corporate citizens. A statement in the annual report, for example, could have an enormous impact on the organization's professional community. In summary, in this initial strategy aligning the corporation with a commitment to ethical responsibility, the CEO is willing to balance the economic objectives of the firm with its social objectives.

Ethical Process and Structure

Although the chief executive's promotion of ethical consciousness is a good first step, it does not go far enough. Professionals also want to see action; otherwise, they will be quick to point out that the firm's social proclamations represent mere lip service. Once employees become aware of the CEO's support of ethical goals, they need to see specific procedures and structures for implementing these goals throughout the enterprise.

Ethical process, then, suggests it is not enough to announce that economic goals will henceforth share the corporate agenda with social goals. What counts is how the organization goes about meeting these goals and what decision-making procedures it adopts in carrying out both its economic and its social policy. Process refers to the treatment of employees, but also of any individual who performs a corporate role or who is affected by corporate behavior. In principle, it might state that everyone will be treated with honesty, fairness, and dignity.

In concrete terms, organizations might set up specific procedures to handle instances of corporate misconduct. Executives and professionals could be held responsible or even fired for such abuses as filing false reports, knowingly marketing dangerous products, failing to monitor improper conduct among associates or subordinates, and so forth. The intent of ethical process is not to encourage snooping and suspicion but to make people aware of the consequences of improper conduct. In some instances, widespread condemnation following an immoral act may be more effective as a symbolic deterrent than actual fines or penalties. Ethical procedures are also not meant to impose artificial standards on people. Professionals in particular need wide latitude in performing their expert roles. Sanctions need to be applied, however, for behavior that is thought to be outside commonly accepted standards of ethical responsibility. Indeed, in some circles, being "professional" is equated with acting in a moral fashion, since the professional is granted enormous influence over the client. Within the organization, setting up standards for moral behavior has the added benefit of preventing outside authorities from imposing legal or ethical constraints on corporate conduct that has not been controlled internally. Otherwise, irresponsible professional behavior can be subject to legal restraint where professional bodies have proven incapable of policing themselves. The accounting profession, as one example, has been investigated over the years by the Securities and Exchange Commission, the Federal Trade Commission, the Internal Revenue Service, the Justice Department, and subcommittees from both houses of Congress. Although widespread wrongdoing among audited companies in the form of improper political contributions, bribes, off-book slush funds, and the like led to the passage in 1977 of the Foreign Corrupt Practices Act, the profession through internal changes in one of its major associations, the American Institute of Certified Public Accountants (AICPA), as well as through changes in accounting principles established by its own Financial Accounting Standards Board (FASB), has sought to prevent further legislative encroachment on its practice.[87]

One way to formulate standards of acceptable ethical behavior in organizations is to issue a code of ethics. Such a code spells out the leadership's position on appropriate behavior in ambiguous circumstances or in situations where there may not be congruity between professional, personal, and corporate standards. Records show that about 75 percent of all U.S. firms indeed have such codes, and the percentage rises to 90 percent among the largest companies. The most common item in these codes is conflict-of-interest provisions, although few provide explicit details on conflict-of-interest situations. Other items concern political contributions, use of inside information, payments to government officials and political parties, gifts, favors, and unrecorded or falsely recorded funds or transactions.[88] The sheer size of corporate entities today and the geographic dispersion of their operations has created a common concern among CEOs for this type of universal statement. A few years ago, former Secretary of the Treasury W. Michael Blumenthal even argued for a general code of ethics for business to ward off the continuing pressure of increased federal legislation.[89]

The obvious problem with any universal code (and this is why the Blumenthal idea foundered) is the specifics of its content. There are also difficult administrative procedures to resolve, such as how and to whom the code should be distributed, how violations are to be monitored, and how penalties are to be enforced. Nevertheless, even at the symbolic level, a code of ethics or of corporate conscience suggests to the corporate community that management is serious about articulating and acting on what it considers responsible ethical behavior.

Another vehicle to affirm management's commitment to ethical standards and procedures is the internal appeals process. It is important that employees, aware that the organization has taken a stand on ethical behavior, have some internal mechanism for voicing their complaints about possible corporate misconduct. It is equally critical that this mechanism assure the employees that they will not suffer any adverse consequences for using the appeals process. Although a mechanism such as this has immediate bearing on how ethical standards are upheld in the organization, it also has a beneficial side effect for management, in that employees given an opportunity to use an internal mechanism for relief will tend to forego reliance on outside sources, such as is associated with "whistle-blowing." An internal process also gives management time to research the issue at stake and seek a remedy to prevent its recurrence. If its research reveals that the complaint is unfounded, it can also use the time to prepare a defense of its actions.

The existence of an appeals process does not force the professional to use it if he or she concludes that doing so will not solve a problem or may lead to reprisals. For example, the professional may believe that bringing a complaint will lead to the destruction of evidence.[90]

The best way to ensure that any internal appeals mechanism works effectively is to see that it abides by commonly accepted standards of due process. There should be a clear method to receive complaints, conduct impartial investigations, define standards of judgment, provide a fair hearing, and reach objective, fair, and responsible decisions. Beyond due process, there are any number of vehicles to implement the appeals process. The traditional formats call for redress through the immediate supervisor, the personnel department, or an open-door appeal to top management. Some policies contain procedures for bypassing a superior believed to be implicated in wrongdoing or one who is unresponsive to a complaint. More formal policies may entail the use of grievance committees, audit committees, or review boards. The membership of these groups varies; it may or may not include, for example, people from outside the firm or the company's chief executives.[91] Some companies have created ombudsman or inspector general roles, assigning one person to receive, investigate, and respond to employee complaints. Finally, participative management systems may in their own right create an atmosphere that encourages open disclosure of most corporate and professional practices. As organizations become increasingly large and decentralized, however, it is possible for professionals who witness ethical misconduct or questionable practices to feel isolated from corporate decision making. They may also feel compromised in revealing certain information to their project manager, group leader, or team leader. Hence the appeals process has to incorporate methods for permitting access to and reporting of information beyond the division or unit level, where necessary.

Among the appeals processes that specifically incorporate professional interests, the procedure installed in mid-1980 by the U.S. Nuclear Regulatory Commission (NRC) stands out.[92] If a professional holds a judgment contrary to NRC practice, he or she submits a written statement to management, which evaluates its merits. The NRC's Office of Management and Program Analysis collects and makes public a quarterly report of all these filed professional opinions. The NRC meanwhile expressly forbids retaliation against any professional who holds a differing opinion. Finally, each year, a Special Review Panel of NRC employees and outsiders reviews the professional opinion process not only to see that it is functioning properly but also to suggest merit awards for those professionals whose opinions "made significant contributions to the agency or to public safety."

Although an appeals process can be a very effective formal mechanism for encouraging ethical corporate practice, it cannot take the place of informal processes that simply provide common means for professionals to question managerial decisions. In Chapter 4, I spoke about the process of "reformism" which in contrast to whistle-blowing allows professionals to operate "on the inside" to change an organizational activity that might be damaging to the corporate community. However, not all professionals are bold enough to fight for moral rights or causes on their own. Besides formal codes of ethics or an appeals process, management can also set up a corporate structure to respond to ethical issues.

One structural adaptation to ethical concerns is the appointment of a staff specialist in a particular social area, for example, affirmative action or environmental policy. The specialist typically gathers information on the organization's activities in the substantive area of concern and matches these data with his or her assessment of external demands. The specialist may also mediate between operating divisions and outside organizations, such as government agencies, which may be pressuring the corporation.[93] To affirm the importance of the function, some organizations elevate the specialist role to an executive position. Regardless of level in the organization, the individual typically fills three broad roles:

1. *advice or counsel*—acting as an internal consultant to the CEO or to operating and functional units and, in this capacity, advising executives on the best way to handle particular ethical issues.

2. *service*—being responsible for the implementation of programs responding to social and ethical problems and providing this service for operating units or the enterprise as a whole.

3. *control*—formulating policies and guidelines that shape the organization's relations with its various publics, as well as monitoring the implementation of these policies and guidelines.[94]

Beyond individual appointments, organizations can establish enlarged structural arrangements to respond to ethical concerns, especially as firms grow in size or participate in markets or services that are particularly vulnerable to ethical dilemmas. Utilities, for example, may face extraordinary pressures as a result of public concerns over nuclear energy or of service considerations arising from their monopolistic status. Some of the alternative structures include:

1. A temporary task force of managers and professionals to handle critical issues as they arise.

2. A permanent committee, composed typically of senior staff, to respond to ethical dilemmas and initiate corporate problem solving.

3. A committee or committees of the board of directors to examine the corporation's ethical behavior and performance and recommend where the firm's responsibilities regarding ethical issues lie.

4. A permanent department to formulate and take the lead in implementing social and ethical policies.

5. Other structures or a combination of the above.

As the particular structural arrangement to be used by the organization in response to ethical issues evolves, management can decide further whether to follow a decentralized or centralized format. Under the decentralized format, each department is assigned responsibility for social issues that fall within its purview. For example, finance might handle investor relations, engineering would be concerned with product safety, marketing would deal with consumer relations, and so on. Under the centralized format, all these functions would originate through one department. The head of this department would typically report to the CEO and coordinate all activities related to external social relations.[95] Most corporate organizations that have developed some sophistication in handling social and ethical issues use both approaches, but the preferred option is to move to more and more decentralization. That would be one way to institutionalize ethical responsibility throughout the organization.

Institutionalization

Assigning the firm's social responsibility to a single individual or unit does not do enough to elicit a full corporate commitment to social or ethical policy.[96] An ethical specialist, for example, can become burdened with moderating individual conflicts within the organization or moving from crisis to crisis. In this third strategy, management attempts to make conformance with the firm's ethical policy a goal for all employees. This entails modifying the organization's procedures, especially those concerned with planning and evaluation, to incorporate social or ethical objectives along with the more traditional economic objectives of the enterprise.

The institutionalization strategy is most appropriately directed at middle-line management. Without the support of line managers, the organization will not be able to deliver on its social contract. A good deal of the action of the firm, including socially relevant activities, takes place at the middle level. For example, an affirmative-action policy is implemented at the department level, where most of the hiring takes place. Unfortunately, much of the work of line managers tends to be subjective and difficult to measure. Nevertheless, they are typically under considerable pressure to conform to their superiors' expectations. It is essential, then, that their social or ethical performance be reviewed as carefully as their economic performance. As Prakash Sethi[97] has said, ethical responsibility should not be represented to the line manager as making a profit and then contributing to social causes. Rather, the line manager should be made aware of what his or her company and particular function are doing *while* making a profit.

The steps used to institutionalize corporate ethical responsibility vary, but experience has taught us to pay attention to particular action points. Institutionalization must follow the prior two strategies outlined in this section. Middle managers or any other employee cannot be expected to heed the call to ethical behavior until they know that the top is serious about it. A corporate social response process starts with the strategic plan of the organization, which describes the mission of the enterprise. It is here that social objectives can be inserted along with the economic objectives of the organization. Next is the structural response, which is ultimately most effective when decentralized to the individual units that are responsible for carrying out the organization's mission. The organization is then ready to institutionalize ethical practice. One of the first steps is to alter the departmental budget to incorporate socially relevant activities. Testing equipment for secondary safety effects may be costly, but including a line item for this function demonstrates the seriousness with which senior management views safety. Expenditures for an internal audit team are also expensive, but demonstrate to the professional accounting staff that the company will not tolerate standards abuses.

A second step in institutionalization is to incorporate ethical responsibilities in the managers' and professionals' job descriptions. Job descriptions should not be so precise as to hinder individual initiative, but they do specify what the jobs require, and hence are a good place to emphasize the importance of ethical considerations in job performance.

Whereas senior management tends to concentrate on strategic planning, middle managers and professional contributors usually focus their planning efforts on the operating level. So, besides incorporating ethical concerns in budgets and job descriptions, department heads, for example, can translate strategic social goals into operating objectives. Middle managers design information and reporting systems essentially to control their operations. These systems contain information relating to anticipated demand for products or services, plant and equipment, capacity utilization, pricing, distribution, staffing, and so forth. Here again, social and ethical considerations can be included as data points for entry into the system. For example, although a company may have a sound affirmative action policy, its plan may call for subcontracting some of its specialized work. Beyond cost criteria, the company could determine whether the potential subcontractors have met base-line affirmative action goals. It should be noted that in many public policy areas, ethical planning considerations have been preempted by government regulations, many of which were initiated because corporations had failed to meet ethical responsibilities.

Perhaps the most critical element in institutionalizing ethical responsibility is the insertion of social or ethical criteria in the performance-evaluation process. Performance appraisals at the middle-management and professional-staff levels are the primary means of controlling human resources at those levels. Only when the staff know that they will be held accountable for their social performance will they be truly free to act on ethical principles and processes in their work. Although performance-evaluation systems vary in many respects, most measure performance against acceptable standards in some way. The socially responsible company ensures that social or ethical measures are included along with other indicators of performance. Hence, corporate attorneys are evaluated not only on the expeditiousness with which they handle claims against the company but also on their identification of corporate abuses that have gone undetected. Mental health professionals are rated not only on the number of acutely disturbed patients under their care but on the quality and dignity of such care. Chemists are rewarded not only for the curative effects of a new compound but for having also scrupulously identified its side effects and interactions.

Flowing from the performance-evaluation system are the rewards to be distributed to organization members. Consistent with the attempt to incorporate ethical standards into performance appraisal, rewards, whether pecuniary or nonpecuniary, should ensue for social performance. The reward system is often contingent on the training and career development functions. Education on social performance expectations and procedures can be provided to managers and professionals. A loan officer, for example, may need not just encouragement but skill development in evaluating a proposal from a minority business to operate in a ghetto area on subsidized funds earmarked for neighborhood development. Beyond training and education, however, rewards for social performance should extend to personal career development, so that the professional who meets ethical as well as economic goals is given a chance to explore advanced or enriched career opportunities in other parts of the organization.

A final step in institutionalizing ethical responsibility is to construct and carry out an actual audit of social performance. The social audit received considerable attention in the press in the early 1970s, and there was even talk at the time of devising a standard social reporting system that would accompany the conventional financial statements issued regularly by all corporations. Thus the public at large, including the investing community, would have information at its disposal on how much a company might have put into quality control, the costs of its emissions, or its expenditures on programs to increase minority worker mobility. Little agreement has emerged, however, on a standard set of indicators that could be used in a social accounting statement, nor has there been much support for an external reporting system. One adaptation that has found some acceptance is the use of footnotes describing social programs and social costs to accompany the financial statements. The American Accounting Association's Committee on Environmental Effects of Organization Behavior, for example, has recommended disclosure of an audited firm's environmental problems, abatement goals and progress, and material effects on its financial position and earnings.[98]

Most companies that have adopted social audits use them for internal reporting purposes, where they can be used to broadcast and control some of the firm's social activities. There are three methods to choose from:

1. *The descriptive or process audit.* In this format, the organization, without adhering to any standard format, simply describes what it is doing and what has been accomplished in the organization's social and ethical activities.

2. *The effort audit.* This audit lists the expenditures and time devoted to various social and ethical activities. It may also include the cost of programs not undertaken but expected or required.

3. *The performance audit.* Although the most difficult and expensive, this type of audit attempts to measure the benefits as well as the costs of social programs. Organizations using performance audits need to devise creative ways of measuring nontraditional social outcomes, such as better air quality, fair advertising, safety, even the value of a human life.

Whatever social audit method is chosen, most companies tend to use only a handful of indicators to evaluate a select number of ethical issues that are seen as relevant to the organization. The social-measurement approach developed in the 1970s at General Electric in a joint effort with the accounting firm of Peat, Marwick, Mitchell and Company is among the most comprehensive designs I have seen.[99] A matrix was developed that matched nine constituencies for which the firm felt a social responsibility with a wide array of ethical-performance factors, many of which were reviewed using hard cost-benefit data.

By the final stage of institutionalization, professionals should feel relatively assured that any concern they have for social justice or for the ethical responsibilities of their organization will not be overlooked. Professionals in these firms need not remain silent when they see mishandling of resources, for they know their opinions will be heard. Not many organizations have institutionalized their ethical consciousness, but professionals might be satisfied with what Robert Ackerman and Raymond Bauer once referred to as "institutionalization of purpose."[100] This corresponds to management's attempt to respond sincerely to professional concerns about questionable corporate practices. Consistent with many of the other strategies introduced in this chapter, it has the effect of making the professional and manager partners in furthering the participative aims and processes of the organization.

Conclusion

Soon, professionals will represent one-fifth of the U.S. labor force. Most of them will be salaried, working in relatively large organizations. Most will be found in service industries, which already account for 70 percent of all U.S. jobs. Since we live in a knowledge-based age, professionals will continue to hold an important position in society, owing to their creative insight and imagination, technical skills, ability to handle increasingly challenging work, and facility in working with information technology.

As prominent members of their organizations, salaried professionals will be in a unique position to affect the course of American enterprise. Whether they use their position to advance their historical role as the soul of society through their commitment to excellence, service, and social justice, or whether they become mere pawns in service to the corporation will depend to a large extent on how they are managed. I have argued throughout this book that it is entirely possible to merge the professional staff's dedication to technical performance in their discipline with a genuine commitment to organizational performance.

One way in which this may be accomplished is through the use by management of mediation strategies derived from the specific cultural differences between management and professionals. The cultural factors that differentiate the parties were displayed in Figure 5-1 as a set of six polarized values, each of which represents a special problem in the management of salaried professionals. Figure C-1 shows the same opposing values, now mediated by a total of twenty-three strategies, each of which has been considered in detail. The mediation strategies are clustered and are symbolically placed between the value dimensions. Their application is thus grounded in an understanding of the not infrequently opposed needs of professionals and managers. Hence, managers considering their use should thoroughly review their derivation as discussed in Chapter 5. Below, they are briefly outlined according to their originating problem.

First is the dual problem of overspecialization, signifying the organizational compartmentalization of professionals who are required to perform fixed tasks apart from other professionals or managers, and of overprofessionalization, which results when professionals pay exclusive attention to their special skills and knowledge without any consideration of organizational goals. The first mediation strategy to respond to this problem is linkage devices, which through such methods as meetings, memos, electronic media, cross-disciplinary placements, and user contact promotes professional access to the corporate culture. The next strategy, open internal labor market policy, stipulates a number of methods, including information on job openings, multiple career paths within the organization, and feedback on job applications, to expand skill and career opportunities within the organization. Organizational socialization through such practices as orientation, realistic previews, and social support eases the transition of professionals, trained under the clean conditions of specialized study in the classroom or laboratory, to the messy, indeterminate problems of organizational life. Finally, mentorship constitutes a strategy for guiding and developing junior professionals while contributing to the broadening process for mature, senior professionals.

Figure C-1 The Mediation Strategies for Merging Professional and Management Values

PROFESSIONALS' COMPLAINTS	MEDIATION STRATEGIES	MANAGEMENT'S COMPLAINTS
Managers who require overspecialization →	Linkage devices Open internal labor market policy Organizational socialization Mentorship	← Professionals who wish to remain overprofessionalized
Managers who underspecify ends but overspecify the means of practice and who expect adherence to the organizational hierarchy →	The dual ladder Transition to management Managing ends not means Professional participation	← Professionals who demand autonomy over and participation in ends as well as means
Managers who maintain close supervision →	Self-management and peer control Professional-administration Management by objectives (MBO) Gatekeeping Professional incentives	← Professionals who resist close supervision by insisting on professional standards of evaluation
Managers who show respect for authority and who believe in formalizing control of professional practice →	Decentralization Matrix Soft control	← Professionals who might defy authority or disregard organizational procedures
Managers who, in the interest of career and teamwork, condone jobs lacking challenge, entrepreneurship, personalness, and stability →	Job enrichment Entrepreneurship Personalness Employment stability	← Professionals who, in the interest of quality of life and individual initiative, display little regard for real-world practice
Managers who strive for corporate efficiency →	Promoting ethical consciousness Ethical process and structure Institutionalization	← Professionals who retain an overriding interest in ethical responsibility

In the second major problem, autonomy, management is faced with the dilemma of allowing professionals to determine the problems they will examine while controlling their services to the organization. The dual-ladder approach has the greatest potential to resolve this problem of any structural accommodation to date. It calls for a conventional managerial ladder of hierarchial positions that lead to increased managerial authority and a second, nonconventional ladder of professional positions that carry comparable prestige in terms of salary, status, and responsibility. In the strategy of transition to management, professionals who are both interested and qualified can increase their influence in the organization. Further, their understanding of the professional culture is likely to be appreciated by their managerial colleagues. A key to resolving the dilemma of autonomy versus control is the strategy of allowing management to control the ends of corporate practice, i.e., the strategic goals and values that shape the organization's mission while allowing the professional to control the means of practice. As I warn in the last mediation strategy on professional participation, however, the operational autonomy granted to the professional needs to be constrained by the criterion of accountability. Explicit methods for inducing professional participation include corporate assignments, attitude surveys, team-building, and, to a lesser extent, financial, legal, or bargaining approaches such as stock-ownership plans, codetermination, or unionization.

A third major problem for management is coping with professionals' distaste for close supervision. Fortunately, professionals can be relied upon to control themselves through self-management as well as through peer control. Second, where training is provided, especially in complex interpersonal communications and managerial problem-solving skills, professionals themselves in administrative and project-management roles can be recruited to supervise other professionals. Although abused in its implementation, the development strategy of management by objectives (MBO) is promoted as an excellent way to promote critical review of professional performance while avoiding the necessity for close supervision. MBO consists in having professionals decide mutually with their managers what the objectives for their jobs are, how long it will take to meet the objectives, and what the criteria should be in evaluating progress toward or achievement of the objectives. A fourth strategy, known as gatekeeping, wherein an influential professional serves as an information conduit between the professional staff within any one organizational department and other departments as well as the outside environment, performs a critical supervisory function. Without the assistance of a gatekeeper, many professionals might lose sight of the latest uses of particular professional technologies, which could have far-reaching effects on the performance of the organizations that employ them. Finally, professional incentives may be used to stimulate professional productivity on behalf of the organization. These incentives incorporate some of the traditional benefits of pay, office space, private secretaries, and access to the top, as well as some academic-like perquisites, such as paper presentations, patents, professional association memberships, and sanctioned bootlegging.

In the fourth problem, formalization, the mediation strategies are designed to fuse the rules and regulations required for the smooth operation of any bureaucracy with professional norms. Some of this can be accomplished by decentralization, which not only tends to reduce formal procedures but brings those that are required closer to professional employees. Decentralization is put into practice in project management, new-venture units, spin-offs, and a structural adaptation discussed in the second strategy, known as the matrix. By combining the disciplinary specialties of professionals with assigned project work, the matrix structure substitutes flexible and interactive behavior for bureaucratic behavior. When working with professionals, formal control methods can also be replaced by soft control, which, as a people-centered approach, elicits commitment to the organization's mission by communicating to professionals a sense of shared purpose.

The problem of real-world practice stems from the professional's interest in individual initiative combined with a commitment to a high quality of life. Can these professional values be merged with the realities of corporate life? Through job enrichment, which focuses professional work on its content, professionals can find fulfillment in multiple settings. The job-enrichment strategy, however, must include diversity, choice, flexibility, mobility, and responsibility. Entrepreneurship, which encourages willing professionals to choose and work on their own projects without constant oversight, is another strategy for stimulating personal and organizational motivation. A third strategy, referred to as personalness, which emphasizes knowledge over organizational politics as the way to obtain corporate rewards, can be a powerful technique for inspiring professionals to commit themselves to real-world problems, especially because of its inherent egalitarian and team-building principles. Finally, in the employment stability strategy, management assures its professional staff of continuous employment as long as the professionals live up to the terms and conditions of their contractual obligations. Employment stability, however, needs to be preceded by so-called buffer or anticipatory strategies, such as overtime, transfers, and subcontracting, so as not to allow the work force to grow faster than the workload.

The last problem emanates from a position this book has taken: that professionals tend to be more interested in ethical responsibility than their managers. Under the stakeholder concept, however, wherein management displays an interest in all of the constituencies of the corporation beyond the ownership, management has begun to align itself with the progressive professional view. Through the initial strategy of promoting ethical consciousness, the top management of the organization raises ethical consciousness by a pronouncement that the organization will be continually responsive to the interests of its various publics. Second, the organization begins to incorporate processes and structures to inquire about and report on its ethical responsibilities, whether it be through a code of ethics, an internal appeals process, or the appointment of a staff specialist or committee to respond to ethical concerns. Finally, under the strategy of institutionalization, the procedures of the organization are modified, especially those concerned with planning and evalution, so as to incorporate social and ethical objectives into the plans of operating management.

These mediation strategies are designed to help management integrate professionals more successfully into organizational life. The ideal is that one day professional accomplishment will become consonant with managerial proficiency. It is my hope that this account will help transform this vision into reality.

Notes

Chapter 1

1. Although first broached by the sociologist, Robert Merton, the problems of cosmopolitan professionals were described in some depth by Alvin W. Gouldner in his famous article, "Cosmopolitans and Locals: Toward an Analysis of Latent Social Roles," *Administrative Science Quarterly* 2 (1957): 281–306, and 3 (1958): 444–80.

2. William Kornhauser, *Scientists in Industry* (Berkeley: University of California Press, 1962), 117–30.

3. Some of the material in this section has been drawn from the author's prior book. See Chapter 1 of Joseph A. Raelin, *The Salaried Professional: How to Make the Most of Your Career* (New York: Praeger Books, 1984).

4. Everett C. Hughes, "Professions," in Kenneth S. Lynn, ed., *The Professions in America* (Boston: Houghton Mifflin Company, 1963), 1–14.

5. Ralph L. Blankenship, "Professions, Colleagues and Organizations," in Ralph L. Blankenship, ed., *Colleagues in Organizations* (New York: John Wiley & Sons, 1977), 21.

6. Seymour B. Sarason, *Work, Aging and Social Change* (New York: The Free Press, 1977).

7. Steven Kerr, Mary Ann Von Glinow, and Janet Schriesheim, "Issues in the Study of Professionals in Organizations: The Case of Scientists and Engineers," *Organizational Behavior and Human Performance* 18 (1977): 329–45.

8. George Ritzer, *Man and His Work: Conflict and Change* (New York: Meredith Corporation, 1972), 53.

9. Richard H. Hall, "Professionalization and Bureaucratization," *American Sociological Review* 22 (1968): 92–104.

10. See, for example, Margali S. Larson, *The Rise of Professionalism* (Berkeley: University of California Press, 1977), and Douglas Klegon, "The Sociology of Professions: An Emerging Perspective," *Sociology of Work and Occupations* 5 (1978): 259–83.

11. John Child and Janet Fulk, "Maintenance of Occupational Control," *Work and Occupations* 9 (1982): 155–92.

12. Kerr, Von Glinow, and Schriesheim, "Professionals in Organizations," 332–39.

13. Kornhauser, *Scientists in Industry*, 5–6.

14. Otis Port, "Where the Jobs Will Be?" *Business Week's Guide to Careers* 3 (1985): 60–63.

15. Harold L. Wilensky, "The Professionalization of Everyone?" *The American Journal of Sociology* 70 (1964): 137–58.

16. Joseph A. Raelin and Betty B. Sokol, "Rethinking the Relationship between Regulation and R&D Lab," *Business Forum* 7 (1982): 11–13.

17. Gouldner, "Cosmopolitans and Locals," 281–306 and 444–80.

18. Joseph A. Raelin, Calvin K. Sholl, and Daniel Leonard, "Why Professionals Turn Sour and What to Do," *Personnel* 62 (1985): 28–41.

19. David J. Cherrington, Spencer J. Condie, and J. Lynn England, "Age and Work Values," *Academy of Management Journal* 22 (1979): 617–23.

20. Joseph A. Raelin, "Work Patterns in the Professional Life-Cycle," *Journal of Occupational Psychology* 58 (1985): 177–87.

21. Wilensky, "The Professionalization of Everyone?" 137–58.

22. See special issue on "The Dilemma of Autonomy vs. Control in the Management of Organizational Professionals," edited by the author, Joseph A. Raelin, *Human Resource Management* 24 (1985): 121–247.

23. W. Richard Scott, "Reactions to Supervision in a Heteronomous Professional Organization," *Administrative Science Quarterly* 10 (1965): 65–81.

24. Mark Abrahamson, "The Integration of Industrial Scientists," *Administrative Science Quarterly* 9 (1964): 208–18.

25. Karl E. Weick, "Educational Organizations as Loosely Coupled Systems." *Administrative Science Quarterly* 21 (1976): 1–19.

26. Douglas T. Hall, "Project Work as an Antidote to Career Plateauing in a Declining Engineering Organization," *Human Resource Management* 24 (1985): 271–92.

27. George A. Miller, "Professionals in Bureaucracy: Alienation among Industrial Scientists and Engineers," *American Sociological Review* 32 (1967): 760–61.

28. Joseph A. Raelin, "An Examination of Deviant/Adaptive Behaviors in the Organizational Careers of Professionals," *Academy of Management Review* 9 (1984): 413–27.

29. Richard C. Hollinger and John P. Clark, *Theft by Employees* (Lexington, Mass.: Lexington Books, 1983).

Chapter 2

1. Frederick W. Taylor, *Scientific Management* (New York: Harper, 1911, republished in New York by W. W. Norton, 1967).

2. Jean-Louis Bouchet, cited in William G. Ouchi, *Theory Z* (New York: Avon Books, 1982), 27.

3. Ralph Katz, "As Research Teams Grow Older," *Research Management* 27 (1984): 23–25.

4. Robert H. Hayes and William Abernathy, "Managing Our Way to Economic Decline," *Harvard Business Review* 58 (1980): 70–71.

5. H. G. Kaufman, *Obsolescence and Professional Career Development* (New York: AMACOM, 1974), 23.

6. Thomas J. Peters and Robert K. Waterman, Jr., *In Search of Excellence* (New York: Harper & Row, 1982), 214–15.

7. The distinction between autonomy over means and autonomy over ends was first presented by Lotte Bailyn in a symposium entitled "The Problem of Autonomy in the Careers of Technical Professionals," delivered at the 44th Annual National Meeting of the Academy of Management, Boston, August 12–15, 1984.

8. *Ibid.*

9. See, for example, Robert Perrucci and Jack Gerstl, *Profession without Community: Engineers in American Society* (New York: Random House, 1969).

10. Kornhauser, *Scientists in Industry,* 63.

11. For a very readable case discussion of the role of strategy making as emergent, see Henry Mintzberg and Alexandra McHugh, "Strategy Formation in an Adhocracy," *Administrative Science Quarterly* 30 (1985): 160–87. Also see accounts of "disjointed incrementalism" in Charles E. Lindblom, "The Science of 'Muddling Through,'" *Public Administration Review* 19 (1959): 79–88, and of "logical incrementalism" in James Brian Quinn, *Strategies for Change: Logical Incrementalism* (Homewood, IL.: Richard D. Irwin, 1980).

12. Thomas Watson, Jr., "A Business and Its Beliefs," *McKinsey Foundation Lecture* (New York: McGraw-Hill Book Company, 1963).

13. This story was recounted in Terrence E. Deal and Allen A. Kennedy, *Corporate Cultures* (Reading, Mass.: Addison-Wesley Publishing Co., 1982), 87–88.

14. These decisions were reported in a study of participation among engineers in John M. Ivancevich, "An Analysis of Participation in Decision Making among Project Engineers," *Academy of Management Journal* 22 (1979): 253–69.

15. Charles C. Manz and Henry P. Sims, "Self-Management as a Substitute for Leadership: A Social Learning Theory Perspective," *Academy of Management Review* 5 (1980): 361–67.

16. Ralph Katz and Michael L. Tushman, "A Longitudinal Study of the Effects of Boundary Spanning Supervision on Turnover and Promotion in Research and Development," *Academy of Management Journal* 26 (1983): 437–56.

17. R. Balachandra and Joseph A. Raelin, "How to Decide When to Abandon a Project," *Research Management* 23 (1980): 24–29.

18. Joseph A. Raelin and R. Balachandra, "R & D Project Termination in High Tech Industries," *IEEE Transactions on Engineering Management* 32 (1985): 16–23.

19. Peter L. Mullins, "Capital Budgeting for Research and Development," *Management Services* 6 (1969): 45–50.

20. Andrew Van de Ven, Andre Delbecq, and R. Koenig, "Determinants of Coordination Modes within Organizations," *American Sociological Review* 41 (1976): 322–38.

21. Raelin, Sholl, and Leonard, "Why Professionals Turn Sour," 28–41.

22. Larry E. Greiner and Alan Scharff, "The Challenge of Cultivating Acounting Firm Executives," *Journal of Accountancy* 150 (1980): 58.

23. Katz and Tushman, "A Longitudinal Study," 453.

24. See, for example, George A. Miller, "Professionals in Bureaucracy: Alienation among Individual Scientists," *American Sociological Review* 32 (1967): 763–65.

25. Michel Domsch, Torsten J. Gerpott, and E. Jochum, "Peer Assessment in Industrial R & D Departments," *R & D Management* 13 (1983): 143–54.

26. Donald C. Pelz and Frank Andrews, *Scientists in Organizations* (Ann Arbor: University of Michigan Press, 1976), 8–34.

27. Peter Blau and W. Richard Scott, *Formal Organizations* (San Francisco: Chandler Publishing Co., 1962), 240.

28. Max Weber, *Theory of Social and Economic Organization* (New York: The Free Press, 1947).

29. Richard Tanner Pascale and Anthony G. Athos, *The Art of Japanese Management* (New York: Warner Books, 1981), 52–55, 104–05.

30. *Ibid.* 90–91.

31. Stanley H. Brown, "How One Man Can Move a Corporation Mountain," *Fortune*, 1 July 1966, 81–83, 163–66.

32. Richard H. Hall was one of the first scholars to note that procedures for recognizing technical competence in an organization would be wholeheartedly approved by professionals. See his "Professionalization and Bureaucratization," *American Sociological Review* 33 (1968): 92–104.

33. See, for example, Paul Freund, "The Legal Profession," *Daedalus* 92 (1963): 689–700; Edward Laumann and John Heinz, "The Organization of Lawyer's Work: Size, Intensity, and Co-Practice of Fields of Law," *American Bar Foundation Research Journal* (Spring 1979): 217–46; and Eve Spangler, *Lawyers for Hire* (New Haven: Yale University Press, 1986).

34. Elizabeth Morrissey and David F. Gillespie, "Technology and the Conflict of Professionals in Bureaucratic Organizations," *The Sociological Quarterly* 16 (1975): 319–32.

35. Frederick Herzberg, Bernard Mausner, and Barbara Bloch Synderman, *The Motivation to Work* (New York: John Wiley & Sons, 1959).

36. See Paul Hersey and Kenneth H. Blanchard's "life-cycle" theory of leadership, in *Management of Organizational Behavior* (Englewood Cliffs, N.J.: Prentice-Hall, 1982), 157.

37. Lee Smith, "The Lures and Limits of Innovation: 3M," *Fortune*, 20 October 1980, 84.

38. See Douglas T. Hall and Roger Mansfield, "Relationships of Age and Seniority with Career Variables of Engineers and Scientists," *Journal of Applied Psychology* 60 (1975): 201–10; and Joseph A. Raelin, "Work Patterns in the Professional Life-Cycle," *Journal of Occupational Psychology* 58 (1985): 177–87.

39. Loving Rush, Jr., "How a Hotelman Got the Red Out of United Airlines," *Fortune*, March 1972, 72–76.

40. Douglas McGregor, *The Human Side of Enterprise* (New York: McGraw-Hill Book Company, 1960).

41. Argyris is an extremely prolific writer. For examples of his ideas on humanistic management, see his *Personality and Organization* (New York: Harper & Row, 1957); *Interpersonal Competence and Organizational Effectiveness* (Homewood, Ill.: Irwin Dorsey Press, 1962); and *Integrating the Individual and the Organization* (New York: John Wiley & Sons, 1964).

42. Pascale and Athos, *Japanese Management*, 150–60.

43. Ouchi, *Theory Z*, 66–69.

44. Deal and Kennedy, *Corporate Cultures*, 8–13.

45. Abraham Maslow, *Motivation and Personality* (New York: Harper & Row, 1954), 13.

46. See, for example, Emile Durkheim, *The Division of Labor in Society* (New York: The Macmillan Co., 1933), 1–31.

47. Conversation with consultant to Hewlett-Packard, Waltham Division.

48. Janet Guyon, "Family Feeling at Delta Creates Loyal Workers, Enmity of Unions," *The Wall Street Journal*, 17 July 1980, 13.

49. Lewis W. Lehr, "Stimulating Technical Innovations—The Role of Top Management," *Research Management* 22 (1979): 23–25.

50. Todd R. La Porte and James L. Wood, "Functional Contributions of Bootlegging and Entrepreneurship in Research Organizations," *Human Organization* 29 (1970): 273–87.

51. Peters and Waterman, *Excellence*, 226.

52. Warren R. Stumpe, "What the Research Manager Should Know about New Product Psychology," *Research Management* 22 (1979): 13–17.

53. Kottcamp, E. H., Jr., and Brian M. Rushton, "Stimulating Technological Innovation—Improving the Corporate Environment." *Research Management* 22 (1979): 19–22.

54. Raelin and Balachandra, "R & D Project Termination," 16–23.

55. Carl Heyel, *Handbook of Industrial Research Management* (New York: Reinhold Publishing Corporation, 1968).

56. James F. Bolt, "Job Security: Its Time Has Come," *Harvard Business Review* 61 (1983): 115–23.

57. *Ibid.*, 120–21.

58. Raelin, *The Salaried Professional.*

59. Bolt, "Job Security," 120.

60. Raelin, "Deviant/Adaptive Behaviors," 413–27.

61. For a full development of these ideas on the job-insecurity crisis, see Leonard Greenhalgh, "Managing the Job Insecurity Crisis," *Human Resource Management* 22 (1983): 431–44.

62. The information in this case was adapted from Robert Zager's article, "Managing Guaranteed Employment," *Harvard Business Review* 56 (1978): 103–15.

63. The information in this case was developed from James F. Bolt, "Job Security," 117–21, and Theodore E. Grosskopf, Jr., "Human Resource Planning under Adversity," *Human Resource Planning* 1 (1978): 45–48.

64. *Ibid.*

Chapter 3

1. Burton J. Bledstein, *The Culture of Professionalism* (New York: Norton Books, 1976).

2. *Ibid.*, 112–13.

3. Jurgen Habermas, *Knowledge and Human Interests* (Boston: Beacon Press, 1968), 77.

4. Bledstein, *Professionalism*, 98–99.

5. *Ibid.*, 102.

6. Donald A. Schön, *The Reflective Practitioner* (New York: Basic Books, 1983), 3–20.

7. *Ibid.*, 12.

8. Joseph A. Raelin, *The Salaried Professional*, 10.

9. Richard H. Hall, "Professionalization and Bureaucratization," *American Sociological Review* 33 (1968): 92–104.

10. Sarason, *Work, Aging and Social Change*, 123–64.

11. Mark Abrahamson, *The Professional in the Organization* (Chicago: Rand McNally, 1967), 17–19.

12. Renee C. Fox, "Training for Uncertainty," in Robert Merton, George Reader, and Patricia L. Kendall eds., *The Student Physician* (Cambridge, Mass.: Harvard University Press, 1957), 215–20.

13. Abrahamson, *The Professional,* 17.

14. Louis H. Orzack, "Work as a Central Life Interest of Professionals," *Social Problems* 6 (1959): 125–32.

15. Abrahamson, *The Professional,* 45.

16. C. F. Cook, "The Troubled Life of the Young Ph.D. in an Industrial Research Lab," *Research Management* 18 (1975): 28–31.

17. *Ibid.,* 28–29.

18. Raelin, *The Salaried Professional.*

19. Cook, "The Troubled Life," 29–31.

20. Nina Toren and Judith King, "Scientists' Orientation Toward Their Work: The Relative Effect of Socialization Versus Situation," *International Journal of Comparative Sociology* 23 (1982): 34–46.

21. Robert Perrucci and Joel E. Gerstl, *Profession without Community: Engineers in American Society* (New York: Random House, 1969), 101.

22. Ralph H. Turner, "The Role and the Person," *American Journal of Sociology* 84 (1978): 1–23.

23. Joseph A. Raelin, "An Analysis of the Work Patterns of the Salaried Professionals over Three Career Stages," *Proceedings of the 44th Annual National Meeting of the Academy of Management,* Boston, August 12–15, 1984.

24. Gene W. Dalton, Paul H. Thompson, and Raymond L. Price, "The Four Stages of Professional Careers—A New Look at Performance by Professionals," Marilyn A. Morgan, ed., *Managing Career Development* (New York: D. Van Nostrand, 1980), 43–60.

25. *Ibid.,* 47.

26. *Ibid.*

27. Raelin, *The Salaried Professional,* 115–19.

28. See, for example, David Cherrington, Spencer J. Condie, and J. Lynn England, "Age and Work Values," *Academy of Management Journal* 22 (1979), 617–23.

29. Phillip E. Hammond and Robert E. Mitchell, "Segmentation of Radicalism—The Case of the Protestant Campus Minister," *American Journal of Sociology* 71 (1965): 133–43.

30. George T. Gmitter, "The Industrial R&D Scientist and His Environment," *Research Management* 9 (1966): 115–31.

31. Thomas S. Kuhn, *The Structure of Scientific Revolutions* (Chicago: University of Chicago Press, 1970).

32. Sheldon Krimsky, "Epistemic Considerations on the Value of Folk Wisdom in Science and Technology," *Policy Studies Review* 3 (1984): 240–62.

33. *Ibid.,* 251–55.

34. Donald C. Pelz and Frank M. Andrews, *Scientists in Organizations* (Ann Arbor: Institute for Social Research, 1976), 8–34; originally published in 1966 by John Wiley & Sons.

35. John A. Byrne, "Up, Up and Away? Expansion Is Threatening the 'Humane' Culture at People Express," *Business Week,* 25 November 1985, 80–94.

36. Edwin O. Smigel, *The Wall Street Lawyer* (New York: The Free Press, 1965), 90–109.

37. James B. Stewart, "Major Banks Loosen Links to Law Firms, Use In-House Counsel," *The Wall Street Journal*, 26 April 1984.

38. These differences were first pointed out by William Kornhauser. See his *Scientists in Industry*, 160–61.

39. Lotte Bailyn, "Autonomy in the Industrial R&D Lab," *Human Resource Management* 24 (1985): 129–46.

40. Allan Cox, *The Cox Report on the American Corporation* (New York: Delacorte Press, 1982), 128. This report intensively examined thirteen diverse, major American corporations.

41. Mary E. W. Goss, "Influence and Authority among Physicians in an Outpatient Clinic," *American Sociological Review* 26 (1961): 39–50.

42. See, for example, Paul Starr, *The Social Transformation of American Medicine* (New York: Basic Books, 1982).

43. Robert W. Avery, "Enculturation in Industrial Research," *IEEE Transactions on Engineering Management* 7 (1960): 20–24.

44. W. Richard Scott, "Professionals in Bureaucracies—Areas of Conflict," in H. M. Vollmer and D. L. Mills, eds., *Professionalization* (Englewood Cliffs, N.J.: Prentice-Hall, 1966), 269–73.

45. W. Richard Scott, "Reactions to Supervision in a Heteronomous Professional Organization," *Administrative Science Quarterly* 10 (1965): 65–81.

46. Alvin W. Gouldner, "Cosmopolitans and Locals: Toward an Analysis of Latent Social Roles—I," *Administrative Science Quarterly* 2 (1957): 299.

47. Kornhauser, *Scientists in Industry*, 73–75.

48. Ronald G. Corwin, "The Professional Employee: A Study of Conflict in Nursing Roles," *American Journal of Sociology* 66 (1961): 604–09.

49. Peter K. Mills et al., "Flexiform: A Model for Professional Service Organizations," *Academy of Management Review* 8 (1983): 118–31.

50. "Can an In-House Lawyer Say 'No' to His Bosses?" *Business Week*, 9 April 1984, 70.

51. Kornhauser, *Scientists in Industry*, 86–90.

52. *Ibid.*, 89–92.

53. See, for example, Charles A. Perrow, "A Framework for the Comparative Analysis of Organizations," *American Sociological Review* 32 (1967): 194–208; and Jerald Hage and Michael Aiken, "Routine Technology, Social Structure, and Organizational Goals," *Administrative Science Quarterly* 14 (1969): 366–76.

54. Michael Aiken and Jerald Hage, "Organizational Alienation: A Comparative Analysis," *American Sociological Review* 31 (1966): 497–507.

55. W. Richard Scott, "Reactions to Supervision," 65–81.

56. James Eisenstein, *Counsel for the United States: U.S. Attorneys in the Political and Legal Systems* (Baltimore: Johns Hopkins University Press, 1978).

57. Abrahamson, *The Professional*, 83.

58. Goss, "Influence and Authority," 39–50.

59. Eve Spangler, *Lawyers for Hire* (New Haven: Yale University Press, 1986), 48–50.

60. Todd R. LaPorte, "Conditions of Strain and Accommodation in Industrial Research Organizations," *Administrative Science Quarterly* 10 (1965): 28.

61. Carl Stephen Guynes, "The Care and Management of EDP Specialists," *Personnel Journal* 58 (1979): 703–06.

62. Corwin, "The Professional Employee," 604–15.

63. Kornhauser, *Scientists in Industry*, 173–77.

64. Don Lebell, "Managing Professionals: The Quiet Conflict," *Personnel Journal* 59 (1980): 569–70.

Chapter 4

1. National Opinion Research Center, *Public Opinion* 3 (1980): 38.
2. Peter L. Berger, "The Worldview of the New Class: Secularity and Its Discontents," in B. Bruce-Briggs, ed., *The New Class?* (New Brunswick, N.J.: Transaction Books, 1979), 49–55.
3. Linda Matchan, "Activating Memories: Baby-Boomers Take Stock Catching 'The Big Chill,'" *Boston Globe*, 31 October 1983.
4. Herbert Sheppard and Neal Herrick, *Where Have All the Robots Gone?* (New York: The Free Press, 1972).
5. U.S. Department of Health, Education, and Welfare, *Work in America: Report of a Special Task Force to the Secretary of Health, Education, and Welfare* (Cambridge, Mass.: MIT Press, 1973).
6. M. R. Cooper et al., "Changing Employee Values: Deepening Discontent," *Harvard Business Review* 57 (1979): 117–25.
7. *Ibid.*, 124.
8. Max Weber, *The Protestant Ethic and the Spirit of Capitalism* (New York: Charles Scribner's Sons, 1958).
9. Amitai Etzioni, *An Immodest Agenda* (New York: McGraw-Hill Book Company, 1981), 3–4.
10. Arnold Mitchell and Christine MacNulty, "Changing Values and Lifestyles," *Long Range Planning* 14 (1981): 37–41.
11. Daniel Yankelovich, *New Rules* (New York: Random House, 1981), 5.
12. Daniel Bell, "The Public Household—On 'Fiscal Sociology' and the Liberal Society," *The Public Interest* 37 (1974): 29–68.
13. William H. Whyte, *The Organization Man* (New York: Simon and Shuster, 1956).
14. Christopher Lasch, *The Culture of Narcissism* (New York: Norton Books, 1978).
15. Yankelovich, *New Rules*, 262–64.
16. Peter Clecak, *America's Quest for the Ideal Self* (New York: Oxford University Press, 1983).
17. *Ibid.*, 17.
18. "The Year of the Yuppie," *Newsweek*, 31 December 1984, 14–24.
19. Rex Weiner and Deanne Stillman, *Woodstock Census* (New York: Viking Press, 1979).
20. Ben H. Bagdikian, "Shaping Media Content: Professional Personnel and Organizational Structure," *Public Opinion Quarterly* 87 (1973): 569–79.
21. Harold Wilensky, "The Professionalization of Everyone?" *American Journal of Sociology* 70 (1964): 137–58.
22. Robert J. S. Ross, "The New Left and the Human Service Professions," *Sociology and Social Welfare* 4 (1977): 694–706.
23. *Ibid.*, 697.
24. Weiner and Stillman, *Woodstock Census*, 190, 201–03.
25. The notion of the New Class was first used by John Kenneth Galbraith in his *The Affluent Society* (Boston: Houghton Mifflin Company, 1968) and then significantly ex-

panded upon by David Bazelon and B. Bruce-Briggs. See David Bazelon, *Power in America: The Politics of the New Class* (New York: New American Library, 1967), and B. Bruce-Briggs, ed., *The New Class?*

26. Daniel Bell, *The Winding Passage* (Cambridge, Mass.: Abt Books, 1980), 144–64.

27. Raelin, *The Salaried Professional*, 10.

28. Everett Carl Ladd, Jr., "Pursuing the New Class: Social Theory and Survey Data," in B. Bruce-Briggs, ed., *The New Class?* 101–22.

29. See, for example, Bell, *The Winding Passage*, 144–64; and David Bazelon, *Power in America*.

30. John K. Galbraith, *The New Industrial State* (Boston: Houghton Mifflin Company, 1967).

31. Irving Kristol, *Two Cheers for Capitalism* (New York: Basic Books, 1978).

32. G. William Domhoff, *Who Rules America?* (Englewood Cliffs, N.J.: Prentice-Hall, 1967).

33. James Burnham, *The Managerial Revolution* (New York: John Day, 1941).

34. C. Wright Mills, *The Power Elite* (London: Oxford University Press, 1956).

35. Alvin W. Gouldner, "Cosmopolitans and Locals," 281–306.

36. Michael Maccoby, "The Managerial Work Ethic in America," in J. Barbash et al., eds., *The Work Ethic—A Critical Analysis* (Madison, Wis.: Industrial Relations Research Association, 1983), 183–96.

37. Joseph A. Raelin, "The Basis for the Professional's Resistance to Managerial Control," *Human Resource Management* 24 (1985): 147–76.

38. Bruce-Briggs, *The New Class?* 191–216.

39. Bell, *The Winding Passage*, 161.

40. Joseph A. Schumpeter, *Capitalism, Socialism, and Democracy* (New York: Harper & Row paperback, 1962), 150–51.

41. Rogene A. Buchholz, "The Work Ethic Reconsidered," *Industrial Relations* 31 (1978): 450–59.

42. Kenneth Keniston, *The Young Radicals: Notes on Committed Youth* (New York: Harcourt, Brace and World, 1968).

43. See Ross, "The New Left," 696; and Bruce C. Johnson, "The Democratic Mirage: Notes Toward a Theory of American Politics," *Berkeley Journal of Sociology* 13 (1968): 104–43.

44. Raelin, Sholl, and Leonard, "Why Professionals Turn Sour," 28–41.

45. Erich Fromm, *Escape from Freedom* (New York: Rinehart, 1941).

46. Mark Mulder, "Power Equalization through Participation," *Administrative Science Quarterly* 16 (1982): 31–38.

47. Rosabeth Moss Kanter, "Dilemmas of Managing Participation," *Organizational Dynamics* 11 (1982): 5–27.

48. Mills et al., "Flexiform," 118–31.

49. See the original Douglas McGregor, *The Human Side of Enterprise* (New York: McGraw-Hill Book Company, 1960) and commentaries by Donald J. Morton, "Theory Y Is Not Participative Management," *Human Resource Management* 14 (1975): 25–28; and Edgar H. Schein, "In Defense of Theory Y," *Organizational Dynamics* 4 (1975): 17–30.

50. Robert A. Solo, "The Crisis of Authority," *Review of Social Economy* 38 (1980): 253–59.

51. Kevin Phillips, "The Balkanization of America," *Harpers*, May 1978, 37–47.

52. David W. Ewing, *Freedom Inside the Organization* (New York: E. P. Dutton, 1977).

53. *Toward Balanced Growth: Quality with Quantity*, A Report of the National Research Staff (Washington, D.C.: U.S. Government Printing Office, 1970).

54. Robert W. Ackerman and Raymond A. Bauer, *Corporate Social Responsiveness* (Reston, Va.: Reston Publishing Co., 1976), 3–5.

55. George A. Steiner, "An Overview of the Changing Business Environment and Its Impact on Business," paper presented at the AACSB on Business/Environment/Public Policy, Summer 1979.

56. Harold M. Williams, "Current Problems in Financial Reporting and Internal Controls," *Internal Auditor*, October 1979, 41.

57. John J. Fialka, "Why Arthur Andersen Was So Slow to Detect Chicanery at Frigitemp," *The Wall Street Journal*, 21 September 1984.

58. For fuller definitions of these terms, see Alfred A. Marcus, "Professional Autonomy as a Basis of Conflict in a Government Agency," *Human Resource Management* 24 (1985): 311–28.

59. Stephen Soloman, "The Corporate Lawyer's Dilemma," *Fortune* 5 November 1979.

60. Alan L. Otten, "States Begin to Protect Employees Who Blow Whistle on Their Firms," *The Wall Street Journal*, 31 December 1984.

61. Ackerman and Bauer, *Corporate Social Responsiveness*, 123–31.

62. See, for example, Norman Podhoretz, "The Adversary Culture and The New Class," in B. Bruce-Briggs, ed., *The New Class?* 19–32.

63. Bell, *The Winding Passage*, 161–64.

64. Lasch, *The Culture of Narcissism*.

65. Bell, *The Winding Passage*.

66. Clecak, *America's Quest*, 271–76.

67. *Ibid.*

68. Abraham Maslow, "A Theory of Metamotivation," in Walt Anderson, ed., *The Age of Protest* (Pacific Palisades, Calif.: Goodyear Publishing Company, 1969), 246–49.

69. Michael Maccoby, *The Gamesman: The New Corporate Leaders* (New York: Simon and Schuster, 1976), 100–22.

70. Lasch, *The Culture of Narcissism*, 186.

71. I am referring, of course, to such popular accounts as Kenneth Blanchard and Spencer Johnson, *The One-Minute Manager* (New York: William Morrow, 1982); Deal and Kennedy, *Corporate Cultures*; Robert Levering, *The 100 Best Companies to Work for in America* (Reading, Mass.: Addison-Wesley Publishing Co., 1984); Peters and Waterman, *Excellence*.

72. Peters and Waterman, *Excellence*, 238.

73. Deal and Kennedy, *Corporate Cultures*, 141–42.

74. Ross, "The New Left," 697.

75. Maccoby, "The Managerial Work Ethic," 190–96.

Chapter 5

1. Elwood S. Buffa, "Making American Manufacturing Productive," *California Management Review* 26 (1984): 29–46.

2. Torsten J. Gerpott and Michel Domsch, "The Concept of Professionalism and the

Management of Salaried Technical Professionals: A Cross-National Perspective," *Human Resource Management* 24 (1985): 207–26.

3. See, for example, Peters and Waterman, *Excellence*; Modesto A. Maidique and R. Hayes, "The Art of High-Technology Management," *Sloan Management Review* 25 (1984): 17–31; and Buffa, "Making American Manufacturing Productive."

4. Mary E. Guy, *Professionals in Organizations: Debunking a Myth* (New York: Praeger, 1985).

5. Alex Freedman, "Du Pont Trims Costs, Bureaucracy to Bolster Competitive Position," *The Wall Street Journal*, 25 September 1985.

6. Theodore M. Alfred, "Checkers or Choice in Manpower Management," *Harvard Business Review* 45 (1967): 157–69.

7. See 230–35 of Raelin, *The Salaried Professional*; and Douglas T. T. Hall and Lynn A. Isabella, "Downward Moves and Career Development," *Organizational Dynamics* 14 (1985): 5–23.

8. Douglas T. Hall, "Project Work as an Antidote to Career Plateauing in a Declining Engineering Organization," *Human Resource Management* 24 (1985): 271–92.

9. J. E. Rosenbaum, "Tournament Mobility: Career Patterns in a Corporation." *Administrative Science Quarterly* 24 (1979): 220–41.

10. John P. Wanous, "Organizational Entry: Newcomers Moving from Outside to Inside," *Psychological Bulletin* 84 (1977): 601–18.

11. Eve Spangler, *Lawyers for Hire* (New Haven: Yale University Press, 1986), 28–69.

12. A concise overview of a three-month orientation program is provided by H. Lon Addams, "Up to Speed in 90 Days: An Orientation Plan," *Personnel Journal* 64 (1985): 35–38.

13. Arthur P. Brief, "Undoing the Educational Process of the Newly Hired Professional," *Personnel Administrator* 27 (1982): 55–58.

14. *Ibid*.

15. Dalton, Thompson, and Price, "The Four Stages of Professional Careers," 43–60.

16. For accounts of some exceptions, see Gerald R. Roche, "Much Ado about Mentors," *Harvard Business Review* 57 (1979): 14–28; Rudi Klaus, "Formalized Mentor Relationships for Management and Executive Development Programs in the Federal Government," *Public Administration Review* 41 (1981): 489–96; and "Everyone Who Makes It Has a Mentor" (interviews with F. L. Lunding, G. E. Clements, and D. S. Perkins), *Harvard Business Review* 56 (1978): 89–101.

17. Raelin, *The Salaried Professional*, 164–68.

18. H. Dudley Dewhirst, "Impact of Organizational Climate on the Desire to Manage among Engineers and Scientists," *Personnel Journal* 50 (1971): 196–203.

19. Raelin, *The Salaried Professional*, 27–34.

20. Howard P. Greenwald, "Scientists and the Need to Manage," *Industrial Relations* 17 (1978): 156–67.

21. Thomas J. Allen and Ralph Katz, "The Dual Ladder: Motivational Solution or Managerial Delusion?" Sloan School working paper no. 1692-85, MIT, August 1985.

22. Hall, "Project Work," 280–84.

23. Laurie M. Roth, "A Critical Examination of the Dual Ladder Approach to Career Development," Center for Research in Career Development, Columbia University, New York, 1982, 10–12.

24. Michael J. C. Martin, *Managing Technological Innovation and Entrepreneurship* (Reston, Va.: Reston Publishing Co., 1984), 216–21.

25. Karen A. Epstein, "The Dual Ladder—Career Paths Are Not Always Equivalent," paper presented at the IEEE Careers Conference, Boston, October 2–4, 1985.

26. Fred. M. Goldner and R. R. Ritti, "Professionalization as Career Immobility," *American Journal of Sociology* 72 (1967): 489–502.

27. H. P. Gunz, "Dual Ladders in Research: A Paradoxical Organization Fix," *R&D Management* 10 (1980): 113–18.

28. Roth, "A Critical Examination," 20–23; also reported in Richard J. Buckles, John W. Sibert, and Raymond J. Hoskk, "How Atlantic Richfield Advances Scientists and Engineers," *AMA Forum* 43 (1984): 29–33.

29. James A. Bayton and Richard L. Chapman, "Making Managers of Scientists and Engineers," *Research Management* 16 (1973): 33–36.

30. Meryl Reis Louis, "Managing Career Transition: A Missing Link in Career Development," *Organizational Dynamics* 10 (1982): 68–77; and Raelin, *The Salaried Professional*, 27–34.

31. Pelz and Andrews, *Scientists in Organizations*, 236–39.

32. Thomas Cummings, "Self-regulating Work Groups: A Socio-technical Synthesis," *Academy of Management Review* 3 (1978): 625–34.

33. Lotte Bailyn, "Autonomy in the Industrial R&D Lab," *Human Resource Management* 24 (1985): 129–46.

34. Irene Unterberger and S. Herbert Unterberger, "Disciplining Professional Employees," *Industrial Relations* 17 (1978): 353–59.

35. Moshe Krausz and Shaul Fox, "Needed: Excellent Engineers, Not Mediocre Managers," *Personnel* 58 (1981): 50–56.

36. C. Guy Suits, "The Manageability of Scientific Research," in J. W. Blood, *The Management of Scientific Talent* (New York: American Management Association, 1963), 22–29.

37. *Ibid.*, 25.

38. Raelin, Sholl, and Leonard, "Why Professionals Turn Sour," 28–41.

39. Aaron J. Nurick, "The Paradox of Participation: Lessons from the Tennessee Valley Authority," *Human Resource Management* 24 (1985): 341–56.

40. R. Bucher and J. Stelling, "Characteristics of Professional Organizations," *Journal of Health and Social Behavior* 10 (1969): 3–15.

41. For an overview of organization development, see Wendell L. French and Cecil H. Bell, Jr., *Organization Development* (Englewood Cliffs, N.J.: Prentice-Hall, 1978); or Edgar F. Huse, *Organization Development and Change* (St. Paul, Minn.: West Publishing Co., 1980).

42. Kanter, "Dilemmas," 5–27.

43. Joseph A. Raelin, "Unionization and Deprofessionalization: Which Comes First?" unpublished manuscript, Boston College School of Management, 1985.

44. Robert E. Davidson, "Professional Conflicts within Organizations," *Sociology and Social Research* 70 (1985): 210–20.

45. Bernard Barber, "Some Problems in the Sociology of the Professions," *Daedalus* 92 (1963): 669–88.

46. Hall, "Project Work," 277–84.

47. For a full list of references on MBO, see Jack N. Kondrasuk. "Studies in MBO Effectiveness," *Academy of Management Review* 6 (1981): 419–30.

48. Thomas J. Allen, *Managing the Flow of Technology* (Cambridge, Mass.: MIT Press, 1977).

49. Katz and Tushman, "Longitudinal Study," 437–56.

50. I. D. Greig, "Basic Motivation and Personality in R & D Management," *R & D Management* 12 (1982): 113–22.

51. Martin, *Managing Technological Innovation*, 224–25.

52. Geraldine Brooks, "Faced with Changing Work Force, TRW Pushes to Raise White-Collar Productivity," *The Wall Street Journal*, 22 September 1983.

53. Lotte Bailyn, "Resolving Contradictions in Technical Careers, or What if I Like Being an Engineer?" *Technology Review* 85 (1982): 40–47.

54. Don Lebell, "Managing Professionals: The Quiet Conflict," *Personnel Journal* 59 (1980): 566–72.

55. Sidney L. Jones, "Professional Development Needs of the Researcher," in J. W. Blood, ed., *Management of Scientific Talent*, 212–14.

56. *Ibid.*, 211.

57. Gloria V. Engel, "The Effect of Bureaucracy on the Professional Autonomy of the Physician," *Journal of Health and Social Behavior* 10 (1969): 30–41.

58. Paul D. Montagna, "Professionalization and Bureaucratization in Large Professional Organizations," *American Journal of Sociology* 74 (1968): 138–45.

59. Dennis W. Organ and Charles N. Greene, "The Effect of Formalization on Professional Involvement: A Compensatory Process Approach," *Administrative Science Quarterly* 26 (1981): 237–52.

60. Deal and Kennedy, *Corporate Cultures*, 178–79.

61. Raymond E. Miles, "The Future of Business Education," *California Management Review* 27 (1985): 63–73.

62. James B. Quinn, "Managing Innovation: Controlled Chaos," *Harvard Business Review* 85 (1985): 73–84.

63. Mills et al., "Flexiform," 118–31.

64. Roland W. Schmitt, "Successful Corporate R & D," *Harvard Business Review* 85 (1985): 124–28.

65. *Business Week*, "Coming of Age at Lotus: Software's Child Prodigy Grows Up," 25 February 1985.

66. Martin, *Managing Technological Innovation*, 316–20.

67. Harvey F. Kolodny, "Evolution to a Matrix Organization," *Academy of Management Review* 4 (1979): 543–53.

68. A similar vignette to this one was presented by Deal and Kennedy, *Corporate Cultures*, 194–5, on the U.S. Park Service, as adapted from Herbert Kaufman, *The Forest Ranger* (Baltimore: Johns Hopkins University Press, 1960). However, in recent years, the Park Service has been the subject of controversy in regard to their below-cost timber sales.

69. Frederick Herzberg, "Herzberg on Motivation for the 80's: Piecing Together Generations of Values," *Industry Week* 203 (1979): 58–62.

70. These criteria were originally suggested by James O'Toole. See his "Work and Love (But Mostly Work)," *Journal of Psychiatric Treatment and Evaluation* 4 (1982): 227–37.

71. Gifford Pinchot III, *Intrapreneuring: Why You Don't Have to Leave the Corporation to Become an Entrepreneur* (New York: Harper and Row, 1985).

72. Howard M. Vollmer, "Professionals' Adaptation to Organizations," In H. M. Vollmer and D. L. Mills, eds., *Professionalization* (Englewood Cliffs, N.J.: Prentice-Hall, 1966), 276–82.

73. William M. Bulkeley, "Computer Engineers Memorialized in Book Seek New Challenges," *The Wall Street Journal*, 20 September 1985.

74. *Business Week*, "Coming of Age."

75. Alison B. Bass, "Managing for Success: The Genentech Story," *Technology Review* 88 (1985): 28–29.

76. Cook, "Troubled Life," 28–31.

77. Work in America Institute, *Employment Security in a Free Economy*, J. M. Rosow and R. Zager, eds. (Scarsdale, N.Y.: Work in America Institute, 1984).

78. Sheldon E. Haber, "The Mobility of Professional Workers and Fair Hiring," *Industrial and Labor Relations Review* 34 (1981): 257–64.

79. Adolph A. Berle and Gardiner C. Means, *The Modern Corporation and Private Property* (New York: The Macmillan Co., 1932).

80. See, for example, John P. Kotter, *The General Managers* (New York: The Free Press, 1982).

81. David W. Ewing, *Freedom inside the Organization* (New York: E. P. Dutton, 1977).

82. Andrew Abbott, "Professional Ethics," *American Journal of Sociology* 88 (1983): 855–85.

83. See, for example, J. Scott Armstrong, "Social Irresponsibility in Management," *Journal of Business Research* 5 (1977): 185–213; and R. Edward Freeman, *Strategic Management: A Stakeholder Approach* (Boston: Pitman Publishing Co., 1984).

84. The three strategies discussed in this section as part of a corporate social policy have been patterned after Ackerman's and Bauer's well-known "social response process." See Ackerman and Bauer, *Corporate Social Responsiveness*, 119–31.

85. "Coal Miners Study Shows Record Can Be Improved When Firms Really Try," *The Wall Street Journal*, 18 January 1973.

86. See, for example, Michel Crozier, *The Bureaucratic Phenomenon* (Chicago: University of Chicago Press, 1964), 133; and Thomas Donaldson, *Corporations and Morality* (Englewood Cliffs, N.J.: Prentice-Hall, 1982), 113.

87. See W. E. Olson, "Is Professionalism Dead?" *Journal of Accountancy* 145 (1978): 78–82; John Child and Janet Fulk, "Maintenance of Occupational Control: The Case of Professions," *Work and Occupations* 9 (1982): 155–92; and Lee Burton, "CPA Firms Diversify, Cut Fees, Steal Clients in Battle for Business," *The Wall Street Journal*, 20 September 1985.

88. Bernard J. White and B. Ruth Montgomery, "Corporate Codes of Conduct," *California Management Review* 23 (1980): 80–87; and Paul M. Hammaker, Alexander Horniman, and Louis Rader, *Standards of Conduct in Business* (Charlottesville, Va.: Center for the Study of Applied Ethics, 1977), 6–10.

89. W. Michael Blumenthal, "Rx for Reducing the Occasion of Corporate Sin," *Advanced Management Journal* 42 (1977): 4–13.

90. Alan F. Westin, ed., *Whistle Blowing! Loyalty and Dissent in the Corporation* (New York: McGraw-Hill Book Company, 1981), 150.

91. William G. Scott, *The Management of Conflict: Appeal Systems in Organizations* (Homewood, Ill.: Richard D. Irwin, 1965).

92. NUREG—0567, "Proposed Policy and Procedures for Differing Professional Opinions," 1979; also cited in Westin, *Whistle Blowing!* 148–49.

93. Robert W. Ackerman, "How Companies Respond to Social Demands," *Harvard Business Review* 51 (1973): 92.

94. Phyllis McGrath, *Managing Corporate External Relations: Changing Perspectives and Responses* (New York: The Conference Board, 1976), 45–56.

95. Fred Luthans, Richard M. Hodgetts, and Kenneth R. Thompson, *Social Issues*

in Business: Strategic and Public Policy Perspectives (New York: The Macmillan Co., 1984), 441–51.

96. Ackerman and Bauer, *Corporate Social Responsiveness*, 374–82.

97. S. Prakash Sethi, "Moving Social Responsibility Down a Peg," *Public Relations Journal* 38 (1982): 25–27.

98. "Report of the Committee on Environmental Effects on Organization Behavior," *Accounting Review*, suppl. to vol. 1008, 1974.

99. Marc J. Epstein, Eric G. Flamholtz, and John J. McDonough, *Corporate Social Performance: The Measurement of Product and Service Contributions* (New York: National Association of Accountants, 1977).

100. Ackerman and Bauer, *Corporate Social Responsiveness*, 124.

Index

About the Author

JOSEPH A. RAELIN is Associate Professor of Administrative Sciences at the Boston College School of Management. His special research interest is in human resource management, where he is recognized for his pioneering work in first-job experiences of youth, part-time employment, the career concerns of professionals, and, most recently, the management of salaried professionals. Besides his teaching responsibilities, Dr. Raelin has managed a number of research grants, most recently a three-year National Science Foundation project that examined the decision-making processes of R&D professionals. His last book is entitled *The Salaried Professional: How to Make the Most of Your Career.*

Dr. Raelin is also a management consultant with over fourteen years of experience working with a wide variety of organizational clients. He has consulted on such organizational topics as team-building, interpersonal communication, leadership, career development, and performance evaluation. Recently, he has specialized in working with managers of professionals, helping to create organizational climates receptive to the mutual goals of managerial proficiency and professional accomplishment.